BORN TO STEAL

BORN TO STEAL

When the Mafia Hit Wall Street

GARY WEISS

WARNER BOOKS

An AOL Time Warner Company

Warner Books, Inc., 1271 Avenue of the Americas, New York, NY 10020
Visit our Web site at www.twbookmark.com.

 An AOL Time Warner Company

Printed in the United States of America

First Printing: May 2003
10   9   8   7   6   5   4   3   2   1

The Library of Congress Cataloging-in-Publication Data:

Weiss, Gary R.
   Born to steal : when the mafia hit Wall Street / Gary Weiss.
      p. cm.
   ISBN 0-446-52857-9
    1. Pasciuto, Louis 2. Stockbrokers—New York (State)—New York—
Biography. 3. Securities fraud—New York (State)—New York. 4. Wall Street. 5.
Mafia—New York (State)—New York. I. Title.

HG4928.5 .W453 2003
364.16'8—dc21
   [B]   2002027243

Book design by Giorgetta Bell McRee

For Anthony and Amanda

acknowledgments

Writing a book while holding a full-time job is a massive undertaking. It requires the same amount of back-breaking toil that was exhibited by Gary Cooper in *Sergeant York,* in the scenes in which he plowed fields at night to save up pennies for a piece of bottom land. Endless hours, lost sleep. Definitely not for me. My thanks go to Stephen B. Shepard, editor-in-chief of *Business Week* magazine, for sparing me that ordeal by generously providing me with the substantial leave of absence that I required to complete this book.

Louis Pasciuto was not a source for any of the articles that I wrote for *Business Week* on stock fraud and the Mob's push into Wall Street. Even so, this book is part of a continuum, if you will, that began with "The Mob on Wall Street" in December 1996, and continued in several other articles that appeared between 1996 and 2000. *BW* showed a special kind of courage in running those stories, particularly the first one—which other media outlets, though in possession of the essential facts, wouldn't touch. My editors at the time, former senior editor Seymour Zucker and chief economist Bill Wolman, were gutsy advocates and supreme wordsmiths. Seymour is a journalist and mentor nonpareil, and in many respects those stories were as much his as they were mine. Kenneth M. Vittor, McGraw Hill's general counsel, steered me from numerous possible legal pitfalls and proved many times that he is as fine an editor as he is a lawyer. Valuable assistance, for those articles and this book, came from Jamie Russell, head of *Business Week*'s Information Center, and her able staff.

I owe a special debt of gratitude to Jerry Capeci, the dean of New York's Mob journalists, for pointing Louis in my direction. Jerry's website, Ganglandnews.com, is the premier source of organized crime information on the Internet, and it proved immensely valuable in double-checking facts and for its treasure trove of Mob lore.

The staff of the North American Securities Administrators Association responded with forbearance to my endless requests for brokerage records. My thanks go to NASAA's executive director, Marc Beauchamp, and his colleagues Cheryl Besl, Jerry Munk, and Ashley Baker.

I also am indebted to Paul Schoeman, assistant U.S. Attorney for the Eastern District of New York, and his colleagues, for their courtesy and assistance.

Many persons whom I cannot name were crucial in verifying Louis's story. They include former chop house brokers and traders and lawyers and wiseguys, organized crime investigators and former regulators. They know who they are, and I hope they know I am grateful. I also cannot thank by name— not because of confidentiality, but because I don't know their names—the cheerful and overworked staffs of the various record rooms of the federal and state courthouses in Manhattan, Brooklyn, Long Island, and New Jersey. I'd have been unable to write this book were it not for their assistance in fetching, often from far-off archives, the voluminous files in their custody. One of the byproducts of stock fraud and organized crime prosecutions, including the vast majority of cases that do not go to trial, is a mountain of correspondence and bail applications and sentencing minutes and hearing transcripts. Such documentation was the principal source for substantial portions of this book, including the chapters describing the early career of Charles Ricottone, and provided substantiation throughout.

Dr. Susan Shapiro, a noted child psychologist, read drafts of the chapters concerning Louis's early life and made valuable comments. Erin Condit also read several draft chapters and offered many useful suggestions. At *Business Week,* Anthony Bianco and John Byrne were generous with their advice and support.

This book would not have seen the light of day were it not for the enthusiasm and advocacy of my agent, the estimable Morton L. Janklow. He and his colleague Luke Janklow patiently steered me through the labyrinthine process of bringing a book to life (which was a bit more complicated for this book, I suspect, than most others). They both went above and beyond the call of duty many times. My thanks also go to their colleagues Bennett Ashley and Richard Morris.

At Warner Books I had the rare good fortune to work with executive editor Rick Horgan, who shares the credit for virtually everything in this book that may seem more than slightly worthwhile. Copyeditor Dave Cole ably rescued me from myself on several occasions, as did Elizabeth A. McNamara of Davis Wright Tremaine, who gave the manuscript a painstaking but sympathetic legal review. Rick's assistant Katharine Rapkin provided valuable assistance as well.

My heartfelt thanks go to members of Louis's family, who were candid and courageous in sharing with me their recollections—no matter how painful. I am grateful to Stefanie Pasciuto, Fran Pasciuto, Nicholas Pasciuto, Louis's sister Nicole, and Stefanie's father and mother, referred to by the pseudonyms George and Barbara Donohue.

I also thank, of course, Louis Pasciuto. We spent many hours together, and they were not always easy. Time alone will determine whether the man who was born to steal has truly left his old life behind him. As of this writing, he certainly has. And I hope that his young son and daughter, when they read this book, will come to understand Louis and the era that he embodied, without losing the love and respect to which their father is entitled. This book is dedicated to them.

author's note

I first met Louis Pasciuto at a restaurant in New York City in December 1999. When I laid eyes on him, I felt like turning around and walking out.

I'd been covering his world for the greater part of a decade. I thought I knew the names of every leading practitioner of stock fraud. I thought I knew the stock promoters, the chop houses, the rogue brokers, and the mobsters. I thought I was an expert. And I'd never heard of Louis Pasciuto.

When Louis called me and we agreed to meet, I ran his name through the usual databases. Nothing. Nobody had ever written a word about him. His regulatory record was no more or less tarnished than most of his ilk. He was, it seemed, quite plain, a total nonentity. And when I got my first glimpse of him, slumped on a seat near the cashier, my fears were realized. He wore a leather jacket and was leafing nervously through a bodybuilding magazine. I thought he was a messenger or a waiter going off duty. He was obviously much too young to know anything or anybody of consequence.

When we shook hands, I noticed something that surprised me. He was nervous. People like him weren't supposed to be nervous. He spoke softly, with a New York street accent so thick I sometimes had difficulty understanding him. But I had no trouble understanding the contents of the large manila envelope he'd brought.

It was an indictment. His indictment. It was impressive.

Louis was not just another crooked broker who'd been rounded up in the crackdown on rogue brokers and their Mob partners. He'd come of age in the Wall Street Mafia.

After talking to him for a while I realized he was different from the scam artists and wiseguys I'd interviewed over the years. He realized what he'd done. He didn't rationalize. He wasn't ashamed, and he wasn't sorry, but he was realistic. He'd been caught.

As I spent hours talking with Louis in that and future meetings, and many more hours checking out his story, my initial misgivings were replaced by a combination of awe and horror. He was as cold and merciless with himself, in telling the story of his own degraded life, as he'd been in removing the life savings of hundreds of investors. He was a confirmed atheist, but before long I realized I was taking his confession.

Even so, it bothered me that Louis was a professional liar— a living, breathing personification of the Liar's Paradox. How could I believe anything this guy said to me? It was the same problem facing federal prosecutors, who were using Louis— and a host of other "cooperators"—as informants and consultants, and preparing them to confront their old pals in court. It's not a new problem. It's been around for as long as criminals have been caught and "turned."

I didn't have to wrestle for very long with the phenomenon of a liar expounding on the art of lying and stealing. Much of what he told me became grist for future indictments and was confirmed by reams of documentation, including the court records of various civil and criminal cases involving Louis's employers and associates. Crucial parts of his story—from the identities of obscure Mafioso to the intimate details of stock fraud—were independently verified by people well outside Louis's orbit.

Louis was a keen observer. He remembered in astonishing detail, down to the clothing people wore and the prices of stock he sold years before. Once I double-checked the price of a stock involved in one of Louis's schemes. Louis had said it was $3.50. The Bloomberg database—which is pretty near infallible—said $2.50. Louis stuck to his guns. He didn't care what Bloomberg said—it was $3.50, not $2.50. I later realized I'd asked for the wrong data. Louis was right.

So this tale is as true as it is ugly. The names of the brokerage firms and companies haven't been changed, and neither have the names of the brokers, their friends, and their favored customers. Only the names of victims, and of Louis's children and his wife's family, have been changed.

None of the companies whose stocks were traded by Louis and his pals were ever implicated in any wrongdoing. There's no evidence that the companies, or any of their employees, were aware that their shares were the subject of illegal stock-manipulation schemes.

In a man musing on objects, attachment to them is conceived.
From attachment springs desire;
from desire springs wrath.
From wrath is utter confoundedness;
from utter confoundedness, whirling memory;
from loss of memory, the loss of the understanding;
from loss of the understanding he perishes.

—*The Bhagavad Gita*
as translated by Jogindranath Mukharj, 1900

Prologue:
Lies and Consequences

Louis Pasciuto was lying on his bunk, staring at the green-painted steel bottom of the bunk above him. Night after night he would lie there, forcing his unwilling mind to go blank as he listened to the snores of the Chinese guy sprawled two and a half feet above him. He would just lie there, sleeping fitfully, until the next cough or snort or moan from the Chinese guy.

For years, Louis's mind had been a well-trained dog. It was a mutt he could get to roll over, jump through burning hoops—and, above all, play dead. But for the past few weeks his mind had become restless, rebellious. It was the only part of Louis Pasciuto not under the direct control of the Hudson County Correctional Center. So he was helpless, despairing, as his thoughts wandered toward his Guys.

Louis hated thinking about his Guys even more than he hated thinking about the future. The past was great. The present sucked, and the future was the present that was going to happen tomorrow. Beyond that—he didn't know and he didn't give a shit. He didn't try to influence it. No point in that. What would happen would happen.

Louis didn't like to plan more than a week or two in advance. A month was his limit. He had no savings, no will, no insurance of any kind. He had no credit cards. He owned no stocks, even though the country was going nuts over stocks, even though he had sold millions of dollars in stocks, much of them before he was old enough to sit in a bar and order a drink.

Louis sat in bars and ordered drinks long before he was old enough to sit in bars and order drinks. For years, Louis had not followed bullshit rules and dumb laws, such as the ones that say you have to pay taxes. He would throw away the notices from the IRS as soon as they arrived. He did not pay parking tickets or traffic tickets. He did not serve on jury duty, vote, or register for the draft.

He did not like restrictions on his freedom of any kind.

He hated moral codes, the racket known as the Church and the fraud known as religion. He had no patience for the misconception known as the conscience. Louis lived a free life, not influenced by such asinine fables.

Louis Pasciuto was a stockbroker. He was twenty-five years old.

For most of his life, and all of his seven years in the literal and spiritual vicinity of Wall Street, Louis had lived as if the rules of society did not exist. But now the rules were crashing down on him, just as surely as if the bunk above him had broken loose from the wall and the Chinese guy had come falling down on his chest.

Louis was a wiry five feet eight inches tall. His prematurely balding head was shaved, his eyes were mahogany-brown, and his lips were curled in a sardonic sneer. He had a lot to sneer about lately. Although Louis believed deeply in breaking every law that stood in the way of a free life, he did not feel any camaraderie with his fellow alleged lawbreakers, the inhabitants of the Hudson County Correctional Center. The other inmates, also accused and/or convicted of various violations of the law, were, in his opinion, scum. Lowlifes. They were muggers, dope addicts, check-kiters, and shoplifters rounded up by law enforcement personnel in the lower-rent districts of northern New Jersey. They were virtually all members of various ethnic minority groups that did not make Louis feel especially warm and fuzzy.

During the day, Louis kept to himself and tried to read, but conditions were not conducive. There were two open tiers of cells facing each other, with a kind of open pit in the center. A TV was always blaring. There were frequent fights about programming selections on the TV, fights of the kind that might break out between siblings with differing tastes, if the siblings were raging maniacs. There was a great deal of noise all the time. The place smelled of disinfectant and perspiration.

It was a familiar odor. He had been here before.

He could do the time, even with the stink and the bad, cheap food and the uniforms and rules that were almost as bad as at St. Joseph-by-the-Sea, the parochial high school that tried unsuccessfully to mold his character. He could withstand prison if he didn't have to think.

When his incarceration began two weeks earlier, he tried to keep his mind on safe ground. Friends and family. That didn't work. He soon learned that there were no safe thinking-subjects in prison. Friends? Shit friends who didn't care if he lived or died. Family? What kind of family didn't visit? Why wasn't anyone taking his calls anymore? Try as he may, he couldn't keep his mind off Stefanie and Anthony, their two-year-old.

Stefanie took his call once. She was okay. The baby was okay. But she was struggling. Nobody was sending her money. One of his so-called friends, Armando, had promised to give her money. She waited, with the baby, at a shopping mall on Staten Island. He stood her up and she waited for an hour like a teenager on a first date at some fucking cineplex.

Now Stefanie wasn't taking his calls anymore.

Charlie was pissed.

The FBI was pissed.

The FBI had knocked on his door just before dawn on October 20, 1999. Louis and Stefanie were asleep in their two-bedroom apartment. They lived in a townhouse attached to other townhouses, lined up with neat geometry in a former rural community called Eltingville, in the southern tier of the New York City borough of Staten Island. Unlike the older, more crowded neighborhoods to the north, crime was low on the south shore of Staten Island. Women could walk the street at night without being bothered. People knew each other. Strangers, be they burglars or FBI men, were conspicuous.

Stefanie was the first to wake from the FBI knocks. She sat up and cursed. More strangers at the door. Over the past few months there had been other predawn knocks. There were a lot of visits by people who didn't like Louis, or wanted something from him. Once, when she wasn't there, the visitors had come by car and tried to smash it through the front door of the garage. She had gotten used to that kind of thing, but not used to it so much that she was willing to continue living with Louis. They were on again, off again, on the rocks.

The FBI men politely removed Louis's computer and gave him time to dress in a sweatshirt and jeans. Then he was escorted in a van directly to the FBI field office at 26 Federal Plaza in Lower Manhattan.

At that point, Louis had to pick between two distasteful alternatives. He chose swiftly.

Having made that choice, the only reasonable choice under the circumstances, Louis called Charlie. Charlie expected his call. Charlie was always available on the phone. That was why he paid Charlie. Charlie was a problem-solver. Of course, the other reason he paid Charlie was that Charlie was a problem-creator as well.

Louis grinned as the FBI tape recorder began humming and Charlie began screaming.

Taping Charlie as he screamed was a labor of love. Charlie loved to scream. When Louis was arrested, the idea of not hearing Charlie scream, of being in a position to not see Charlie's phone number in his pager, gave him a feeling of serenity.

His hatred of Charlie was combined with another emotion. Fear. After a few days fear overcame hate and he stopped cooperating. So his bond was revoked and he was transported to the HCCC, where federal defendants awaiting trial were housed when the Metropolitan Correctional Center was filled up. Or at least that was the explanation. Louis theorized that he was sent to the HCCC, and not the allegedly less unpleasant MCC, because the federal government, for a growing list of reasons, did not like him.

The feds kept him in HCCC, he theorized, because Louis knew about the Guys. He knew why they were on Wall Street. He knew their names. He knew the scams that had fed them.

So there he was, three weeks after his arrest, two weeks after he was sent to the HCCC, lying on his bunk and listening to the snores and thinking about the Guys. The Guys could get him out of there. Charlie was his Guy, but there were plenty of others who had come into his life over the years. Ralph. Phil. Sonny. Frank. John. John. Two Johns—the Turk and the Irishman. Elmo. There were so many Guys, and they were so different in age, appearance, and ostensible socioeconomic strata. Carmine was a fruit man. Sonny was a media icon long before Guys became media icons. Phil was educated and Frank wore a mink jacket. Ralph was from Pennsylvania. Whoever they were, it was always first names and nicknames. Cigar. Dogs. Fat Man. As if they were schoolkids. And they traveled in gangs, like schoolkids and prisoners. Gangs of fat, stupid, violent, middle-aged men. Not *Goodfellas*. Not *The Godfather*. At times they seemed to Louis to be a kind of weird amalgam: *The Sunshine Boys* meets *The Warriors*.

To the Guys, Louis was a piggy bank they would crack open, literally if need be, when necessary to get money. Louis would fill his piggy bank with other people's money. When he had the money it always seemed to go somewhere, and quickly. Most of it went to his debts, because Louis gambled and was the most inept gambler since Staten Island was settled in 1670-something.

A lot of it went to Charlie, but never enough.

All he needed were a few more scores. All he had to do was get out. Maybe he could give the FBI some Guys, and get out.

The Chinese guy stopped snoring, and for just a little while he was doing what he loved. Stealing.

Louis went to Arizona to steal from Joe Welch just a couple of months before he was arrested. He went to steal but not to rob. There is a difference. A robber uses a gun. Louis never used a gun when he stole. He didn't have to.

Joe Welch lived in northeast Tucson, on a side road off a side road off a side road. A dirt road. Since this was the desert Southwest, the street where he lived had a weird-sounding name—Tonolea Trail. When Louis heard it he thought he had misunderstood. Tana-what? Tana-lay? As in fuck? Louis hated the Southwest. He hated the desert. He hated dirt roads. He hated dirt. Period. He liked clean things, objects and places that were tidy and familiar, and people whose reactions were predictable. Large, clean apartments. Old men.

Joe Welch was an old man. Old men liked Louis and he got along with them, joked with them, cursed at them, let them curse at him. Knew what made them tick. You had to have that kind of knowledge, that kind of rapport, if you were going to steal from old men who had a lot of money—the only old men worth knowing.

Louis hated the desert but he loved the people of Arizona, as long as they lived where the cacti outnumbered the people. Phoenix was bad. Tucson was small enough to be good. Small towns, ranchers—they were the best. He loved rural America. Their young men and even their professionals were fine. His kind of people. But the World War II generation was, for Louis, truly the Greatest Generation. And when they died—

well, that could be awesome. It was so easy, so utterly cool, to steal from the dead. He had done it before, and he hoped, and prayed, even though he was an atheist, that he would do it again.

Soon Joe Welch would die. But Louis didn't know that as he arrived at Tucson International Airport and waited for Joe Welch to pick him up. Most clients wouldn't have picked up their brokers at the airport, but Louis and Joe had a special rapport. They were friends, almost. Father and son, or grandson, almost.

Joe Welch was eighty-five years old. He had a $10 million account at Smith Barney. Louis wanted all of it.

Louis knew the financial needs of men that age—particularly men old enough to die soon. He knew what kind of investments would meet their special requirements. He had plenty of experience.

By the time he met Joe Welch in the summer of 1999, Louis had been a broker for the greater part of seven years and had worked at seventeen brokerage houses. The bull market had been constant background noise for most of his life. It had begun when Louis was in grade school. He never knew a bear market. And since he rarely put his clients' money in anything resembling an investment, he never really knew the bull market either. But he knew how to sell stocks. When it came to selling stocks, no one was better.

He knew precisely the kind of stocks to sell to Joe Welch and the other persons who had the misfortune to be clients of United Capital Consulting Corporation. Certificates of deposit, mutual funds, and other easily liquidated, conservative investments were not for them. Louis preferred moneymaking opportunities that would appeal to the youthful zest in even the most wizened old fart.

Walt Disney Company, for instance. Great company. Louis had designed a superb trading strategy for Welch, and his other clients, involving that particular stock. They were not aware of this strategy, though Louis was such a terrific sales-man that he probably could have sold them on it anyway. What he did was simple: He took their money. That was it. How much more superb could you get?

Louis applied that same straightforward if not honest ap-proach to every aspect of his brief career as United Capital's chief executive officer and sole employee. For example, every small brokerage firm must have a larger firm to handle client accounts. So Louis informed his clients that United Capital's accounts were in the custody of a perfectly respectable corpo-ration called Penson Financial Services. But instead of actually contacting Penson and opening the accounts, which would have presented problems since Louis was not actually buying stock for his clients, Louis just went ahead and made copies of Penson's forms and made believe he was dealing with Pen-son. So the nonexistent Disney shares were put in nonexistent Penson accounts.

He had other great things for his clients. The hot invest-ment vehicle of the 1990s was high on his list—initial public offerings, or IPOs, when companies sell stock to the public for the first time. The public loved IPOs. IPO investors would buy the shares, and the shares would turn into something better than gold. It was in all the papers. Everybody was talking about IPOs. The blabbermouths on CNBC were constantly hyping them.

So Louis had a fine IPO at United Capital. He sold Welch and other clients shares in the IPO of "Goldman Sacks." Great name. Not Goldman Sachs, the investment bank that was ac-tually going public. Louis changed the spelling of the name. He figured that maybe, if he ever got caught, using a phony name somehow would make it less serious.

The Goldman Sacks IPO was Joe Welch's first investment at United Capital. Then came the Disney "shares." Welch sent a $48,000 check, by Federal Express priority-one overnight delivery, directly to Louis's "corporate headquarters" in Eltingville.

Joe Welch's checks came often, which made him a terrific client. In the weeks before the visit to Tucson, Louis had called Joe Welch with other opportunities as they arose. Trading situations, for instance. If a stock traded at a certain price. Louis said he could "buy" the stock for a few bucks less than its price in the market. Then he would "sell" the stock. Instant "profits" for Joe Welch—instant cash for Louis, who would follow the standard procedure of taking Welch's money and keeping it.

After the first $300,000 from Welch, Louis was ready to go to Arizona to lay the groundwork for getting the rest of the $10 million just sitting in that goddamn Smith Barney account.

He had to look the part. No problem.

In the morning, as he prepared to leave for the airport, Louis put on his platinum Rolex Presidential. This was not the Oyster, which the losers and wannabes wear. This was top-of-the-line, with a square-diamond bagette bezel. It had cost him $17,000 and it *looked* as if it cost him that much. To get money, even if you are desperate for money as he was, you have to look as if you have money already. His suit was a custom fit. The tailor had come to his office and measured it to his body. Pinstripes. Suitably conservative. The suits had cost him $2,000 each but you need a custom suit, you have to have one, if a suit is going to look really good. In a regular suit the ass would be a little baggy but the waist would be tight. Custom suits fit the body perfectly. Not that Louis was a freak or anything. He would look great in an off-the-rack suit. He was 160 pounds of solid muscle. Louis made good first impressions. He was somber, sensitive when in the right mood. He spoke with a New York accent, a street accent, but his manner was deferential, respectful. Not arrogant. He was a New York broker but he didn't act the part. Strangers quickly noticed the taste so evident in his tailored Armani suits, his clean-cut appearance, his manners. In moments of greenback-driven passion at some of the firms where he had worked, Louis would tear off his shirt, revealing a muscular back covered with a panoply of tattoos, with "Native New Yorker" in Old English lettering and an ebullient, sprawling dragon covering the left shoulder. But the tattoos were well hidden under his $300 Hugo Boss shirts, with "LAP" on the cuff.

Rich people dressed that way. Or so he thought until Joe Welch pulled up in his rusting heap of a wreck.

"He had a torn dungaree jacket on. He had Air Force pins all over his jacket, wore loafers and shitty pants. A fifteen-million-dollar guy looked like a bum on the street," said Louis.

Louis felt relieved when he arrived, a nauseating half-hour drive later, at Tonolea Trail. It was quite a spread. Louis judged people by their possessions, and his estimation of Welch immediately rose. Welch lived in a beautiful split-level house with an in-ground pool. Louis loved beautiful houses. He loved in-ground pools. He looked in Joe Welch's in-ground pool. It was empty, except for the rats. Louis's opinion of Joe Welch returned to equilibrium. He concentrated on the task at hand. "This pathetic bastard—I'm gonna rob him blind," he said to himself.

Louis tried to be honest with himself, because it was impossible to be honest with anyone else. He was going to steal from Joe Welch. That was why he came to Arizona. He had to focus on that. He wasn't there to hike in Sabino Canyon—he hated the outdoors with a passion anyway—and he didn't go there to buy cactus jam or Indian tamales outside the San Xavier Mission or visit the prairie dog colony at the Arizona-Sonora Desert Museum.

After ushering Louis inside his sprawling unkempt house, Joe Welch introduced Louis to his young Asian wife. Louis had always marveled at the ability of money to lure women, and his esteem for the female-grabbing power of greenbacks was instantly enhanced. The woman was approximately one-third of Welch's age.

After dinner, Louis hinted to Joe that it might be time for business. Instead came more torture. Music. "He starts playing the piano. So I'm sitting in the chair, I'm a professional, I got my legs crossed. 'Play for me, Joe. I love the piano.' I say, 'I'm a fan of the piano.'

"He sits at his piano and he's horrible. And at the end of the thing, I remember I went, 'Bravo! Bravo, Joe.'"

It was time for business. Louis moved his chair close to Welch, knowing that physical proximity bespoke intimacy, the intimacy required to steal large sums of money.

"He's sitting at his couch, and out of respect, to make him think we're really going to talk about something serious, I say, 'Is it okay if I talk in front of your wife?' Like we were about to split the world today. And so he says, 'Would you feel more comfortable if she wasn't around?' I say, 'Actually, Joe, I would. No disrespect, but I would.' He says, 'Honey, can you leave us alone a little bit?'

"We talked our business, and that was it. He sat at the table and wrote out a check for two hundred thousand dollars."

After that, Louis was so filled with sheer pleasure that he practically ran the seven miles back to the airport. At a stopover in some dipshit city, Louis took out the check and stared at it, reveling in the kind of pride a painter would feel if he could roll up the canvas and stick it in his wallet. Louis was not a thief; he was an artist. He was a hero of his own fantasies. He was like the firemen who extract victims from car wrecks, except that instead of the Jaws of Life he used his tongue, and instead of mangled corpses he extracted large checks from old men with wives who were about to inherit $200,000 less than before.

Louis was staring at the check, in the airport bar, when a man walked up to him and began speaking to him. It was no problem. Louis loved talking to strangers, or anyone else he might be able to use. The man asked him what he did for a living. Louis told him: An investment banker. Where? Prudential. The family business, Prudential.

"He says, 'Oh, you look young, you must be successful.' I remember saying, 'You know, my father's very high up in Prudential,'" Louis recalled. It was wonderful, working for such a fine and reputable firm. Louis Pasciuto, the young executive, scion of a long line of Prudential executives, left the airport bar and completed his trip back to Staten Island.

Charlie was pleased by the proceeds from Tucson. Louis had done his job. He had taken from Joe Welch. Now it was time for Charlie to do his job, which was to take from Louis. And the Guy above Charlie would take from Charlie. And so on, up to the top of an amorphous but rigidly defined pyramid of Guys.

Charlie Ricottone was his partner in life and in business. He was a stern taskmaster, a father figure and elder brother. He was precise and neat, neater than Louis ever could be or ever would want to be. Charlie had been to prison and did not care. Being a Guy meant there was no shame attached to going to prison. There was no stigma in having a criminal record. On the contrary, it was expected. And the federal government was obliging. More and more Guys were being incarcerated, and many of them were being incarcerated because they were the life partners of guys like Louis.

Louis came to Brooklyn and gave Charlie his share of the money from United Capital and Charlie didn't hit him. It was a relief. Louis never raised a hand to Charlie when he got slapped around. His father, Nick, pumped iron but didn't step in when Charlie smacked Louis right there, right in front of him. You don't raise your hand to Charlie, or Ralph or Phil or the Fat Man, just as you don't raise your hand to your priest. Or your father.

The FBI agents assigned to Louis, John Brosnan and Kevin

Barrows, really wanted Charlie and were seriously annoyed that Louis had cooperated and then changed his mind. They didn't threaten him. They didn't have to. Louis knew that he was facing years in prison. Maybe three, maybe five or ten. It all depended on the sentencing guidelines and the prosecutor and the judge—and him.

At his arraignment on October 20 he was charged with one count of securities fraud stemming from his investment strategies at United Capital. But that was just an opening salvo, and he knew it. They had more charges in store for him unless he gave them Charlie and the others. Everybody. Guys. Brokers. No exceptions.

At the time he made the taped phone call to Charlie shortly after his arrest, their relationship had been undergoing severe stress. United Capital was a thing of the past, and Louis was not giving Charlie money anymore. It was a promise he had made to himself, and he did not share it with Charlie at the time. All Charlie knew was that Louis was in a slump. It was an extended slump—over two months—so Charlie was in a bad mood when Louis called him with the tape recorder running, and Louis put him in a worse mood by goading him, to the great pleasure of the FBI men in attendance. Louis knew how to push Charlie's buttons and Charlie said things that were profane, and threatening, and might tend to incriminate him.

Louis called Charlie from jail after he decided to not cooperate. He was pleading now, apologetic, but it was too late. "I decided I ain't doing nothing for you," Charlie said. He could see Charlie at the pizzeria on Kings Highway, in his jogging suit, smoking his Cubans. They had to be Cuban, even if they burned like crabgrass.

Charlie was hurt. He had been spurned. Louis never laid a hand on Stefanie. But to Charlie he was a wife and he was abused and fucked. Louis didn't take it personally. That's how Guys were. They got into a relationship with you. They weren't policemen for crooks—the media got it all wrong. They didn't need psychologists, like the TV mobsters. They *were* psychologists. They burrowed into your mind.

Louis could not forget the Guys if he tried, even if he tried as hard as the feds wanted him to remember. But he couldn't recall all the places he had worked. They were hard to remember because they were so unimportant, so interchangeable. He had worked at so many places with meaningless names on the door that it would take some memory-jogging to get him to recite their names—and Louis had a terrific memory.

To refresh his memory, the feds showed Louis a list of the places he had worked. The number dazzled them. He was at each place for months sometimes, or sometimes for only a few weeks, extracting cash and moving on, fast, when the "product" ran out.

Some of the places where Louis worked were real in the physical sense, in that they had offices and receptionists and desks and phones. These were the chop houses. Chop houses looked like brokerages, in much the same way as a sewer pipe superficially resembles a water pipe. The chop houses were registered with the regulators. Some were in business for months, even years. And the stocks they sold existed. They were usually, but not always, pieces of garbage.

Late in his career he worked at bucket shops. United Capital was a bucket shop. Bucket shops pretended to sell stocks. Outfits with that simple business model were around in the days when elevated trains whipped around the S-curve at Coenties Slip. Bucket shops had a majestic history. They were an old-money, Gilded-Age-era ripoff.

The chop houses of the 1990s committed thievery on a scale that had never been seen before. And it took place out in the open. One estimate was $10 billion a year. It could have been more, or it could have been less. No one really knew how much was stolen. You can't count what you can't see.

The chop houses and bucket shops were the best-known secret on Wall Street.

Now the guys in the chop houses and bucket shops, and the Guys who took their money, were starting to go to jail.

How did they get him? The question gnawed at Louis.

Someone had turned. The FBI knew all the places he'd worked, whether he was on the books or not. They knew about the Guys. They knew about the nominee accounts. They knew the names he had put on some of those accounts. Nicholas Pasciuto. Stefanie Pasciuto. They had him.

They had surveillance pictures of him with Charlie. They weren't good pictures. But they were clear enough.

He thought about Roy Ageloff, his first mentor. Roy of the pastel suits and the cigarettes and the cursing. Father-figure Roy. Fun-filled Roy, the unofficial chief executive officer of Hanover Sterling & Company. Roy had recruited him, trained him, taken him from a gas station on Amboy Road and molded him into what he had become. He owed it all to Roy. It was a debt he could never repay. He loved Roy. They all did—all of the chop house kids.

Roy had been indicted the year before. Multiple counts. Could Roy have turned cooperator? Louis didn't believe it. Roy was a Jew who liked to hang out with Guys. He dressed like a Guy and talked like a Guy and beat up people like a Guy. Even when he was under indictment, he was arrested in Florida for head-butting a guy who mouthed off at him. That was Roy—he didn't take shit from anybody. But the government had dipped him in a Mt. Vesuvius of manure. So now that he faced a long prison term, was he going to turn rat—like a Guy?

Nowadays everybody was turning. Ratting. Louis hated the word because he knew that he had no choice. He knew that not cooperating would be silly. Stupid. Who was going to do time to protect him? Nobody could protect him. His friend and father-in-law George couldn't help and neither could his parents. They had bailed him out and gone bankrupt loaning him money.

> I know in my heart things are going to turn around the right way.

His mother put those words on a birthday card, in her neat, even, penmanship-book handwriting.

> I love you with all my heart and soul. You're my first and you will always be. Listen don't be mad if I can't accept the calls. They are expensive and I can't afford them.

He wasn't mad.

> It hurts me more than you not to talk.

He read those words again and again. *It hurts me more than you not to talk.* That was his situation. The words were true. He would hurt himself by not talking. That was a fact. So were the other words. He read them again. *You're my first and you will always be.*

He was the first and he will always be.

He didn't want to tell the truth, not at first. But in the weeks and months and years that followed, Louis told the truth. He talked about the Guys and the brokers—from Roy and the gas station to Joe Welch in Tucson. He went back to his old friends, wearing a concealed tape recorder and transmitter. He recounted, in merciless detail, all the chop houses and bucket shops—the seventeen he didn't want to remember. He remembered the names. The guys and the Guys behind it all. They were his friends, his enemies, his creditors. His family.

It was the truth. It was the first consequence Louis ever encountered in his twenty-five years: telling the truth.

part one

SANTA CLAUS

CHAPTER ONE

Louis always knew that Santa Claus was a crock of shit. As far back as he could remember, he didn't buy into the Santa thing. Back when he wasn't big enough to stand up, maybe then he believed all that garbage. But by the time he was five he knew where the presents came from. He saw them in the upstairs closet. When they brought out Uncle Sal on Christmas Eve he could see through the glued-on white beard. What did they think he was, an idiot? He knew there was no Santa Claus and no Tooth Fairy and no Easter Bunny and no God.

Jesus walked on water? A snake told Eve not to eat the apple? Kiss my ass, he'd say. It was all a fable, to give people faith. A good thing, for sure. Louis would go to church with his grandmother when he was a little kid. And after she died he would go there to light candles for her. But it was respect for his grandmother. It wasn't as if he were looking up in the sky and talking to her. When you're dead, you're dead. You live for the present, the here-and-now.

Louis knew better than to buy into all that horseshit about the soul and afterlife. He knew very early there were no eternal consequences for what one does in this life, and no code of conduct that was dictated to everybody from God. Sure there were Ten Commandments. Somebody sat down one day and wrote them out. Moses never came down some mountain holding on to them like two bags of groceries from Food Emporium.

Where is this Heaven and Hell? He couldn't see them. What Louis could believe in were the things he could hold in his hands, the things other people had, the things he wanted, and the things that money could buy.

His parents tried hard to teach him otherwise. Years later, Louis exonerated his parents. They were honest. They tried to teach him right from wrong. Not just knowing right from wrong, but doing right when it was easier to do wrong. Louis always knew what was right. But he didn't care. His parents would set an example, the way parents are supposed to according to the self-help books, and he didn't care.

Take the time when he was a little kid, with his mother at a neighborhood bowling alley in Staten Island. He found a pay envelope with $500 in cash. He picked it up and brought it to his mother.

"I would have put it in my pocket when I was ten. I must have been eight," Louis recalls. "So I went to my mother and I said, 'Ma, I found this on the floor outside,' and she brought it to the lost and found. And I remember I was thinking like, 'This is stupid.' I was old enough to know this would get me a lot of baseball cards. But she made me give it back. She says, 'This is somebody's paycheck. This is what they make in a week.' I said, 'I hear you. But they dropped it. Finders keepers.'"

Maybe it was an Oedipal thing, or Jupiter misaligned with Mars. Maybe his mother had bumped into a doorknob or drank too much coffee while she was pregnant with Louis. Maybe it was all these things or none. Maybe there was no reason. All he knows, all anyone ever knew, was that Louis was a thief all his life. It began as a realization early in his life that money was something he was supposed to have. Giving back money someone else had lost made no sense at all. It followed, when he started to think this way, that he really didn't care about the guy who lost the money. The guy would get another paycheck. He could spare it. Or maybe not. "I might get a little feeling, like, 'Ehh, poor guy.' That's all I'd get," said Louis. "That's all I've ever gotten on Wall Street. Sometimes I'd feel real bad. But it wouldn't last long. I'd say to myself, 'Ehh, poor guy. What are you going to do?' Then I'd think of the money I was getting, and I'm thinking, 'Fuck him.'"

Louis wanted to be his own Santa Claus. He couldn't see Heaven or Hell. But he could see numbers. He believed in numbers.

Louis was fascinated with numbers. He saw numbers recur, and he saw patterns in the numbers in his life. Phone numbers repeating house numbers repeating phone numbers. He was born on the twentieth, his grandmother died on the twentieth, he got arrested on the twentieth; he was married on the twenty-seventh, his son was born on the twenty-seventh. Also Tuesdays: He was born on a Tuesday, and he would get money on Tuesdays. It was uncanny. It would always happen. On Tuesdays, when he was on the Street, they'd come with the cash. Maybe not always on Tuesday, but enough that he noticed. The bills would come in paper bags, and he would put them in neat stacks. He would count them fast, with his thumb, like a teller.

The money would come from people, not from God.

Thus it was strict biology, pure chemical interaction, that placed Louis Anthony Pasciuto on this planet on November 20, 1973. Louis's parents were from Bensonhurst, a largely Italian neighborhood in Brooklyn just to the north of Coney Island. Nicholas Pasciuto, Jr., was a handsome, bright kid, a good street athlete, and not wildly ambitious. He worked in a printing shop. He met Fran Surrobbo, a petite brunette, at a club in Manhattan. They were married five months before Louis was born. It meant Nick couldn't go to Baruch College, where he had just registered. It meant he would still be a printer when he was past fifty.

Tough. He had to do the right thing.

FRAN PASCIUTO: "My grandmother, mother, mother-in-law—when they saw Louis their eyes used to sparkle. He never did any wrong in their eyes. Always gave him a lot of attention. Oh, he was tough. Louis was tough, even when small. A lot of energy, very headstrong. When he has his mind made up you couldn't talk him out of it. He was the type of child when he wanted something, he had to get what he wanted. As a young kid he was like that. Very high energy. Smart."

NICK PASCIUTO: "He got a lot of attention, no question about it. He was like the Number One, the Messiah. He always wanted one hundred percent attention. He didn't demand it but his actions required attention. He was a handful, no doubt about it . . . I guess he had a normal life, as far as I was concerned. He was always mannerable. We raised him up to be mannerable and respectful and all that."

Years later, Louis thought back to his earliest memory—getting his head stuck in the bars of the iron fence outside their building in Brooklyn. He did it once and then he did it again—and each time his parents would have to call for the fire department. He remembered his head stuck in the bars and the big red fire truck. All the commotion. All the attention.

He also remembered the yelling. Screaming. Cursing.

The yelling started as far back as he can remember, when he was a little kid, and continued when Louis was five and the Pasciutos moved to a semidetached two-family house in the Great Kills section of Staten Island. A sister, Nicole, was born two years after they moved to Great Kills. Despite the seven-year age difference, Nicole and Louis bonded early.

Louis: "We spent most of the time by ourselves, not wanting to be around them. They argued every morning, every night. My father was sort of like me. He used to like to go out and not come back. Couldn't sit still. Had ants in his pants. I don't think if there was no child involved they would have got married because they were always fighting. My aunt says they were fighting when they were dating. My father would wander off. It's just like the same traits as me because that's the way I am. That's the way I was with my marriage, or even dating Stefanie. I was always lying to her about something. . . . My mother always used to say that. 'You're just like your fucking father!'

"Something would always happen. The bus was stuck. Cab crashed. He fell in the Hudson River, he had to swim home. Some stupid shit. So he would leave on a Friday, say he was working late, not go home until, like, Sunday. So he would say he was coming home at five o'clock from work and he'd be home at nine o'clock."

Nick: "I was never home, working fourteen, sixteen hours a day. . . . After work when I got the time I would get the chance to maybe hang out with the guys, something like that. So either way I was coming home late, whether I got done early at work or I got done late at work. Then I would go basically straight home. If I was done early I would go out with the salespeople, we go have a couple drinks, dinner, just hang out, then go home. Never got home early enough. The kids were just asleep. That went on for years.

"There was always tension and a lot of arguing with his mother. You drink, you do this. Drugs, this, that, whatever. That went on a majority of many years. Arguments and stuff like that. So I would figure not to come home the next day. . . . [Laughing.] If you're damned if you do and damned if you don't—when I do I don't want to be damned. That's what made me want to hang out. During the week, I'll be honest with you, I never looked to go home."

Louis emerged from the pressure cooker of the Pasciuto household as what might be known today as a "difficult child." But on Staten Island in those days he was known as a "brat"—at least, outside of the Pasciuto household. He was also known as a "monster."

Louis would not dispute those characterizations.

No matter what Nick and Fran wanted, Louis was not going to do it. They disagreed with each other on just about everything. So why should he be any different?

LOUIS: "I didn't listen because I had my own opinion about things. My dad used to tell me you could go out from five o'-clock at night and you have to be back at twelve. I used to say, 'Dad, that's seven hours. What's the difference if I leave at eleven and come back at six in the morning? It's still the same seven hours!' I used to try to make them believe it. I used to sell him into fucking believing that. Or I'll even come home at four, so I'm only going to be out five hours. I'm out two hours less. You got two hours on me, I used to tell him. What's better than that? It didn't work. But I would leave anyway."

Nick tried hard not to be like his own father, who had been a stern taskmaster before leaving the family when Nick was ten. He tried to be Louis's friend even as Louis got worse and worse, more and more defiant. The family car stolen and wrecked when he was seventeen and not even licensed. He got a beating for that but it was no big deal. Boys will be boys. Besides, times were changing. Kids showed no respect. Nick's father had demanded respect. "Lots of times he'd smack you around just in case you did something wrong," said Nick. "That means, if I do something wrong, he already hit me for it. I didn't want to be that way with Louis."

Nick tried not to hit. It was tough.

NICK: "Having no respect for authority. That's basically what it turned out to be. There was no rules but Louis's rules. I had rules too. 'But those are your rules, Dad. This is what I do.' Okay. That's it. But I can tell you one thing, when you do it your way, those rules—they're not going to work. It's going to come back and bite you in the ass. He comes back with, I'm old, I'm this. I'm a man. Okay. Very nice. [Laughing.] It was so many years of not being like my father did with me, where I had like no opinion. I gave you the chance to give your opinion and I gave my opinion and you shit on it. So you know what? I'm not going to waste my breath on it. Just don't break my balls, don't break your mother's balls. Go kill yourself."

Since Louis was a rebellious kid, Nick and Fran were glad that they didn't live in Bensonhurst. In Staten Island, they could keep an eye on him and keep him off the streets, and away from the people nobody liked to talk about.

Everybody knew them. They were in the family. They were cousins and uncles. Friends. People down the block. Nick used to shine shoes at the Club 62 on Fort Hamilton Parkway, where the men in the tailored suits would give him $30 tips— at a time when his father took home $50 a week. It was hard to grow up in Bensonhurst and not know Guys.

Fran and Nick had friends, relatives, in that life. They weren't proud of them, didn't boast about them. They were just there. Friends like Gerard and Butchie. Relatives like Fran's Uncle Joe. And it wasn't an Italian phenomenon, really. Jewish people of the over-sixty generation have similar memories—of Uncle Morris the bookie, of gangsters on street corners of neighborhoods like Brownsville. But the old working-class, second-generation Eastern European Jewish neighborhoods were dying or gone by the 1960s, while Italian neighborhoods, and their Guys, were growing and thriving through the twenty-first century. Plenty of street kids were still hoping to become Guys. The glamour, the perks, the advantages of being a Guy have never gone away in places like Bensonhurst.

Guys broke the law and got away with it. That was a powerful thing in Brooklyn in the 1960s. It appealed to a lot of neighborhood kids who didn't have much else to admire.

NICK: "All the biggest gangsters came from that neighborhood. You knew what they were. You knew how they got their money. And you knew what you were. You were a nine-to-fiver and they were a gangster. I disagreed with their philosophy. I don't believe in people shaking down their own kind. I never respected them for that. I had friends that were big people. I never really hung out with them. I would say hello and goodbye. I disagreed with them. . . . You want to rip off a corporation, you want to rip off big gamblers. Whatever else they want to get into, it's a different story. Never ever do you ever get involved with drugs or shaking down your own people. I just totally disrespected those people for that."

LOUIS: "All my father's friends were somewhat connected. But my father was never into that. He just used to say, 'Fuck that.' My father's like a very straight-up guy. He's one of the most honest people I've ever met. If he tells you 'X,' it's 'X.' If he tells you 'Y,' it's 'Y.' That's it. When he does business there's no manipulating. He's totally not like the way I am. So he just never wanted to be involved in that. But he had friends. His friend Butchie was a Persico. I started seeing Butchie when I was young, like maybe sixteen. But I used to not like Butchie because my mother used to say, 'Fucking Butchie'—she thought he was a bad influence on my father. They'd go out and he wouldn't come home."

But Nick had friends Fran liked. Gerard was one of them. As a kid, Louis would stare, goggle-eyed, as Gerard would drive up in the newest Benz and emerge in a long mink jacket, dangling gold jewelry like a rig of a pint-sized Clydesdale. Gerard had a way of talking, with his hands. He had attitude, self-confidence. Gerard owned a printing company and spent time in prison when Louis was ten. It was no major shame, but not discussed.

Louis had no aspirations to be a Guy. But he wanted everything that the Guys had. He found a way.

Louis: "I was maybe ten years old. Me and my friends would go into town, and we would go and buy baseball cards. And they'd be buying, like, Mattingly, eleven dollars, and I could never get it. My mother just wasn't giving me the money. The kids up the block, they always had money. They had forty, fifty, and I had four dollars. I was always the guy with the short end of the stick.

"My father had change up in his closet that he was saving, quarters and stuff, so I would take three dollars. I would always say to myself, 'I'll put it back. When my mother gives me the five next week, I'll get quarters and put it back.' But then I would take three more and then three more. I used to start putting nickels in the jar to make it look higher."

Fran: "When Louis was a young child I never had money missing from my pocketbook and it was always around. I used to keep money on the table. He didn't steal. Not that I know of. He never mentioned to me. My pocketbook was always around, I had money on the table, his friends used to come in. When he was younger, things were always around. I never had anything missing—jewelry, nothing."

LOUIS: "I was slick. I was sly, so it was hard for them to catch me. If I took money out of my mother's wallet, if she had like three tens and twelve singles, I'd take like two singles and a ten. I wouldn't take two tens. I would split it up so she would be, like, 'Well, maybe I spent that ten.'

"From as early as I can remember I did everything I had to do to get everything I wanted. If I wanted that baseball card, I'm getting that baseball card. I didn't care what I had to do."

Such as steal. Just as the Bible says. Thou shalt steal.

CHAPTER TWO

Whenever Roy Ageloff pulled into the Getty station on Amboy Road in the fall of 1992, he would never let the scrawny kid gas-station attendant fill the tank of whatever he happened to be driving on that particular day. Roy was damned if he was going to let the finish on his Benz or his Ferrari or his Lexus be ruined by some stupid kid with long hair and an attitude. So Roy would take a rag, wrap it around the nozzle, and fill it himself. Not a drop spilled. It made the kid, an eighteen-year-old Louis Pasciuto, absolutely furious.

Roy was thirty-three, stocky, and with a pencil-thin mustache that lined the rim of his lip. He wore his dark brown hair slicked back. He lived right up the road and around a corner. And what he did for a living—well, Louis was dying to know but didn't dare ask. Since the guy paid in cash, he didn't even know his name. Louis would have guessed he was Italian, a tough Italian—half-a-wiseguy, maybe. If Roy had known that, he would have been a very happy man.

Roy Ageloff carefully cultivated and nurtured his image of toughness and possible Italian origin. Sure he was a Jew, with a white-collar job and parents in Florida. But his attitude exuded the kind of guy he wanted to be, a "don't fuck with Roy Ageloff" kind of attitude. Roy gives fucks, he doesn't take them. He gives ulcers, he doesn't get them. Roy gives beatings, he doesn't take them.

It wasn't just the cars that dazzled Louis. It was everything about Roy and the heavyset young guy who usually sat next to him, who he later learned was named Joe DiBella. There was the way Roy dressed. Louis had never seen anybody dress so sharp. Roy dressed in the color and smell and taste of the money he was making, the money so obvious from the cars he drove. Roy wore bright electric-blue suits, but never with some dumb blue tie. He'd always wear a contrasting tie—a pink shirt with a green tie. A yellow suit with a red tie. And the shoes. They'd knock Louis out. Blue shoes. Yellow shoes. On a scrub they'd look moronic. But they looked cool on Roy. And he was a down-to-earth guy, no stuffed shirt. When he came by for gas they would joke around, usually about how Roy would never let Louis fill the tank for him.

Still, it annoyed Louis. So one day he challenged Roy on that issue. There was no need for this. He could be trusted with the nozzle. Hell, he could be trusted, period. Ask anybody.

Louis liked his job. It was boring, though, particularly when he had to work night shift. Fishing money out of the floor safe with a clothes hanger—that broke the monotony. So did putting down the wrong numbers from the gas pumps, so the last money of his shift would go into his pocket and not the register. True, the guy on the shift after him always got stuck, because it showed him pumping more gas than he really did. But that was his problem.

And then there was the real perk of working at the Getty station—Louis's favorite customer. He was the credit card guy. A youngish guy, maybe thirty or so, with a chubby face and always in a rush, like a coke-head. Louis never knew his name, and the names on the credit cards would change every now and then. It was a simple, beautiful scam. If during his shift Louis pumped, say, thirty gallons for people paying cash—maybe $50 or so—he would ring up credit-card-guy charge slips for all or most of that gas. They would split the $50 in the cash register, and replace the cash with $50 in credit card slips.

Louis could have told Roy about that, if he dared. He didn't know it, but Roy would have been impressed. What Roy could tell, by just chatting with Louis, was that he was glib and facile, convincing and sharp. It was a gift. It worked wonders with the owner.

"I was charging forty to fifty a night with the credit card guy," said Louis. "After a while I started getting crazy, charging, like, eighty dollars worth of gas on one slip. And the owner says, 'What kind of car does he have?' and I say, 'He came in with three cars. He had his mother and his wife. They fill up twice a week.' I used to tell him he used to leave me his credit card because he lived down the block and he'd go back and get his other two cars. He'd leave his credit card, go back, get the car, get the gas, go back for his other car. He wanted it all on one charge, I used to tell him."

The owner believed him. Of course. People want to believe the more palatable of two alternatives—when Alternative A is you're a sucker, you've hired a thief, and Alternative B is you're smart, you've hired a trustworthy kid and the customer fills up three gas tanks at a time.

What wasn't there to like about a job like that? Between the money out of the floor and the gauge numbers and the credit card guy, he was pulling in maybe $300 a week. Not enough for the kind of Ferrari Roy was driving. Louis wanted to touch it.

Roy liked that kind of spirit, within reason. "I want to tell you one thing, kid. If you spill anything on the car you're going to fucking wear it," he told Louis. After he pumped the gas, not spilling a drop, Roy said, "I'll see you tomorrow." He liked the job Louis had done. Louis was flattered. Roy could have gone to any other gas station on Amboy Road, and he was coming to this one.

Who was this guy? Louis was dying to know. What did he do for a living?

Roy was driving the Ferrari when he came the following day. And they talked, and Louis didn't ask what he did for a living. The next time, a few days later, he came in a Lexus. Louis shot him the question. Roy answered without hesitation.

"We kill people," said Roy.

Louis knew he had to be joking. They didn't really kill people, did they?

"Okay, sign me up," Louis replied. "If I can get a Ferrari I can kill people too."

"So what do you do, kid?" Roy asked him. When Louis told him he was studying to be an accountant at the College of Staten Island, Roy looked as if he were about to throw up. "What do you want to be, a fat accountant? Fuck that shit," Roy told him. "Take my number. Call me tomorrow. Tell them Lou Getty is on the phone."

Fran hit the ceiling when she heard about Roy Ageloff. Louis should stay in school, and not get a job with some guy who drove a nice car.

Fran always knew that if Louis applied himself, he would excel. He was good with numbers, good with math. This was the era when kids with mathematical aptitude could do well on Wall Street. In the early 1990s, "rocket science" was the rage. Derivatives were in the news. They were financial techniques to reduce risk and make money, usually designed by applying complex mathematical formulas. Even the *Daily News* had articles on how bright math majors were getting jobs right out of college.

But Fran never seriously considered a Wall Street career for Louis. Had anyone ever suggested that, she would have given him a dirty look. Fran knew Wall Street. She had worked there when she was about Louis's age during his time at the Getty station. She didn't like Wall Street.

When Fran graduated from New Utrecht High School in the mid-1960s, she got a job as a clerk at a brokerage firm. It paid well. But she didn't like the atmosphere. It was crude, as in a locker room, there was plenty of foul language, and people were treated in a nasty way. And there was something else, something more than the atmosphere. A neighbor who worked on Wall Street told her that the people in those cavernous 1920s office buildings, with their fancy lobbies and shoe-shine men and candy shops, were . . . well, he wasn't too specific. "My neighbor said don't do it," said Fran. "You don't want to get stuck in that world, he said. 'Be careful, you'll get into trouble. It can lead to trouble,' he used to tell me. 'You'll do things you're not supposed to do. Be smart.'"

Fran never learned exactly what the neighbor meant by "trouble." She never asked and he never volunteered just what he meant. She didn't really care. It was none of her business. Wall Street was not a genteel place, not a proper place for a girl from a conservative Catholic family. It was a rough-and-tumble world, with its own way of doing things.

You might say that on Wall Street there were three ways of doing things—a right way, a wrong way, and a Wall Street way. The foul language Fran experienced, what later generations might even call sexism, might even sue over—well, that was just one aspect of Wall Street's moral twilight.

Ethics and profits were not always compatible on Wall Street. One had to give way. It was a dilemma everywhere, even on the floor of the New York Stock Exchange. For years, the tales circulated, to be occasionally confirmed by indictments and regulatory actions, none of which really meant a damn. Floor brokers at the stock exchanges routinely traded for their own profit, even though they were supposed to just execute trades for other people. They did it right out in the open, in front of exchange officials who were supposed to be watching, and in front of the public—quite literally. The illicit trading would take place right underneath the visitors' gallery and, in more recent years, under the gaze of TV cameras from business news shows.

You might say that the floor brokers had a hanger to pull out money from the safe in the exchange floor—and with nobody noticing or caring. Floor brokers are the men—there are very few women among them—who act basically as couriers, seeing to it that large mutual funds and pension funds get their trades filled on the exchange floor. But because they fill that function, and because they hang out on the exchange floor all day, they get all kinds of information that the general public doesn't have. If you are a floor broker, and you know a trade is about to take place that is going to lift the price of a stock, should you slip in a trade of your own first? You can do it, and maybe get away with it. Nobody will notice. Everybody's doing it. And if you feel that everybody's doing it is wrong, and decide to blow the whistle by notifying the government or the regulators—well, you might just as well put a target on your rear end and say, "Kick me." You will be unemployable on Wall Street—permanently.

Fran had been briefly exposed to a subculture almost as tight, almost as suspicious of outsiders and governmental authority, as Bensonhurst. Through bull market and bear, that was one aspect of Wall Street that never changed. The government was the enemy. Regulators hamper the Street in the pursuit of its one and only goal—making money.

So if you worked on Wall Street, you kept your mouth shut. You didn't embezzle. That would be wrong. You didn't blow the whistle on people who cut corners. That would be right—but dumb. Instead, you didn't steal but you didn't get all upset if people violated a few idiotic regulations nobody enforced. That was the Wall Street Way.

For the floor brokers, the Wall Street Way was the only

way. How else were those guys to make a living? What were they going to do, drive a cab?

One American Stock Exchange floor broker had to do just that when he lost his job. He wasn't ashamed. He was a blue-collar guy with kids to support. Lots of guys like him on Wall Street by the early 1990s. Ambitious, working-class guys. Street guys.

CHAPTER THREE

By the time he met Louis in the fall of 1992, Roy Ageloff had made his move. It was long overdue. People may not have been making fun of him—nobody did that, ever—but they could have, if they saw how he lived. It was absurd. Imagine the head of Hanover Sterling, one of Wall's Street's fastest-growing brokerage houses, living in a subdivision. Living in one of those three-story two-tone jobs, with red brick at the bottom and faux-wood-grain white shingles at the top, three cruddy floors with tiny energy-efficient windows looking out on other tiny windows and other two-tone cookie-cutter houses. So he moved from the cruddy townhouse-rowed subdivision street called Blythe to the awesome Ardsley Street in the section of Staten Island called Richmondtown.

He could afford it. He could afford practically anything if he set his mind to it. And Roy Ageloff was very ambitious when it came to setting his nimble and unrestrained mind.

This was going to be Hanover Sterling's first full year of operation. He had a sweet deal. He was pulling in 45 percent of the trading profits. That amounted to a million or so bucks a year, and he declared every penny of it to the IRS. Roy Ageloff could make big-time money legally, for that was the beauty of Wall Street, which had jobs for the up-and-comers and the silver-spoon crowd alike. Roy was no silver-spoon baby. He was a guy from a lower middle-class family. And now he had arrived. Hanover had arrived.

Every morning he drove out of the garage of his beautiful, big, wide, brick, massively windowed new house at 163 Ardsley Street, and drove in one of his gorgeous new cars over to Clarke and the expressway and the bridge to the city. He came in to the office whenever he wanted. He was boss. Not boss on paper, but the real boss. The paper boss, Lowell Schatzer, had a little office near the front entrance. Roy had the corner office, with a view looking northeast over the bridges, over the Fulton Fish Market, toward Queens and the majestic Midtown skyline.

What a house it was. It had to be big. People, in his world, judged you on what you owned, how you dressed, how you lived. His new house was twice the size of both halves of the house on Blythe. It had huge vaultlike windows etched in a fine Beaux Arts pattern. There was a gazebo to the side of the house. Out front, cast-iron street lamps. Big ones with hanging white globes, five for each lamp, the kind that public buildings used to have in the days when public buildings were built to impress the public. Roy's house wasn't a mansion but rather an institution in only the best sense of the word. It could have been a small-town city hall or maybe a library or courthouse somewhere, in a town with a historic preservation movement.

What a transition for a kid from Brooklyn. He grew up there. Was proud of it. He was from Midwood, the Brooklyn of tough Jews, and Roy was a tough Jew. His house in Midwood, a two-family house—the Ageloffs had the left side—was shabby and had TV antennas on the top and was a short block north of Kings Highway, the main shopping street. Through the 1970s, one of the borough's last hangouts for tough Jews was still going strong on Kings Highway, out by the D-train station. It was the last of the old

Jewish cafeterias in Brooklyn, Dubrow's. The Irish had bars, the Italians had social clubs, while the Jews had candy stores and cafeterias. But the neighborhood got older, the tough Jews died or moved to Florida, just as Roy's parents did. The cafeteria closed. All the old Jewish cafeterias in the city closed, quietly, unnoticed and unmourned, by the mid-1980s. The last, another Dubrow's, shut in 1985. It was on Seventh Avenue, in the Garment District, where there were still a few aging, tough Jews.

Roy might have gone into the garment business fifty years before. But the barriers had come down. Democracy had come to Wall Street. Working-class guys were in the front office. They were manning trading desks and working on the floor of the New York Stock Exchange and selling people terrific little stocks, penny stocks. You didn't need an MBA to succeed in penny stocks or squatting at a trading desk or screaming out orders on the exchange floor. What you needed were the kind of inborn characteristics that come from being on the street. The ability to talk, to persuade, and maybe to lead. Roy had all that. He was a powerhouse broker. Okay, not educated. He failed the Series 7 test—that's the one all the brokers had to take, testing you on dividend yields and ethics and other crap—twice before he passed. But everybody on Wall Street knew that the Series 7 didn't measure what you really needed to become a broker—which was in your guts as much as it was in your head.

Roy got his start on Wall Street at an outfit that employed guys like him—guys who could sell. Guys who knew the gambling mentality because investors were really gamblers at heart, so many of them. He got his training at a place called J. T. Moran & Company. When Roy knew him, in 1987 and 1988, John T. Moran was a young guy, in his early thirties. He had just started the firm a year before. He had a respectable background. He was a man of moderation—a nonsmoker.

"He had very loyal employees," said one former Moran broker who worked at the firm in the 1980s. "But he'd always use the analogy: 'Whoever's not producing, and selling so many shares of this stock or that stock or that bond, was only a footstep away from that hot dog stand outside. Now, what would you rather do,' he'd say. 'Be Giussepe at that hot dog stand or here being a stockbroker selling stocks?' They were always 'tomorrow' stocks. Not making money today, but tomorrow—just you wait and see."

Moran's brokers could sell that kind of hope. Blue chips were yesterday stocks. Penny stocks were stocks for the future. Dream stocks. Not dreary, dull, boring stocks like utilities that paid penny-ante dividends. These were little companies, start-ups, fresh companies. Sure, they hadn't started making money. Of course not. Neither did IBM and GM when they were starting out, neither did Thomas Edison before he got that lightbulb in the stores.

They didn't cost in the pennies, really. "Penny stock" was like a lot of dumb Wall Street expressions, this one coming from the old days when penny stocks literally cost in the pennies. By the 1980s, all that a "penny stock" was, in the generally used definition of the term, was a stock that sold for under $5. And they weren't always "stocks" at all, but very often they were sold to the public as "units." A unit included a share of stock and something called a "warrant," which is basically a piece of paper that you can convert into stock at a specific price in a specified period of time. Kind of Wall Street's version of those nice coupons the A&P sometimes gives you on the back of the checkout receipt—buy five more rolls of toilet paper at 50 cents off!

What great stocks. Brokers like Roy could sell them because these stocks sold themselves. There was Phonetel, which had pay phones in a bunch of terrific shopping centers in Ohio. There was Hygolet Brill, which made a brand-new type of toilet seat, specially hygienic, satisfying a need of many people on the go. There was another outfit that sold respirators for people and horses alike—a company as clean and fresh as the air itself. And then there was Moran. The company was underwriting its own debt, selling bonds in the company to the public. Getting a piece of a mint company like Moran was maybe the biggest thing the company had to offer at all. Every broker has to sell himself, and so was Moran. Selling himself. Literally.

Roy moved on to another firm in April 1988—you had to keep moving, keep seeking opportunities—but Moran kept on growing, kept on getting brokers and customers and stocks to sell. By 1989 it wasn't a small brokerage anymore. It was becoming one of the biggest brokerage firms on Wall Street that sold stocks to the public, one of the top twenty, with three hundred brokers.

Moran never got much bad press or publicity of any kind. So it came as something of a surprise when the firm shut down at the beginning of 1990. But the real shocker came on June 26, 1991, when John Moran was indicted by a federal grand jury in Brooklyn. The indictment said that Moran used brokers to push stock on the public at inflated prices— including the shares of his own holding company, the one that was issuing the bonds, J. T. Moran Financial. Moran and three other top Moran officials pleaded guilty.

Moran's stocks were basically selling at prices that John Moran determined. It was a bit like a horse race in which the fillies in win, place, and show are all predetermined, and where even the amounts paid out at the pari-mutuel windows are fixed in advance. Stocks were easier to dope than any horse, because Thoroughbreds have minds of their own and can run out of control, no matter what the jockeys want. A stock is not like that. A stock can be controlled more surely than any fifteen-hundred-pound filly. A stock is more like a trotter. A horse at a trot can be controlled. For years the trotters had a bad rap among gamblers, a rap that they were fixed maybe a little too often. Penny stocks had that kind of rap. Blinder Robinson & Company and First Jersey Securities, which glommed most of the publicity, and other outfits like Hibbard Brown and Investors Center, gave penny stocks that kind of reputation.

Moran was just as big as First Jersey and Blinder, and he never received a fraction of the attention while he was still in business. There were a few penny stock prosecutions here and there, some people actually being sent to jail. But Blinder Robinson's Meyer Blinder and First Jersey's boss Robert Brennan kept prosecutors at bay for years, and they were overshadowed by other financial miscreants. This was the time when the insider trading/arbitrageur/junk bond scandals were dominating the financial news, when Michael Milken and Drexel Burnham Lambert and Ivan Boesky and Dennis Levine were all mired in the public consciousness as a kind of massive pinstriped mélange. Penny stock scamsters, who actually ripped off the public, were definitely not on the front burner—when they were on the stove at all.

Stay out of the papers. It was a lesson Ageloff could have learned if he had been paying attention. He was a small fry at J. T. Moran, and his name never surfaced at the time, but if he was game he would have found the key to success, or at least to nonfailure, in his world: Avoid publicity. Don't attract SEC attention. Keep out of the limelight and, if possible, out of the brokerage entirely. Don't put your name on the books at all—at least not as a manager, not if you can avoid it. And there were other lessons, lessons that Moran didn't learn, but that Roy did, after he was boss.

They were not lessons that Louis had to learn—or even know about—when he was at Hanover. In fact, when he first started work at Hanover he only faintly knew that Wall Street existed. He knew that it was a street way downtown, and that his mother used to work there. He also knew that his mother didn't want him to work there. Not that he cared.

In fact, Louis didn't have the slightest idea what business Roy was in. But he knew that Hanover Sterling had to be a cool place. From the little he saw of Roy, he saw that Roy would be a good guy to work for. He had a kind of charisma, a magnetism. Louis knew that even from the short time he had seen Roy at the gas station.

First he had to get a suit. Louis had one his mother had gone with him to buy a couple of years before, but he had outgrown it and the thing was stupid anyway, out of style. So Louis went to Oaktree in the Staten Island Mall and bought a nice $90 suit. Navy blue. Nice material. But Oaktree brand, cheap. It still had its factory creases the following day, when he took the Staten Island Rapid Transit to the ferry terminal at St. George.

If Louis had looked carefully at the skyline on the way over on the ferry, he could have seen 88 Pine Street. You could just make it out, if the sun angle was right. Pine was the first street north of Wall, and its name went back to the days when maybe there really were trees in Lower Manhattan, as well as a wall. Pine was a narrow vestige of the old Dutch days, barely four car-widths wide. The Hanover habitat was a block from the East River waterfront, where Pine intersects with Water Street, which is spacious and used to have an El train before the Third Avenue El was shut down in the early 1950s.

In those days, the organized crime of the waterfront—the shakedowns, the loan-sharking, the strong-arm rackets—were about as alien to Wall Street as the burly, tough-talking longshoremen who had their own separate world down by the Wall Street waterfront. They existed, for all purposes and intents, on a separate planet from the men in suits in the offices high above, on Wall and the adjoining streets. But there were intersections. Confluences of interest. For years, the Street was beset by Mob-linked securities-theft rings, with one, never apprehended, operated by a crew calling itself the "Forty Thieves" that worked out of a bar across South Street from the fish market.

Elsewhere in the city, Guys occasionally surfaced in stock scams. A Brooklyn gangster named Carmine Lombardozzi made the papers in the 1960s as the "The Doctor"—the Mob's Wall Street "financial wizard" and "money launderer." "Johnny Dio" Dioguardi, an old-school Garment District gangster best known for supposedly blinding columnist Victor Riesel, was sent to prison in 1973 for his role in a stock-manipulation scheme.

The Mob's early stock scams were small operations, profitable but scattered. The Street's potential was never exploited. It wasn't anything like the fish market, which was a franchise handed down from father to son to cousin over the decades. By the early 1990s the Mob's days in the Fulton Fish Market were numbered. But they were not over just yet. The last Guys in charge of the Fulton market, Alphonse "Allie Shades" Malangone and Alan Longo and Vincent Romano, would park their cars downstairs from 88 Pine, in the lot where the Hanover brokers parked their cars, and not pose as they got their blurry pictures taken by the cops. Roy could look down and see them. And that made sense. I. M. Pei, the noted Japanese architect, designed 88 Pine for the men in the suits, to look down, literally and in every other way, on the waterfront directly below. In the words of the *AIA Guide to New York City*, this "white, crisp elegance of aluminum and glass" was "the classiest new building in Lower Manhattan."

When Hanover moved to 88 Pine in June 1992, it was one of the very few times that Hanover made the papers back then. The *New York Law Journal* reported that this "stock brokerage firm" had relocated to Pine from 5 Hanover Square. "This was an excellent opportunity for Hanover Sterling to acquire the space it needed to accommodate its continuing growth," the leasing agent was quoted as saying. The *Law Journal* went on to point out that "the company has doubled in size in the past few years."

Louis was entering a growth business.

CHAPTER FOUR

Louis had no idea where he was.

He arrived at 88 Pine Street at about nine-thirty. It was a large building and Roy worked in an office that seemed to employ a lot of people. That was about all he could figure out.

"I was scared," said Louis. "I got out of the elevator and at the end of the hall there's a big reception area. I ask the lady behind the desk, 'What is this place?' And she says it's a brokerage firm. So I say, 'I'm here to see Mr. Ageloff.' And she says he ain't in yet. Take a seat. So I sat there. I'm dying. And the girl says to me, 'He's always late like this.' So I'm waiting. I see people walking back and forth. Nobody's saying anything to me."

There wasn't much traffic in and out. The secretary spent most of her time making personal calls, and Louis leafed through a copy of *Crain's New York Business* that happened to be there. It was not a recent issue. It would not be interesting to Louis, or understandable, even if it were still warm from the presses. Louis tried reading it but then put it down and stared at the wall.

Roy arrived shortly before noon. He passed Louis without saying anything. Five unbearable minutes went by before the receptionist told Louis to walk down the corridor until the far hallway, and then turn left.

Roy's office was in the corner facing the East River. It was the kind of view you had to pay to see at the World Trade Center or Empire State Building.

"Sit down. I want to introduce you to somebody," said Roy. He walked outside and came back with a guy he introduced as Mark Savoca.

Mark was a young guy, just twenty-three. They shook hands. Mark asked Louis to come with him. They left Roy's office, walked past the receptionist, and Mark pushed the button for the elevator. They waited. The elevator arrived.

Louis had no idea what Mark was doing, and the thought passed his mind that he must have done something they didn't like and now was getting his ass kicked out of the building.

When the elevator reached the lobby, Mark walked toward the revolving doors. Louis followed. Mark was acting as if he didn't care whether Louis came or not.

It was cold, with gusts of icy wet air from the East River. Mark walked ahead, not saying anything. They went up Water Street, north toward the Seaport. In the parking lot across a side street from 88 Pine, Mark stopped and pointed. It was a Stealth. "I been doing this for a year and this is what I've gotten," said Mark.

Louis practically collapsed. A Dodge Stealth! What the fuck! Even though it was only a $30,000 car, Louis was impressed. Whoa! "A Dodge Stealth is the biggest car at that time. A Dodge Stealth is awesome," said Louis, recalling the moment.

"He says to me, 'When I came in here I had nothing. I couldn't even afford a car or an apartment. But now I live in Manhattan. I have a beautiful apartment. I have a Dodge Stealth and I go out to dinner seven days a week.' He says it took him a year to go on his own. The first month he was on his own he made fifteen, sixteen grand."

That was the highlight of the day—the Stealth. Louis could get a car, an apartment, a life. He wouldn't have to wait until he was thirty or forty. He wouldn't have to flip burgers at the goddamn McDonald's, as he did one lousy summer, or stack boxes at Consumers Warehouse. He hated jobs like that, with their dumb rules and their moronic supervisors, guys he hated, guys who hated him because he sneered at their dumb way of doing things. At McDonald's they had asinine rules for fixing burgers. The way they did it the bun was cold when he put on the burger. He wanted to heat the bun first. Got into a big fight. Lost his job. It was the same in high school, at St. Josephs-by-the-Sea. He aced calculus classes without studying and he would tell the teacher that there was more than one way to solve the problem, no one right way. But she always wanted it done her way. The bitch.

At Hanover Sterling he could get great stuff and still be young and not have to put up with stupid middle-aged ass-holes telling him what to do. Everybody there was young and cool.

Back upstairs, Mark flipped through a midnight-black three-ring binder—his "client book." He went through the procedures Louis would have to follow if he wanted a Stealth and an apartment of his own. You get yourself clients, you call up "leads"—potential customers—you tell them your name, and you pitch them stocks. And if they buy, they're your clients.

"But I don't know what he's talking about. I never heard of Wall Street in my life. I didn't know what a 'client' was, never mind a 'new issue.' He walks me around the boardroom, shows me what everybody does. He shows me the quote ma-chines. Meanwhile, I don't have any concept of what he's showing me," said Louis.

But Louis wasn't dumb. For an hour and a half he just sat there listening while Mark was on the phone, pitching people.

Louis paid attention. It was easy. All his life he had been a good talker. All he had to do was talk.

After a while he was summoned back to see Roy.

"You interested?" Roy asked him.

Louis was interested. The only problem was that he had just started a semester at the College of Staten Island.

Roy asked him how much it cost. Louis told him—$900.

Roy reached into his pocket, took out a money clip, and peeled off nine $100 bills. "Come back at seven in the morning," said Roy.

It was pitch-black out when Louis got up the next morning. There were still bums on the ferry. It was cold, miserable, but Louis would have gone to Hanover Sterling stark naked if Roy had asked him.

Louis was put to work in the "boardroom." It was a weird use of the word, which most people associate with long tables surrounded by retired rear admirals and other members of corporate boards of directors. In the chop houses, the boardrooms were big rooms for all the brokers and cold-callers. Every firm had its own arrangement. At Hanover the desks were arranged in clusters, and people would work together in teams. Well, "teams" is what they called them most places on Wall Street. The chop houses called them "crews." And the guys in the crews were all very much like Louis.

These were kids from the boroughs and the close-in suburbs. Kids who had gone to community college or no college at all. White "ethnics," the Manhattan snobs would call them. Guys who spoke with New York accents. In Manhattan, people didn't talk like that anymore if they could help it. If you had any kind of standing in Manhattan, you worked hard to eradicate that way of talking. Not Roy. Not the kids in the boardrooms.

Years ago the kids in the boardrooms couldn't have made it into the front office. If they had worked hard and gotten MBAs maybe they could have gotten assistant-trader gigs at second-tier firms. But these kids didn't have MBAs. Some of them could barely read. They couldn't have gotten any firm to hire them as brokers, not when it was the 1980s and the market was booming and the Street was filled with ambitious preppies trying to make it in the business. Kids without fancy college degrees could have made it only to the back office, slogging along as clerks like Fran Pasciuto, or maybe working in the offices where brokerage trades are executed. But the penny stock era, the era that was coming to an end in the early 1990s, started to put the street kids in the front offices.

Now the chop house era was beginning and the street kids were everywhere. Hanover Sterling was at the forefront of this socioeconomic-demographic revolution on Wall Street. In the boroughs and the burbs, word was spreading, fed by word of mouth and ads in the city's tabloids. The Street was looking for ambitious kids from the street.

Stefanie Donohue was excited about Louis's new job.

They had met the year before, in the record-hot summer of 1991. Louis had just graduated from Sea, Stefanie from Tottenville High School. The Donohues could afford Sea but felt its rules and its uniforms and its discipline weren't necessary. Stefanie and her brothers were nice kids. They could be trusted. Stefanie and Louis were about as different as any two people could be and still be in the same species.

Stefanie's family was comfortably middle class, quiet, maybe a little repressed in an Irish Catholic way. But a little repression wouldn't have done Louis any harm—which might have been the appeal. George Donohue was a retired policeman who ran a bar on Coney Island Avenue in Midwood, the neighborhood where Roy Ageloff had spent his formative years. By the time George wound up at the Seventieth Precinct, the Jewish population was being fast supplanted by a kind of polyglot stew of nationalities—resulting in some interesting grocery stores and a boring array of domestic strife and postmidnight mayhem. There were Russians and Pakistanis and Arabs and Haitians. George served in plainclothes most of his time at the Seven-oh.

George was a Brooklyn boy himself, and his family wasn't exactly prosperous, but George did well for himself. He was proud of what he had overcome, what he had accomplished, but he didn't boast. He served in Vietnam as a military policeman but didn't like to talk about it. George didn't talk much. He didn't have to. A glance was enough. Voices weren't raised much in the Donohue household. George had a "don't give me any shit" glance that could sting as hard as the back of a hand. George wasn't old-country strict but he wasn't going to let his kids run around like skells—and they didn't. Gender roles were unambiguous. Generational differences were not bridged. The kids weren't pals. They were offspring. End of discussion.

Well, not really end of discussion. George had another old-fashioned virtue: loyalty. The Donohue kids could get into trouble, even bad trouble at times, but the love was unconditional. You were part of the family. You made mistakes, you screwed up, but you could always come home. George had known misfortune in those close to him. He didn't like to talk about it. But it showed up in the way he acted. No kid of his, no one close to him, was ever going to be without support.

So as a teenager, Stefanie's normal rebellion was muted. She worked. She obeyed. She had values. Her life revolved around close friends and a close family. She did normal things on summer nights. Bars. Clubs.

STEFANIE: "I was at a bar on Bay Street, which is where a lot of kids hung out. I was at the bar with two of my friends. A friend of his, Mike, comes up to me with two of his friends and says, 'You know my friend Lou?' I say I don't know him.

"Mike says, 'He wants to meet you.'

"I say, 'I don't care.'

"'Do you want to hang out with him?'

"'I don't know.'

"Louis was about twenty-five feet away. He looked like a skinny kid. He had long hair, punky clothes on. His pants were below his belt. He was wearing a little T-shirt. A hat down to his nose. He was with a group of kids. I knew a lot of his friends, kids he went to school with at Sea."

LOUIS: "I just had a mad attraction to her from the first time I saw her. It was that innocent look. Very innocent. She had blond hair—I love blondes. Tall, five-eight. And she was very, like, quiet. It was nice. To me, in my eyes she was beautiful. Like I'm very attracted to her. She was Irish. I had mainly gone with Italian girls. She went to public school. Maybe her parents didn't have the money.

"Usually I would hang out with the girl, go with the girl and not think about them. But with Stefanie, I was thinking about her. The next day I was, like, 'I got to call this girl.' When I went home I told my friend Mike Layden, I said 'Mike, I want to make this girl my girlfriend.'"

STEFANIE: "I thought he was nice and everything—cute. The next night I saw him we exchanged numbers. But then he didn't want to go home. He said, 'Can you drop me off at my friend Mike's house?' I thought it was strange, so I said, 'Where's Mike? Where was he tonight?' And he says, 'Oh, he didn't come out.' And I said, 'You're living with this friend?'

"I thought it was strange. So he says, 'My mother, we got into a fight, so she threw me out and I'm staying here for a couple of days.' He gave me Mike's number and his house number, and I gave him my number. I thought it was a little odd that he was thrown out."

Louis had a girlfriend with a loving family, a source of stability and limits in her life. Stefanie had a boyfriend who was a bit wild and on the edge, something that was absent in her stable and sane and loving but, maybe, slightly dull family.

They had a normal courtship, the Italian street kid and the cloistered Irish girl. Their lives were happy. Their parents approved.

CHAPTER FIVE

I do not like them, Sam-I-Am. I do not like Green Eggs and Ham.

The first time he read from *Green Eggs and Ham* at Hanover Sterling, Louis thought it was dumb. He wasn't mad. He was just annoyed, a little, but he accepted it. It was okay. Not much of a price to pay if he was going to make good money. He hadn't read Dr. Seuss since he was a kid, and maybe not even then—not out loud anyway. Roy would have them read from it at the meetings they had in the morning. And you did what Roy told you to do.

So they would read *Green Eggs and Ham*. They would take turns reading lines from it. That's not the only weird shit Roy would do in the morning. Sometimes he would have one of the brokers, Benny Salmonese, "do the monkey."

"Benny's a big, stocky guy—looks like a monkey," said Louis. "So Roy would have him stand in the middle of everybody, all the hundred brokers, and act like a monkey. That's the kind of place it was—crazy." Crazy—but fun. Crazy—but lots of money. And that's what mattered.

He had never had a job he liked, never gotten up early for anybody. But yes! He could do it! He had it, he had a job that offered him what he wanted, and he was motivated. He belonged. He could get up early. He could take the ferry and do what other people told him to do. Imagine that—somebody actually told him to do something and he didn't rebel against it.

In the past he did not like it, would not do what other people told him. Would not do it in his school, would not do it in his home, would not do it anywhere. But now he did it in an office, now he did it in a firm, now he did it for Roy.

I do so like green eggs and ham!

He loved Hanover. "Those were the best times that I can remember," said Louis. "Every day was a great day. Roy was nothing but fun." Sure, it was tough. He would have to drag himself out of bed very early, five, to make it to the Great Kills station of the Staten Island Rapid Transit and then the ferry and then the walk to Pine Street. And then—*Green Eggs and Ham.* Every morning. It was a ritual, a crazy fun ritual. Who knew why Roy did it? Nobody asked him and he wouldn't have said if anyone had asked. Maybe it was just fucking off. Or maybe it was Roy's way of letting them know every day that they were going to do what Roy wanted, even if that meant eating green or black or blue eggs and ham. Sure, the *Green Eggs and Ham* readings were kid stuff. Roy had kids of his own and the brokers were a bit like his kids too.

Most of the brokers and cold-callers at Hanover were just out of high school like Louis. Hanover was a Staten Island outfit. Roy was from Staten Island, and so was his partner Bobby Catoggio and so was Lowell Schatzer, who was on the papers as president of Hanover Sterling. Nobody paid much attention to Lowell.

It was a different kind of Wall Street. Spirited. "'Buy fucking Porter!' If you walk into Shearson Lehman, they'll be sitting there, quiet. We were, like, yelling, 'Yaaaaaaaaah!' It was crazy," said Louis. "We'd work from seven in the morning to eleven at night, nonstop. Pump those phones, man. It was awesome. Best training I ever had, there." But this was no button-down operation. He learned that fast. "Always some-body smoking a joint downstairs. Everybody'd get stoned during lunch," said Louis.

Sure, Roy had to make a fist every now and then. The bro-kers had to be kept in line. It was like St. Joseph-by-the-Sea. Tough kids. Corporal punishment.

"Every day, people would get beat up," said Louis. "One kid never used to wear a shirt and tie. One day Roy broke his nose. Right at the meeting. 'Come here.' Crack! Punched him right in his face. Kid's nose was all bleeding. He was crying. But Roy and Bobby ran the joint. That was it. Everybody was petrified of him. I couldn't even go into Roy's office without getting abused. I used to, like, stick my head in and he'd go, 'You little Staten Island fag, get the fuck in here!'"

But Louis didn't mind. It was okay. Roy yelled and hit but so did his father. People in authority yelled and hit. Besides, at Hanover he never got smacked—which made Roy an im-provement over his father. Wasn't necessary. Louis didn't need to get smacked. He didn't give Roy shit the way he gave his father shit, and the way he gave the priests at Sea shit. Why would he? No cause for that. He was making money. He was really diligent, not "put-on-an-act" diligent.

He started out like everybody else, making cold calls but not selling anything. "Qualifying leads," it was called. The "leads" being customers, the "qualifying" meaning that the cold-callers wanted to find out if there was any point in call-ing these people. You don't sell stock to a guy who owns noth-ing but mutual funds, any more than you'd get on the phone and peddle ham hocks to those bearded Hassidic guys Louis saw when he drove through Borough Park. Only beginners qualified leads. Louis wasn't a beginner for very long.

"So on my first day I went to the kid Chris Girodet. I walked in, sat down, he handed me the leads and explained what to do. Now I still have no idea what I'm doing. He says, 'Here's a stack of these leads'—he's explaining it to me. 'Call the number, ask for this guy. If he gets on the phone, you tell him, "This is Chris Girodet from Hanover Sterling. What I'd like to do is send you out some information, and get to know what kind of investor you are.' This is not a sales call, you tell him right away, or they would hang up the phone," said Louis.

It was easy. All he was doing was feeling people out, prepping them for the brokers. But Louis was paying attention. He was listening. He heard the way the brokers were pitching stock. He could do that.

But Chris Girodet didn't want him to do that. He just wanted Louis to qualify leads. He didn't give a shit about schooling him, what the rest of the Street would call mentoring. Louis knew that he wasn't going to get a Stealth and an apartment, not as a cold-caller. He had to move up.

Fortunately, Roy took a liking to Louis. After a while he introduced him to the best broker at the firm, Chris Wolf, and one day he had Louis hang out in the office with Chris and his partner Rocco Basile. Louis listened to them pitch for an hour or two.

Louis was in the presence of genius.

"Man, he was good. Definitely one of the best salesmen I've seen. Chris is about five feet four or five. Long, pushed-back hair. Good-looking kid. Real name's not Wolf. It's Italian. He's an Italian kid. Changed his name to Wolf for his Series 7 broker license. That's the name he chose to do business. Great name, Chris Wolf. Jewish much better than Italian last name," said Louis.

"So I listened to him, and he had this thing that he did when he opened accounts. Somebody would say I'm not interested, blah blah blah. Chris would say, 'Okay, take care.' Then Chris would call them back thirty seconds later and he'd say, 'You know, Bob, I just gave you that investment opportunity and I'd be an asshole to let you off the phone. It's an outstanding situation. All I'm looking is for you to buy one share or a thousand shares—it don't matter. It's not the dollar amount. Give me a chance to show you percentage gains. Because you know and I know that if I show you forty percent on paper, I'm going to be the broker you're going to be doing business with year-round.' Blah blah blah. So you beat him up till he buys the stock."

Louis paid attention. The next morning he called one of his leads and pitched him. He used the whole spiel, and after the guy hung up he did a callback and talked about being an asshole to let him off the phone. Blah blah blah.

It worked. The guy bought a thousand shares.

"I get off the phone and I'm screaming, 'A thousand shares! I opened a thousand shares!' And then Chris Girodet came over and he's mad I used his name and opened an account. I went to Roy. I said, 'Roy, I opened an account. I took the pitch, I pitched the account, I opened it.' And Roy comes out of his office and says to Chris, 'If this kid wants to open accounts, he opens accounts. This is my protégé.'

"He cut my tie—that's what they do when you open your first account. They cut your tie. It's like a traditional thing. So I'm walking around with no tie. It's great. I opened my first account. And I opened an account every day since then."

At this point Louis hadn't passed the Series 7, which is the test, administered by the National Association of Securities Dealers, or NASD, that gives brokers the solemn right to sell stocks to the public. He also wasn't supposed to be using Chris Girodet's name. During his pitch he guaranteed profits, which was another no-no. But at Hanover Sterling, all this fell under the category of "big fucking deal."

After that, Louis became a pitching fiend. Pitching to everybody. Pitching to himself in the mirror. Pitching to Stefanie, to his father.

Louis was a natural at getting people to do things. He had been manipulating people since he was a kid. He had the knack, the instinct.

"How are they going to say no to me? 'Grab a pen. Grab a pen.' I'd say it sixty times. 'Grab a pen. Grab a pen.' And that would be it. They would grab a pen, and then I would rip them to shreds. And then they'd be like, 'Oh, I don't really want any.' I'd say, 'Of course you don't want any.' Sometimes I used to fucking kill them. 'Of course you don't want any. You're in Texas. You don't know anything about the market. You probably don't have a TV antenna down there.'"

Selling was an interactive thing. That's why scripts were dumb. With scripts you talked "at" people. To sell, you had to get into the other guy's head. You had to engage in a dialogue. Talking with, not talking at. He was now in the realm of the kind of relationship that would define his life—the relationship between thief and victim.

That was the division of the world. The takers and the taken. Louis was planting himself firmly on the side that was going to prevail.

CHAPTER SIX

Benny Salmonese didn't have any problem with "doing the monkey." It was okay with him. Most things were okay with Benny. That was the kind of guy he was. Easygoing. Benny was a jovial, hefty Brooklyn kid, half Italian and half Puerto Rican, and he had grown up on the streets of Bensonhurst. He was also hardworking. A talented salesman. A people person, in a street-kid kind of way.

"Benny was cool. Benny had a unique style on the phone. It was like, 'Heyyyyyyyyyy'—somebody would pick up the phone, and he'd be like 'Heyyyyyyyyyyyyy, Ben Salmonese here. Hanover Sterling.' We used to listen to him and he'd sit with the phone down on the desk, and he wouldn't touch the phone. He'd just bend over and talk into it. I started doing that too. I got that from him. I didn't pitch like him but I started doing that," said Louis.

Benny was Louis's best friend at Hanover. He tried to learn from Benny just as he tried to learn from everybody. Louis was becoming something that no one could ever have dreamed that he would be—a workaholic. It was a disease that was sweeping Wall Street in the early 1990s. Not that Louis cared—he and the rest of the Hanover kids had about as much to do with the rest of Wall Street as they did with the

Paris Bourse—even though Wall Street, the literal Wall Street, was so close that they could walk to it holding their breath and not get winded. The Hanover kids were a couple of blocks from the pinstriped young preppies who filled the trainee programs at J. P. Morgan and Merrill Lynch and Nomura but they were from different class backgrounds, different neighborhoods, and different schools—if they had bothered to finish school. They were an old-style New York neighborhood mix of Italians and Jews, almost all guys, while the white shoe firms were populated by suburban WASPs and out-of-towners and Jews from the East Side and a growing and increasingly slightly tolerated number of young women with short hair and tailored suits. Bedford vs. Massapequa. Yale vs. St. John's. You could see the difference from a distance, and you could hear the difference without seeing the difference.

What the Hanover kids had in common with the rest of the Street was a kind of all-encompassing, obsessive love of money. It was a great deal to have in common. For Louis, anyone who came in the way of that love affair would not be welcome no matter who it might be—whether it was the government or his fellow brokers. Not all of them shared his love of money and his desire to work hard for money. Not all of them paid him what he was owed. Some wanted to stiff him. Some of them, he complained to Roy, were thieves. After going through a succession of deadbeat broker bosses, Roy put him with the honest (to Louis), hardworking power broker John Lembo. But Chris and Rocco remained his pals and role models.

Louis didn't want anything to do with scrubs, guys who weren't into the money the way he was. John Lembo, Chris Wolf, and Rocco Basile—they were top brokers, and young. There were like him. They knew their business. They were committed. "None of the rest were into it," said Louis. "One guy they assigned me to, he didn't want to come in on Saturdays. I wanted to come in on Saturdays and work. I couldn't unless the broker that I was working for was there. I was always the last one there. Roy used to come back from going out, and I'd be the only one left, with like two other people."

The checks were announced every month. "Chris Wolf, he's not even twenty-three at the time, getting a $112,000 check— in a month! Other kids were getting checks, twenty-year-old kids were getting checks for $20,000, $26,000 for the month. Roy used to pass out the checks and announce the names. 'Joe Blow, $110,600!' And everybody would be like, 'Yaaaay, Joe!'

"Roy used to make the whole firm go into the boardroom and hand out the checks. He'd be like, 'Chris Girodet, $16,400. John Lembo, $21,300.' Rocco and Chris Wolf always got the most money. 'Rocco Basile $110,000. Chris Wolf $112,000—$40,000 in fines.' He would be fined a lot. It would come off his commissions. Fines—coming in no tie, $5,000. Coming in late, $3,000 fine. Roy used to fine him left and right. Because he wouldn't listen to Roy. But Roy would never fire Chris because he was a powerhouse."

Chris didn't even care about the fines. "Whatever," he'd say. That attitude, shrugging at fines the size of his father's annual paycheck, pumped up Louis. He wanted to get $112,000 checks. He wanted to get that attitude toward money.

Roy wanted people producing and he wanted to keep their spirits up—and in check. Even though he had never spent a day in a school like Sea, he seemed to have an instinctive knack for managing kids from parochial schools.

"Everybody took lunch at the same time. Literally the whole firm was going downstairs. You took lunch from twelve to one. Roy better not find you eating lunch after one o'clock, or he'd rip your head off. He used to throw it out. He'd throw out people's breakfasts too. He used to come to the desk, see someone eating breakfast after eight o'clock, used to take the fucking bagel out of his mouth, throw it in the garbage. And say, 'Before seven-thirty. Otherwise, don't eat.' Later on I treated my cold-callers like that. I used to throw their lunches out. Or not give them lunch. I got a lot of my ways from him."

Roy imbued Hanover with a corporate culture, a mind-set that was infectious. It was a tough place to work. A hard place to work. A hard place, with hard people.

A Guy named Fat George used to come up to Hanover and yell at Roy now and then. Roy would close the door, roll down the blinds, and you could hear the yelling. Muffled screaming. It was a kind of angry screaming, sort of the way people yell when they are being screwed by a car dealer and the manager isn't able to do anything to make it better and the customer has lost it, and is ready to march off to the attorney general. That kind of screaming. "He'd always be yelling at Roy, 'WHAT THE FUCK!' 'THIS IS WHAT YOU MAKE THE KIDS DO!' 'THIS IS FUCKING NUTS!' 'IT'S LIKE A FUCKING HOODLUM AREA HERE!'" And Roy would take it. You could always hear Fat George through the closed glass doors but you could never hear Roy yelling back. "When you shut the blinds you always knew there were gangsters there," said Louis.

There were the rumors that Roy had people behind him. Guys. That a Guy named Allie Shades—Alphonse Malagone, the Genovese family skipper from the Fulton Fish Market a few blocks away—was the power behind Hanover.

But they were only rumors and Louis didn't give a shit about rumors. If there were really Guys behind the scenes at Hanover, he would have to see them with his own two eyes if he was going to believe it.

And even if it was true, so what?

part two

FUCK-YOU MONEY

CHAPTER SEVEN

Chris Wolf had to get his safe back. Someone had taken it and it had to be returned. If the safe was not returned, someone was going to get shot. It didn't matter how many people were around. Black Dom and the rest of them were going to use those machine guns.

The trouble began at the due dilly the night before. If the due dilly hadn't been a fiasco, they wouldn't have stolen the safe and—well, it was a mess, no question. Louis had seen his share of messes. Had caused some. But the mess that began at the due dilly party for Porter McLeod was a mess to end all messes.

Due dillies were always fun. This one was for a company called Porter McLeod National Retail Inc., which was about to go public in July 1993, using Hanover as the underwriter. Louis, who spent many hours describing its virtues to potential investors, hadn't the slightest recollection, some years later, as to what the company did or even what industry it was in. In fact, Porter McLeod performed a function vital to American retailers. The company was a general contractor, based in Denver, that provided construction services mainly for national retail firms—building and renovating stores throughout the country. Without outfits like Porter McLeod, stores wouldn't open and, hell, the whole economy could grind to a halt. It was an easy sell. Not that what Porter McLeod did, or if it did anything, mattered one bit. What mattered was that Louis made money from it, and that Lawrence Taylor was at the due dilly.

A former star linebacker with the New York Giants, Lawrence Taylor was a regular at Hanover in the spring of '93. An IPO for his company, All-Pro, was underwritten by Hanover, so he was a frequent visitor to 88 Pine, meeting often with Roy, who was the big Pied Piper for deals at Hanover Sterling. It was always a treat to see the beefy, fire-plug-necked Taylor. The kids at Hanover were devoted sports fans and Louis was genuinely starstruck. Hanging out with Lawrence Taylor was one of the best things about working at Hanover Sterling. Right up there with the money and the due dillies.

Due dillies are enshrined in the securities laws. But like all Wall Street concepts, particularly the ones required by the securities laws, "due diligence" had a special meaning at Hanover Sterling, and was a lot more fun than the Wall Street way of doing things.

When a company is preparing to sell its stock to the public, it has to do so, except in the smallest cases, through an underwriter. That's a fancy name for an investment bank, which is a fancy name for a brokerage house that raises money for companies by selling their stock. The underwriter is subject to all kinds of awful lawsuits unless it "had, after reasonable investigation, reasonable ground to believe and did believe" that there was nothing serious missing from the registration statement. That is the law of the land—so decrees the Securities Act of 1933.

At Hanover, a due dilly meant only one thing—party time!

"You heard 'due dilly,' and it would be like, 'Yeahhhhhhh!' Due dillies were a fucking bash. You went to a due diligence to meet the people who owned the company, and they were supposed to explain to you about the company, tell you what was going on. But that never happened. We'd never do it in an office where a couple of people from the company would make a presentation. It was either in a boat, in Trump Tower, or in Atlantic City. It was always like a huge thing. Roy would have the company pay for it. We weren't celebrating that we were taking a company public, we were celebrating that we were going to make fucking loot," said Louis.

The Porter McLeod due dilly was on a yacht that could barely squeeze into the boat basin at Battery Park City. It was about thirty yards long, with three decks, a dance floor with a live band, two bars, girls nobody had ever seen before, and bedrooms for the girls if the due dilly had lasted long enough. Great food for everybody. The food and the girls were always terrific at due dillies.

After a short speech from Roy, which pumped everybody up the way it always did, the party began, the dance music echoing off the empty Hudson River piers. The boat went up-river at a leisurely pace. It wasn't going anywhere in particular. Just another cruise for another brokerage house. The party was on for about an hour and a half, just started warming up, when Chris Wolf decided to have some fun.

Louis was hanging out at the stern. Music was blaring from the dance floor.

"They're smoking joints on the back of the boat, and this kid Tony was sitting on the railing of the boat," said Louis. "Chris Wolf and this kid John Claudino ran up behind him and flung him off the boat. So he's down in the water.

"As soon as they threw the kid off the boat, everybody ran off the deck. We all went inside. It was like, 'Holy shit.' I mean, he flung the kid off the boat, really flung him. He was in the water awhile. They threw the life saver to him, but they couldn't get him in. They didn't want to bring the boat to him. It wasn't a normal boat. You're not going to bring a ninety-foot boat close to somebody. They'd run him over. The captain was turning around in the water. The Coast Guard came and pulled him out. It was a fucking mess.

"When we got back to the dock, forget about it. Coast Guard, fire department, ambulances, police. People ran off the boat. It was ridiculous."

Lawrence Taylor was hustled away. Louis read in the paper the next day that he wasn't in New York at all that night, but was someplace out of town. It didn't matter. Nobody was talking. No repercussions. No lawsuits. No complaints. The cops tried questioning people, but they didn't get anywhere. The Hanover kids took care of things themselves.

Later that night, Tony's friends tracked down Chris Wolf on lower Broadway.

"I heard they pulled up in a limousine. Chris was walking," says Louis. "One of Tony's friends throws him through a plate-glass window, jumped back in the limo, and pulled away. Chris had a scar across his face for five years after that. He had to get plastic surgery. That scar went from the top of his head all the way down to the bottom of his chin."

At about the time Chris was getting tossed through that window, Louis was also on lower Broadway, bonding with Roy. It was a rare experience, and he savored it.

"When I left the dock, everybody scattered all over the place," said Louis. "People were going here, people were going there, and for some reason Roy just let me go in the limo with him. We took a ride, and we got out and went to Morgan Williams, a bar on Broadway. That's when I found out he used to do mad 'ludes. He handed me a handful of quaaludes and made me hold them for him. That was the first time I really interacted with Roy, went drinking and partying with him. After that the relationship became more, like, not so business. Now he knew me. Now he remembered."

Throwing Chris through the plate-glass window might have evened the score for most people. But the situation escalated the following day.

Louis got in late—seven-thirty. But instead of Roy yelling at him or locking him out, he was sitting in Chris's office. He appeared stressed out. Chris was there, his face covered with bandages and stitches. "I just wandered by the office nonchalantly and Roy says, 'Get me a coffee,'" Louis recalled. He had never seen Roy look so upset before, not even after he had been with Fat George for three hours.

"Usually Hanover Sterling at seven-thirty is like twelve o'-clock in the afternoon, packed. Instead it was just me, Benny and four other guys. Benny says to me, 'They stole Chris's safe.' He's telling me, 'Let's get the fuck out of here!' What happened was—and this was bad—whoever Tony's friends were, they went up and they took Chris Wolf's safe out of his office. Chris would keep money and his client book and other shit in there. Supposedly he had four, five hundred thousand dollars in the safe," said Louis.

Louis got the coffee for Roy, who closed the door. Louis was sitting back at his desk for about five minutes when about a half dozen Guys came walking into the boardroom toward Chris's office. They were carrying submachine guns—Tech Nines. They went in Chris's office and closed the door.

"They were standing there waiting for their safe. I heard later that Chris told Roy that he'd blow up the place if he didn't get his safe back. Black Dom Dionisio was up there, and so was Rico Locascio. They were all up there with him—Dom, Rico, John Claudino, Joe Temperino. All the boys. Chris figured Roy probably knew who took the safe. He didn't want to know who it was. He just wanted to get it back," said Louis.

Black Dom and Rico were both hooked up with a crew in the Colombo family. Black Dom was a nephew of Wild Bill Cutolo, a Colombo skipper. Louis had heard about Dom. What he didn't know then, what he only found out later, was that even though Dom and Rico were there for Chris Wolf, they weren't there for Chris the way Tony's friends had been there for Tony.

It wasn't friendship. It was the same for Chris's crew, his cold-callers. It wasn't friendship for them either. They made money with Chris. Roy could yell at them and fine them and push them around. Somebody could toss Chris through a window. That was okay, no problem. But stealing Chris's safe was out of line.

"Chris Wolf had a crew of psycho kids from Brooklyn. They were just street kids, street-thug kids who came up to Hanover to work. They were nuts. They would have wrestling matches every night after work. From five to six o'clock they would have a wrestling match in Chris's office, between two people in the office. They all bet on it, who would win. Joe Di-Bella and Chris, they would bet five, ten grand on who would win. Then they would take everybody out for drinks," said Louis.

Louis just sat there and read one of the pitches he found on a table. He read it again and again. He looked up long enough to see Bobby Catoggio come by. The door opened and Bobby was pulled in. The door closed again. Louis knew Roy and Bobby were in trouble, but he did the right thing. He minded his own business.

After a while Louis started working the phones—after all, that's what it was all about. Working the phones, making money. Nothing he could do to help Roy. Not with Rico and Black Dom there. Rico and Black Dom were muscle. The bad-news dudes. They said Black Dom was part black. But nobody made too big a deal of it. Some of the boys called him "Nigger Dom," but never to his face. Not to the face of a guy who was six-foot-six of solid muscle.

So Louis did his job and didn't look up and minded his own business. And then—it ended. The guys with the submachine guns left. He looked up—it must have been around lunchtime—and the crisis was over. Sometime later he found out that the safe had been returned.

If Roy was close to Guys, why didn't he call in his Guys to deal with Black Dom and the rest? Was there a reason *not* to have a Guy go to bat for you? Louis thought about that afterward. But it was none of his business.

The boat-toss/glass-throw/safe-stealing incident was forgotten. Everybody went back to work. It was no big deal. Nobody lost any money. That was the most important thing. That was the moral of the story. Money meant you could do anything. Throw people off boats. Throw people through plate-glass windows. Money was more than power. It was a way of life. It was life itself.

The chop house kids were earning a special kind of money. Fuck-you money. It was another concept Louis picked up from Roy and Chris, as they both used the phrase on occasion.

Outside of the chop houses, the term simply meant a sum of money so large that you could tell people—your boss, for example—"fuck you." But it was "fuck you" as in saying to the boss, "Fuck you, I have so much money I don't need you anymore." That's not quite what "fuck-you money" meant in the chop houses. It's meaning was in the realm of giving, not receiving. "It would be like, 'Here's a lot of money. Fuck you. You'll do anything for money,'" said Louis.

Chris gave a demonstration of fuck-you money one winter at Hunter Mountain. That's a ski area that was popular with the chop house kids, kind of a Hamptons with snow, and it was in the Catskill Mountains, over a hundred miles from New York.

"There was this kid Mario," said Louis. "Chris paid the kid forty grand to walk back from Hunter Mountain. He was in the Marines or something. So it was like, fuck-you money. It was for Chris. 'Here's forty grand. Walk back. Fuck you. I can make you do anything I want for a little money. Fuck you.'"

Until Hanover, Louis had lived his life saying "fuck you" without much to show for it, including consequences. Hanover Sterling taught him that he could make a ton of money, not have consequences—and still say "fuck you."

At Hanover, working for the best brokers in the shop, Louis was a star pupil. He was an amazing listener. He picked up from the brokers the best of their techniques and made them his own.

Great as they were, Chris and Rocco and Roy and the rest of the chop house brokers couldn't have accumulated all that fuck-you money without a lot of help.

Nobody helped the chop house brokers more than the people who were supposed to stop them.

CHAPTER EIGHT

Massood Gilani was known to the brokers he dealt with as unfailingly professional and courteous, and always sartorially impeccable. Louis never met this lean, dapper man with a black mustache, but other brokers recalled him with affection. "I used to call him Blue Suede Shoes," said a former chop house broker. "He was always nattily dressed. Real likable."

In 1993, twenty-four years after he emigrated from Iran, Gilani was fifty-four years old and could take satisfaction that he was moving, slowly but inexorably, toward fulfilling the immigrant's version of the American dream. He was a respected professional—an accountant. In his various jobs he had always been conscientious, hardworking, and happy. By the early 1990s he had acquired a sensitive if not prestigious position: compliance examiner in the Special Investigations Unit of the National Association of Securities Dealers, the primary regulator of securities firms in the United States. He worked in the Whitehall Street offices of the NASD's District 10, which had jurisdiction over the hundreds of brokerage firms based in New York.

Gilani was responsible for seeing to it that brokers didn't rip off customers. He took his job seriously. He wasn't in it for the money. Gilani was not paid "fuck you" money. Like most of the officials assigned to investigate the nation's most so-phisticated brokerage firms, he was paid considerably less than the babes who sat behind the tall desks in the chop house reception areas. In 1993 he was paid $34,800 before with-holdings. In 1994 he was promoted to senior compliance ex-aminer and his salary was increased to $38,280.

Like most NASD examiners, even the ones in the elite Special Investigations Unit, Gilani had no Wall Street experience before joining the NASD. He had no experience as an investigator. But it didn't take particularly strong investigative skills to see that some of the firms in District 10 stank worse than the Fulton Fish Market at high noon in July. Or that the worst of them was the one just down the street from the Fulton Market.

Gilani's job included investigating customer complaints. And a disproportionate share of the complaints concerned Hanover.

In the brokerage business, there are complaints and then there are *complaints*. It's not unusual for customers to blame brokers for their own bad stock picks, or for buying stocks for customers that weren't right for them—"unsuitability" is the complaint that brokers get in such instances. That means a broker is not supposed to sell pork belly futures to an old lady about to enter a nursing home. Complaints like that can be serious, or they can be unjustified grousing by customers who are blaming their brokers for their own poor judgment.

But then there are the *complaints*. Such as the ones that came from customers who opened up their statements and found stocks they didn't order.

Complaints like that aren't a sign that the firm is being a wee bit aggressive in its sales practices. They are red flags. When they happen over and over again, they mean the firm is in business to steal.

They are *complaints*.

Hanover got *complaints*.

Usually those complaints would have been locked away in a file drawer, forgotten. And they would have stayed there, gathering dust, if Gilani hadn't gone down the path of becoming a disgruntled employee and then, as so often happens to disgruntled employees, getting fired and becoming a disgruntled former employee.

The lawsuit Gilani filed in late 1996 opened a rare window onto the internal workings of the NASD. His suit claimed he was a victim of racial discrimination. It also claimed that the public was a victim of the NASD. One of the things Gilani alleged in the suit was that he recommended action against Hanover Sterling and that the NASD didn't do anything.

In March 1993, as Louis learned his trade at Hanover, Gilani was assigned to investigate customer complaints of unauthorized trading at Hanover Sterling. Gilani believed that formal action should be taken in most cases. But Gilani's supervisor did nothing.

Between June and September 1993 Gilani was assigned to investigate seven complaints against Hanover brokers. They involved unauthorized trading—*complaints*. Again he recommended formal action—including two against "a principal of the firm" not named in the suit. And again, the NASD did nothing.

Between October 1993 and June 1994 Gilani was assigned thirty-one more customer complaints against Hanover. Gilani saw a pattern of misconduct and a weirdly passive attitude by Hanover management. He recommended a full-scale investigation. According to the suit, his supervisor "told Gilani to 'mind his own business.'"

Gilani went over his supervisor's head, to a NASD assistant director.

Again, nothing.

Gilani was persistent. The suit paints a picture of a man repeatedly, and with intriguingly little impact, banging his head against a brick wall:

"Between June 1994 and February 1995 Gilani met with [his supervisor and the NASD assistant director] on at least five different occasions to express his grave concern about Hanover as a brokerage firm and the irreparable harm it was wreaking on its customers and on the markets the NASD was entrusted to protect. . . . Senior members of the NASD instructed Gilani to perform his job and to leave management decisions to the NASD's management," his suit alleged.

In all fairness to the NASD, it should be noted that the NASD denied Gilani's allegations quite vigorously at the time. The NASD said that Gilani was justifiably fired. He was, among other things alleged in the NASD's defense, a "disruptive" guy who wasn't a team player.

Gilani was too conscientious.

As soon as Gilani filed his suit, the NASD embarked on its "too conscientious" defense. In March 1998, he was called by the NASD lawyers to provide sworn pretrial testimony. The NASD's lawyers were interested in two fusses Gilani made when he worked there, and their questioning brought out how ridiculously conscientious Gilani had been.

Fuss No. 1 involved one of the cases he had submitted to his supervisor for action. Gilani was upset that he had recommended action against a broker and nothing had been done. The deposition doesn't identify the broker or brokerage. It does say that the broker didn't obey a NASD request for information—which is grounds to be automatically barred from Wall Street, forever.

The broker wasn't barred. In fact, nothing happened to him. Why was that? Because somehow the entire case file—a huge amount of paperwork—was "lost."

"I said, what do you mean?" Gilani testified. "This was a case with seventeen exhibits this high. It wasn't just one folder you could lose."

This got Gilani mad, which was why the NASD lawyers

wanted the file-loss episode brought out. "Team players" just didn't make a fuss about things like disappearing files.

Fuss No. 2 involved another incident concerning another unnamed broker and brokerage firm. The broker had stolen from a client ("misappropriated," in NASD-speak). The broker had also risked an automatic bar from Wall Street by not responding to information requests. Gilani had recommended action, the NASD had done nothing, and—aha!—that upset Gilani.

"Did you disrupt the meeting or not, Mr. Gilani?" a NASD lawyer asked.

"No. No," Gilani responded.

"Did you disrupt the meeting or not?" the lawyer persisted.

"No. No. I asked what happened . . . why was this case filed without action [concerning] the underlying violative act, and the fact that the rep also failed to appear for the interview. The combination of those are sufficient to bar a man from the industry," Gilani replied.

"You were very agitated when you said that. Weren't you, Mr. Gilani?" said the NASD lawyer.

At the time, the NASD was portraying itself as a regulatory William Tecumseh Sherman, waging scorched-earth warfare against stock fraud. Its public image was on the line, and this "examiners mustn't get agitated" line of defense simply was not going to do the NASD any good. Gilani was a major embarrassment. He had to be silenced. He was.

When Gilani filed his suit, which was in October 1996, he spoke freely about his experiences with journalists. Gilani's complaint was even posted on his lawyers' website.

Gilani's suit dragged on through the courts for a little over two years until February 25, 1999, when his lawyers filed a one-sentence stipulation and order agreeing that "all claims asserted in this action are hereby voluntarily dismissed with prejudice and on the merits." Translation: Gilani was settling the suit. And, suddenly, the window that Gilani had opened on the NASD slammed shut.

Massood Gilani was no longer able to talk about his experiences at the NASD. Several years later, his lawyer said that Gilani's ability to speak now required the permission of the NASD—and the NASD wasn't giving permission.*

So all that remains in the public record is a sheaf of legal papers in a courthouse archive, and its portrayal of a NASD that worked hard to keep all those *complaints* from disrupting the daily routine at 88 Pine.

Well, not all. Other glimpses of life at the NASD in the early 1990s have emerged now and then. Such as the account of a person who worked there when Hanover applied for its first set of papers from the NASD. He is familiar with how it happened. And he was always puzzled by it.

He's not a Massood Gilani. He wasn't fired and doesn't have an ax to grind against the NASD. But still, he wonders what the hell happened.

When Ageloff, Catoggio, and Schatzer organized Hanover Sterling in 1991, they were rejected. "Initially they were turned down, the NASD didn't like their backgrounds," says this person. "And then all of a sudden it got accepted. And I could never figure out how they got approved. I was surprised."

As the years went on, Louis had his own experiences with the NASD. They were always good experiences. Or at least, they weren't bad experiences. But in the early stages of his career he didn't have any experiences at all. The NASD and Securities and Exchange Commission acted as if he didn't exist. They didn't have any official record of Louis except as an "assistant." And they didn't have the foggiest idea how he, and the other "assistants" and brokers, made a living.

---

*Despite repeated requests, the NASD would not make its staffers available to discuss its oversight of Hanover and other chop houses during the 1990s.

CHAPTER NINE

At Hanover, the money was in the rips.

Sometimes they were called chops. But call them what you want, they were where the money was. They were known informally at the chop houses as "commissions," but they weren't anything of the kind.

Rips were the huge sums that the brokers earned from the stocks they sold. Ordinary stocks generated commissions for brokers. Ordinary Nasdaq stocks had "markups"—a reasonable profit for the broker and his firm. Chop stocks had rips.

Rips performed several functions.

They were motivators, without which brokers would not have been willing to push stocks that had all the appeal of wet tree bark.

They kept the conscience quiet. They kept stirrings of the phony emotion called "guilt" from wafting out of the toilet bowls of their souls.

Nobody knew how the term originated. Nobody cared.

The rips were announced each morning. Bobby Catoggio, in his capacity as trader—the guy who brought the stocks into Hanover—would make the announcement. One stock, Mr. Jay's, was selling for about $8 and its rip was $1.50, which meant that Hanover had the stock on its books for about $5 and split the $3 profit 50-50 with the broker.

The difference between a rip and a markup was subtle.

A $3 markup for the broker and the firm would not be so bad if this was a $100 stock. That's a 3 percent markup. Reasonable. There are no hard and fast definitions of excess markups, but more than 5 percent is a red flag and more than 10 percent will almost invariably result in a visit, sooner or later, from a grim-visaged, Syms-suited NASD examiner.

But Mr. Jay's sold for about $8. If it cost Hanover $5, that looks a lot like a 60 percent markup, doesn't it? Nope.

Rips weren't markups—if the chop houses were careful. It was all a question of timing. If a firm bought a stock at $5 and immediately sold it for $8, that would be a huge markup and that Syms suit would appear at the door. But if the firm waited a little while, and $5 was no longer the "prevailing market price"—voilà! It wasn't a markup anymore. It was a "trading profit." A rip. What made it even easier was that the house controlled the "prevailing market price" of the stock.

So the brokers were paid vast sums and the regulators, who were looking for excessive markups, didn't notice.

True, rips weren't foolproof, no matter how long the firms waited. Sometimes they got careless and the rips really were excessive markups. Since the brokers usually got the stock up to $8 (or whatever) by fibbing about it, they could be prosecuted for that. But the $1.50 that went to the broker—the "rip"—was at least superficially legal and, above all, was invisible to everybody, regulators and customers alike.

The brokerage would add on a few cents' commission. "The customer thinks he's only paying three cents a share commission, which is very reasonable. A good commission. He'd be happy about that," said Louis.

"That's how they made a ton of money at Hanover, because

the brokers' 'buying power'* was astronomical. The brokers could put away a million shares of stock in two days," said Louis. A million shares times $1.50, or more, is nice money.

"We would get crazy rips at Hanover. Eagle Vision was eleven with seven [a rip of $7 on an $11 stock]. It was paper—a Bulletin Board piece-of-shit paper stock. They were probably writing the certificates."

That's what chop stocks were all about—paper. Moving paper. The brokers moved paper, stocks that were often barely worth the paper they were written on, if they were still written on paper—and they often weren't, because by now stock certificates were being phased out. So the investors didn't even have nice stock certificates to use as wallpaper, as in the old vaudeville routine.

Louis wanted rips. He wasn't getting them. Roy wouldn't let him have his own client book. He wouldn't let him become a broker. That was going to have to change, and fast. Louis was getting serious with Stefanie, and he knew how much women cost. He was prepared to pay.

The summer of 1993 was hot, but it wasn't hot enough—not for Louis it wasn't. People were making money all around him at Hanover. Big money. And he wasn't getting any of it.

When Louis started at Hanover, the best brokers were making about $100,000 a month and it seemed great at the time. But that was just the beginning. The payouts went up and up: $200,000, $300,000. Half a million. And up. Louis was so frustrated, seeing other guys make money, that he quietly seethed.

But still, he was making good money for a teenager who had just dropped out of community college. Fifteen hundred a week, on average, meant that he and Stefanie could go out to

*Brokers sold stocks, of course. But since they had to technically buy them from the firm, their ability to sell stocks was referred to, counterintuitively, as "buying power."

nicer restaurants. He could afford cabs. Cabs were awesome. He never took a cab in Staten Island. But after a few months at Hanover he could afford to take a cab from the ferry to 88 Pine, even though it was only a five-minute walk away. Some people might call that a nice, brisk walk in the morning. But Louis didn't want to take a nice, brisk walk when hundreds of people were having the same nice, brisk walk off the ferry, crowding together, smelling in the morning like perfume and Right Guard and smelling at night like sweat and ass. The ferry stank, a piss and gasoline smell, and the bay smelled from dead fish and God knows what.

Louis hated bad smells and he hated crowds and he hated subways. At night he started taking a car service back home. It cost him fifty bucks a night. He didn't care. He could afford it.

At Hanover he could order cigarettes from downstairs. Condoms if he wanted them. A guy came by and shined the brokers' shoes, maybe the same guy who came to the investment banks and shined the Yalies' shoes. A shoe is a shoe. Money is money.

To get money, he would have to become a broker.

As he worked at Hanover he saw Chris become famous in the chop house world as half of the team of "Chris and Rocco"—the other half being Rocco Basile. So why shouldn't there be a Louis and—whoever? A "Louis and Benny," maybe?

Benny Salmonese would be a great partner. They had talked about teaming up. It was a bullshit talk, the way guys yammer away when they've had a couple of beers. But it made sense. Benny was no scrub—he worked late too. And Benny's strengths offset Louis's weaknesses, and vice versa. Benny was a few years older, a smooth talker, a deal-maker, a conciliator. Louis was still a teenager, rough around the edges as No. 3 sandpaper—and he didn't have a broker license.

Louis took the NASD test for the first time when he was at Hanover. He didn't study. He got a 40.

License, bullshit. Why shouldn't he make money? Why shouldn't he have a client book? He could get clients. It was only fair.

Benny had a license. Perfect. They could both use it. They could both be Benny.

That was the plan. Now they had to execute it. They *had* to execute it.

Benny went to a little brokerage called Robert Todd Financial Corporation in July 1993. Louis had never heard about it but Massood Gilani, over at the NASD, sure had—just as well as he knew Hanover and just as well as he knew John Lembo, one of the most complained-about brokers at the most-complained about brokerage. Gilani's District Management Information System Cause Examination Examiner Log for District 10 showed that Robert Todd was one of the little firms in Manhattan that was getting *complaints*. January 15, 1993—"unauthorized transaction." January 20, 1993—"failure to execute sell order." Red flags, no action. Todd stayed open. Benny, and soon Louis, would be in no danger of their livelihood being interrupted.

"After Benny got to Robert Todd, I don't hear from him for a few weeks," said Louis. "Then one day he calls. 'Louie, it's Benny.' I didn't really think he'd call. Once he left Hanover I thought he was gone. He left three weeks, four weeks before he even called me. He says, 'What are you doing?' 'I'm working, what do you think I'm doing?' And he says, 'Can you take lunch? Can you come up here? I want to talk to you.' He wasn't going to talk on the phones at Hanover, because Roy could sometimes listen in on the calls if he wanted. He could come right into your phone. You'd pick up the phone and Roy would be like, 'Get off the phone!'"

They worked out a great deal—great for Louis, great for Benny, great for Todd. Todd got 30 percent of the payout—in other words, 30 percent of the rips Benny and Louis were to generate. Louis and Benny agreed to split the remaining 70 percent. Louis got 40 percent of their share if he brought in more than $100,000 in rips. Otherwise he got 30 percent.

Robert Todd was in the eastern part of Midtown Manhattan, in a building at 50th Street and Third Avenue grandly named the Crystal Pavilion. It was one of the newest of the new office towers that were built on Third Avenue since the mid-1950s, when the Third Avenue El was torn down. The El was a great backdrop for filmmakers, particularly if they were making noir tales of greed and betrayal—movies such as *Side Street*, which Anthony Mann filmed back in 1950 in a run-down tenement at 850 Third Avenue, right down the street from the Crystal Pavilion. *Side Street* was about a part-time postman who stole thousands of dollars in a moment of impulsive greed.

Third Avenue was a perfect backdrop for a fifties morality tale. It was run-down but decent, a vivid contrast with the bourgeois hypocrisy of the era, epitomized by an aerial view of Wall Street that began the film. Years later, filmmakers would have to look elsewhere to find that kind of melodramatic contrast. Blue-collar Third Avenue was gone, retreating to the outer boroughs and suburbs in the 1960s and 1970s. When Louis and Benny and the other Todd brokers came to the Crystal Pavilion in September 1993, a bit of blue collar came back to Third Avenue.

A spit throw from the fictional angst of *Side Street,* Louis might have had his own, real-life moral dilemma. A lot of people in his position would have been wracked by guilt. Here he was, getting thousands of dollars a week in ill-gotten money—money that he needed to break out of his own blue-collar world, money that he didn't take on impulse, but was removing with growing skill and calculation, by dint of hard work.

Louis had no angst, no existential crisis. He never gave

much thought to the morality of what he was doing. Like not letting customers sell stock.

"I started realizing that you couldn't get out, that it was all bullshit," said Louis. "Even though the price was twenty, it didn't matter, you couldn't get out at twenty. I knew they were lousy companies. But at Hanover I wasn't sure about anything yet. Once I got to Robert Todd, that was it. I knew that it was all bullshit. And I just treated it that way. I didn't give a shit. I just wanted the money. It didn't matter to me."

In the movie that Anthony Mann filmed down the street forty-three years before, the hero wound up back in the arms of his wife—bloodied and beaten, but with his integrity restored. It was a simple solution to a simple moral problem. But in Wall Street of the early 1990s, moral dilemmas were never simple. Brokerage and stock exchange executives, men of patrician backgrounds who held chop house brokers in contempt, turned a blind eye to the insane overhyping of stocks by analysts, and the web of conflicts of interest that would become a full-blown scandal in 2002. Across town, the rips of the chop houses were also nonissues. Complaints about rips—the heart and soul of the chop houses—never crossed Massood Gilani's desk. No reason they would. Customers didn't know about the rips. But the rips were not hidden so well that the NASD and SEC wouldn't have found them if the NASD and SEC were looking, or if the NASD and SEC had given a damn. "The SEC guy would look at the ticket and say, 'Oh, he marked it up an eighth [13 cents a share]. He did it right.' He didn't know about the $4 rip that we made," said Louis.

Louis was in a world where the outer parameters of acceptable behavior were determined not by right or wrong, but by what the NASD and SEC saw and what they didn't see or didn't want to see. The regulators saw the unauthorized trades and no-sales rules because people complained. They didn't see, and didn't want to see, the unregistered brokers and the rips—or at least, they didn't see them while the unregistered brokers were working and the rips were being charged.

Sure the regulators acted decisively against the chop houses—after they went out of business. If World War II had been fought like that, the Allies would have stormed the beaches of Normandy during the Korean War.

Todd was never seriously threatened by regulators during its existence. It nurtured Louis, transforming him from a well-off kid into a rich adult.

CHAPTER TEN

After Louis started pulling down good money at Todd, the first thing he did was buy a brand-new Jeep Wrangler. A beauty. Nick Pasciuto signed the papers because Louis didn't have a credit rating.

The second thing he did was move out.

Louis moved to Tottenville, a neighborhood at the tip of Staten Island, where he rented a small apartment in a row house. The first night was bliss. Silence. No screaming. No criticism. He dropped down onto the bed, after a long day of hard work at Todd, and slept.

Fran Pasciuto was upset. She was not an overly protective mother, not by any stretch of the imagination. But she worried and she had a sixth sense, an instinct of sorts that kicked in when Louis was in trouble. She could tell when there was a problem. Fran's sixth sense told her that Louis should not move out of the family's house in Staten Island. He should stay where he was. At home.

But there was no convincing Louis once he made up his mind. It was enough to make any mother feel as if things were spinning out of control.

"I couldn't handle it too well," said Fran. "I thought he should be home. When he moved out it was a whole different lifestyle. Whatever he was doing—partying, drinking, going out, having a good time—it was a world that I was never in, never used to, so for me it was crazy.

"Louis and Stefanie used to come for dinner on Sunday. I used to say, 'What's going on?' He'd say, 'Ma! Don't worry about it. What are you worried about?' I think Nicky knew more of what was going on than I did. . . . He was gambling, going to Atlantic City a lot, he'd be betting on football games. And I used to get crazy. I'd say, 'Where are you getting this from? Nobody ever gambled in this house. All of a sudden now you become the gambler?' I said, 'We never went to Atlantic City. We never bet on football games. Your father never bet or gambled.' Where was this coming from? This was like shocking. I didn't know where it was coming from. It came out of left field. . . .

"I don't know if it's part of the Wall Street thing. All the kids, young guys, I really don't know. But that used to make me crazy. All the gambling, Atlantic City. I was shocked. Really shocked. Crazy. Like I said, we never went for that. I can count on one hand the times I've been to Atlantic City. I hate it. I really hate it. I think I'm the only person in the world who hates it! I used to go as a kid, because of the rides, the boardwalk, the convention center. We used to go for that—for the rides."

The Donohues loved Atlantic City, and they took Louis along. It was a typical future-in-law power struggle, and the Donohues were winning. The trips to Atlantic City were the clincher. "When I got there and I seen it for the first time," said Louis, "I was like 'Holy shit!' I think we arrived out there at about six o'clock. It was getting dark so you could see the lights. It was really cool. I says, 'This place is two hours away from Manhattan?' I felt like I'd never seen the world, never been out of the city. I'd been to the Jersey shore, but never to Atlantic City. This was fascinating shit. Those hotels were sick. The Taj Mahal was insane.

"Right away that first time I won five hundred dollars at roulette. So naturally I wanted to go back again. I left there and I says, 'We got to go back.' This is too easy if I could win five hundred every time I come there. It's fucking crazy. I was figuring shit out. 'I can make fifteen hundred a week at Hanover plus five hundred at Atlantic City, that's two thousand a week.' That's what I was thinking."

Louis's lucky streak was running in all parts of his life. He had a new career, a new car, a great girlfriend with a great family, and even a new pastime that was obviously going to pay dividends in the future.

It wasn't just the money. It was the fun. The rush he felt when he put his money on the table. And it was great how Atlantic City was such a short ride away. Soon he started going there by himself. Zooming down the Garden State Parkway in his brand-new Beemer. He got the BMW right after he moved to the apartment. Having two cars was nice. And Stefanie really liked Beemers.

The wisdom of his move to Todd was confirmed during his first month there, when he took home about $10,000. But after the initial glow wore off, he realized he and Benny had a problem. A corporate culture issue.

The brokers at Todd were a mixed bag. Aside from Benny there was a powerhouse young broker, Marco Fiore, plus other brokers who were in it for the right reasons. Louis liked to work with the right people—hungry kids who wanted to make money. But for the most part, the brokers and cold-callers at Todd had all the energy of a mouse turd on a subway platform.

"When I walked in that first day, the only one I heard on the phone was Benny. Everybody else was on the phone, but they were sitting down. At Hanover, if you sat in a chair, Roy used to put paper clips in the rubber bands and fold them back, and if you're sitting down you get shot in the head," said Louis.

"When you're up, when you stand, you project more. My cold-callers never sat down. I'd take the chairs out of the room. You have to stand up. You can move your hands around, walk around. Used to get my cold-callers twenty-foot cords, and the chairs that I had were uncomfortable for them. I didn't want them to sit down. I got wooden folding chairs. When you sit down you get lazy. When you stand up, you go. It's a numbers game. Got to keep dialing that phone."

Louis had to get some new cold-callers—and fast. The firm was going to pay for ten cold-callers, so Louis and Benny had to start recruiting.

At nineteen, Louis was one of the younger middle managers on Wall Street—and surely one of the very few, at that or any other time, who was listed in the NASD's Central Records Depository as an "assistant." By law, brokerage house managers had to hold not only the Series 7 broker license, but also the Series 24 license required for individuals with the task of managing others. Such formalities were obeyed by the chop houses only when it wasn't too inconvenient.

"They were going to pay for ten cold-caller salaries, so we put an ad in the paper and that's how we found Sally Leads, Chris Ray, Pete Restivo, everybody. We had ads in the *Post,* the *News,* the *Times.* Didn't do the *Staten Island Advance.* Benny didn't like the kids from Staten Island. He thought they were fucking thugs. They were. They were not good workers. Some of them were good, but most were like punks. I hated hiring kids from Staten Island. Too close to home anyway. They'd come to your house when you owed them money. It was a pain in the ass," said Louis.

The crew system fostered unit cohesiveness, intramural competition, and loyalty. Louis and Benny hired kids who were very much like themselves—hungry outer-borough kids, mainly Italian and Jewish.

"Me and Benny used to do the interviews. They'd come in, and we'd ask them stupid questions—Roy Ageloff questions. 'Why you here?' 'I seen the ad in the paper.' 'You know what this is? You sell stock here. Can you be on the phone all day?' I wouldn't even know what the hell to ask," said Louis.

"And then if we thought they had potential we hired them. Give them a shot. And make them work too. Work hard. We kept them if they worked hard. Some of them would come in and they'd say, 'Oh, it's not for me. It's only a hundred a week,' blah blah blah. The ones that didn't complain, some of them said, 'Can I make money if I open accounts?' Some of them were just determined. They wanted to do it."

For the ones with potential, persuading them to take the job wasn't too hard. All Louis had to do was tell the truth:

"I used to tell them, 'I'm nineteen years old. I got my own apartment. I got a car. I make ten grand, fifteen grand a month.'"

CHAPTER ELEVEN

"Half these people, you could hear it in their voice. They're willing to send the money. They'd give signs. I'd really pay attention to what they said, because a lot of the times it was a sign that they were willing to invest.

"A guy would say, 'How exactly do you spell that?' I'd know he was done right after he said that. I knew he was interested. Or, 'What kind of commission do you charge?' I'd say, 'Nothing.' Yes, absolutely nothing except for a two-point chop I won't tell you about. It was weird. These people were just naïve. I guess they just didn't know anything out there. Probably still don't know.

"To this day, I would bet any sum of money that people are still stupid. I used to tell Benny we could make a million dollars by getting a million leads, we hire thirty cold-callers, and have them just calling everybody, and ask them for ten dollars. Ten dollars in a check by mail. And I bet you any amount of money that after five months we'd accumulate a million bucks. We ask them for ten dollars and if they send a dollar it would be good enough. Call a million people. That's how stupid these people are.

"We had stacks of leads from Shearson Lehman, D. H. Blair. We wound up getting Hanover leads; we got Hanover microfiche, which was big. And it was a great edge for us, because on the microfiche we would get the statement, so you would see the stocks that they bought. And I'd say, 'Remember the last time I spoke with you, you told me you owned Mr. Jay's and Porter McLeod at Hanover Sterling?' It would give you, like, an edge. 'How are those stocks doing?' 'Ehh, they're doing shit.' 'Well, why don't you transfer that account over to me, work with a real guy?' They would do it. They would fill out ACAT [account transfer] forms.

"I would never call anybody who lived in Jersey or New York. Never. My best states were Utah, Texas, Arizona, Virginia. Michigan was one of my favorite states too. Michigan was good. Stupid people up in Michigan. California too. Not Los Angeles but on the outskirts of California. Sacramento. Utah was my favorite state. I think that was my top state. Because they were completely fucking retarded. They have like nine wives, they're Mormons. They're retards. You call them from New York, and they're like, 'Where are you?' And I'd say, 'I'm a spit throw away from the New York Stock Exchange.' And they'd say, 'Really! How is it up there in New York?'

"They're fascinated by the whole concept of it. Utah, Arizona, Texas—but only certain parts of Texas. Dallas, never. San Antonio, never. Houston, no. Parts of Texas like Fort Worth. Just shithole parts of Texas. I would never call big cities. I would never call Salt Lake City. Because these were big cities; people would know better. I'd call towns. Rural places, not suburbs.

"I used to see Dallas on the lead, I'd go, 'Nope.' Places like Fort Worth were okay. I went to Fort Worth once. Went into the store, asked the lady for five packs of Marlboro. Her kids are running around barefoot. She went, 'Fahv packs a Marlboro?' Like people bought a cigarette at a time. I wanted five packs and she almost dropped dead. She says, 'Fawteen dollars,' like it's the biggest sale of the century.

"In the more eastern states, people were closer in touch. When you called out West, it's just a different fucking world out there. And some of the South people too, like Tennessee. I had this guy, an old black guy from out there. This guy was good. We lost him money. I remember him calling up, he had this black Tennessee accent, and he says, 'I'll tell you, boy, you fucking New Yorkers, man. You lose me all my money.' I remember him calling up, and he had this old scratch in his voice.

"The furthest I'd been was Ocean City, New Jersey. I didn't even know these people existed out there, out in the country, or even had money. It was actually fascinating for me at first. I used to tell Stefanie and my mother, 'I spoke to somebody in like Montana, Ma!' Then it became like a ritual, like second nature to me. And then I used to know what to say to a guy who lived in Utah. Or I would know the different ways to talk to these people. And if they were old or if they were young how to talk to them. Like the old men, I used to hard-sell them. Pump them up. Because they used to like it, the old men. I'd say, 'Come on, Bob! What the fuck! Grab your balls!'

"Old men I used to treat like that. And they'd go, 'Ahh, you fucking New York broker!' They'd be like crazy old men. The young guys I used to talk to in a more sincere, greedy kind of way.

"I used to love talking to the old guys. They were my favorite. Because they used to abuse you and send you the money too. They'd be like, 'Ehh, you're busting my balls! I'll send you the goddamn hundred grand.' It was like a comedy. It was. But it's the truth. It's sad but it's funny.

"They'd call up and they'd say, 'You charged me thirty bucks too much on the commission,' and I'd say, 'I'll send you a personal check for that thirty bucks,' and I would send it to them. And they would get the thirty bucks. And they'd say, 'Wow, that was great. I'll send you a hundred thousand now.'

"Just dumb. I'm not saying I was such a great salesman that people would send me money, because yeah, I was a good salesman, but come on! I would get off the phone with some of these people after they sent me a hundred thousand and I'd say, 'What the fuck is wrong with this guy? Is he a retard?' And they would call back the next day and ask, 'Did you get that check? I sent it out.' Yeah, I got it, I spent it already. I just bought myself a new car. So obviously I got it, right?

"I would give them my home number, and it would be like the best thing that ever happened. 'Only a picked few of my clients get my home number.' Since you sent me over a half a million, and you actually hooked up my phone line for me. These people were just naïve to the world I guess, you know. They live in the boondocks of Texas or Arizona, where dirt roads lead to their house. They just don't know no better.

"I don't know if it's greed. I don't know what it is with these people. Why would you send somebody half a million dollars? Us being New Yorkers, somebody tells us we're going to make a million dollars, we'd say, 'Get the fuck out of here. Right, give me the half a million and then I'll give you half a million.' We're very shrewd. But they're not shrewd. It used to surprise me how the fuck they got their money. Like, how did this idiot get fifteen million? What did he do for this fifteen million? Because he's a complete moron. If he's sending people a million dollars over the phone, he's not going to have that fifteen million for long.

"We used to get attorneys to send us a couple of hundred thousand. We had an attorney in Utah. This guy Alan, I forget his last name. He was an attorney, like a trial attorney. We got him at Robert Todd. Supposed to be a smart guy, sends us seven hundred thousand for fucking dogshit stocks. Over the phone without meeting us. He's an attorney. He should be more shrewd than that to be an attorney. Boy, I'd hate to be in fucking Utah having him represent me.

"Sometimes their wives would pick up the phone, and they'd tell me, 'He's out in the crop.' Out in the field in their crop. Sometimes they couldn't even get him, and I used to picture this guy having like six hundred acres of land, and his wife saying, 'The New York broker called,' and him saying, 'You didn't tell me! Gee!' And him running to the phone, from six miles out in the field, running back to the phone.

"And I used to laugh about it too. I used to cover the phone and say, 'She's getting him. He's fucking four miles out in the field. He's gonna run back to the phone, Ben. Watch.' And I used to know that if he came to the phone at that particular moment, if she got him to come to the phone, he's done! He's good for a hundred grand. Came all the way from his fields to the phone.

"They'd be farmers, or they'd be retired and have all this money. We had this guy, John Kiwalski. He was in computers and he actually engineered computers for some company. He sent us like three hundred thousand. I used to ask him about himself, and he had a wife, two kids, three kids. He had a nice house. I always asked them what kind of car they drove, and I would write it down. Because you know how the guy is living. He had a Jaguar. And I remember pitching this guy and saying to myself, 'This guy's got to be a smart guy. He builds computers.' But he can't even find the stocks I'm giving him on the computer.

"They'd say that—'I couldn't find that stock in the paper.' And I'd say, 'Well, it only goes in the paper if it trades more than a hundred thousand shares.' That's not true! And they would believe it. Or I'd say, 'What paper you looking in?' They'd say, 'I'm looking in the *New York Times*,' and I'd say, 'No, you have to get the *Journal*.' They'd say they couldn't get the *Journal* out there, and I'd say I'd send them a copy of the *Journal*. And I'd never send it. Just a fucking joke.

"The best client Benny and me had at Robert Todd was Stormin' Norman. That's what we called him, Stormin' Norman. Stormin' was like eighty-nine. We used to call up and he'd say, 'Yeahhhh, how's my account?' Talking like he's dying. And we used to keep pushing him for more money. He used to call up and say, 'We need some money back down here.' And I'd say, 'I need another fifty from you to even start to send you money back.' He was from someplace out West. He was good, Stormin' Norman. We had like two hundred thousand of his money, lost him like ninety thousand.

"He was a nasty old man. But he liked me. He liked me on the phone. When I used to call him, he'd say, 'Ehhhhhhh, what are you doing up there in that New York shithole?' He was a crazy old man. And I just started calling him 'Stormin' Norman.' I'd say, 'Stormin!' And he would send money like it was going out of style. I got checks from him that I didn't even ask him for. And then I would do trades in his account, and he would get a bill, and not remember that he didn't even tell me to do the trade. He'd get a bill for like forty-six thousand, he'd call me up and say, 'Hey, I got a bill here for forty-six from you guys up there.' And I'd say, 'Stormin', last week you told me to do the trade,' and he'd go, 'I'll send the check, then.' And he'd just send a check.

"It was ridiculous. Where did these people come from? I used to say, 'Ben, this is crazy, man.' Stormin' was in Pacific Rim Entertainment, and Net Optix, two Robert Todd stocks. And then we put him in California Quartz warrants. They were a dollar, we were getting paid something like thirty cents.

"So one day I called him up. Somebody answers the phone and says, 'Norman passed on.' And I say, 'Ohhh.' I was really upset about it, you know? Me and Benny almost cried. We wrote sixty tickets on his account not even ten minutes after we got off the phone. I says, 'Benny, UT [unauthorized trade] him. The whole account.'

"We UT'd his account, we went and we celebrated. I re-member we were cheering, 'Stormin' Norman! He's dead!' We just wrote tickets and churned his account. Sold, bought, sold, bought, and just made commissions. The account got down to about thirty grand and we made all the rest in commissions. People called, and I said, 'I'll send you out the account statement.' And that was that. Dead issue.

"Norman was dead, and that was that."

CHAPTER TWELVE

The chop house brokers and cold-callers lived in their own ex-blue-color, upwardly mobile nouveau-everything world, separated from the rest of the Street—the Real Wall Street—by differences in class and education, and by the fact that the chop house brokers just didn't give a shit about anything outside the chop house world.

They didn't care about blue chips or high tech. They didn't know bonds from urinal mints. The Dow Jones Industrial Average meant nothing to them, and Louis always believed that the brokers on the Real Wall Street never knew what they were talking about, half the time, when they went mouthing off on the subject of the "market."

"We weren't brokers like they were," said Louis. "We couldn't even have a conversation with half these fucking brokers. We'd come into contact with them at Moran's and shit, but we just didn't have a conversation with them. Sometimes Benny used to get drunk and I used to see him remotely try to have a conversation with some broker. They would talk about market shit and we didn't know what the fuck they were talking about. Options and shit. What's an option? A future? I never heard of a future in my life.

"They were really investing clients' money to make the

clients gain wealth. We weren't doing that. We were investing the clients' money so *we* could gain wealth. They were making money, but they were making two percent a year off an account. If a guy had ten million in an account, they're taking two hundred thousand every year. If we had ten million in an account, we were making like two million a month. Different story."

Not knowing about the market or stocks or money market funds put Louis in a bind. He had a problem that would have surprised his clients, because it contradicted everything he was telling them: Louis didn't know what to do with his money.

In the beginning, at Hanover, he used to spindle the bills very tight and put them in a mayonnaise jar in his room. The first couple of checks from Todd went to the Jeep and then the apartment and then the BMW, but there was still a lot of money left over. When you're nineteen and don't know how to invest and are from a family that has never had a lot of money—well, that is not a small issue.

After being at Todd a few months, Louis put away his mayonnaise jar for good. He didn't find a great stock or a top-notch mutual fund. He was a teenager, and Louis did what teenagers do with money. He spent it. At Todd, under Benny's tutelage, he began to find cool stuff to buy, great things to do.

Entertainment, for instance. The chop house kids loved to avail themselves of New York's cultural scene, particularly its strip joints.

Strip joints and chop houses served very similar functions. Chop houses took money from people to satisfy their fantasies of greed—fantasies that were almost never realized. Strip joints took money from the public, and from a lot of chop house brokers, to satisfy their fantasies of sex—fantasies that were also not realized very often. But they were realized often enough that Louis and his friends didn't mind spending hundreds or even thousands of dollars a night. Louis didn't grow up with the time-worn attitude that strip joints were for dirty old men who couldn't get laid, who retreated to some quiet corner to pleasure themselves after watching the only naked women who came into their lives.

By the early 1990s, strip joints were becoming cool. Celebrities were going to strip joints. Howard Stern, who hosted the morning talk-radio show Louis and the other chop house kids adored, was always talking about his trips to Scores, the strip joint in the shadow of the 59th Street Bridge.

Still, in the beginning, strip joints were disappointing. Strip joints were a con. Louis didn't like being conned. But he started going to them anyway once the Todd money started flowing. He and Benny began with grubby strip joints near their Midtown offices, but after a while they started going to the mother of all strip joints, Scores.

"At first Benny says 'Scores is too much. We're going to start spending like five thousand.' But then we started making money. We went one night for a party because we had a good month. We had a three-hundred-thousand-buck month at Robert Todd, so we went to Scores. We ran a sixty-four-hundred-dollar tab. Cristal—five bottles, six bottles, maybe. I must have spent fifteen hundred on this one girl. Samantha. But she wouldn't give me the time of day. Kept on giving her money, and I used to try to make her come home but she wouldn't come."

Money went a lot farther back home on Staten Island. Over there he was the Man.

At Sea—St. Joseph-by-the-Sea in Tottenville—he was the skinny kid with the stormy home life who never had any money. The kid who was so incorrigible, cared so little for their rules, that the priests had him in permanent detention year after year and even during summer recess. He was the least likely to succeed. Louie the Louse, they used to call him. Lou-natic. It wasn't meant in a mean way. Louis would laugh about it.

He wasn't laughing anymore. Nobody was laughing on

Staten Island. Not with his money. Not when everybody knew that he was big on Wall Street and that one of the kids he used to hang out with at Sea, Mike Layden, now worked for him as a cold-caller at Robert Todd. Mike would let Louis stay at his place when his mother used to kick him out. He was staying at Mike's place when he first met Stefanie. It was embarrassing. Louis didn't have to be embarrassed anymore, not when Mike was running errands for him.

Most of his friends were still in an extended adolescence, going to school, getting money from Daddy. Louis was still a kid but Middle America was handsomely subsidizing his adolescence. Very few teenagers had that kind of allowance. Nick and Fran never gave him much money anyway (except for dumb things parents care about like the two loans they had to take out for his college education). Now Louis made his own money. He drove to work. And Mike Layden or another cold-caller, the eager young kid he called Sally Leads, would park the car.

"Everybody knew me. People I didn't even know, didn't talk to in school, used to see me in a restaurant or something and they'd come over to me and say, 'Hey, Lou, what's going on? I hear you're doing really well.' Blah blah blah. Then a lot of the girls that I couldn't get in high school, they were coming around town. I'd be in clubs and they'd be all over me.

"To the friends that I knew from Staten Island—I was the Man. They're going to school, and I was the boss—all-around boss, no-matter-what boss. At work and at home. I'd say, 'Mike, come pick me up.' He'd come pick me up. I was the boss. Ran the shop. Forget about it.

"My friend Joe Favo, I went to school with him, and I started working on Wall Street and I'd still go out with him all the time. He seen me get the Jeep, get the BMW, and he was still going to school. He'd say, 'What the fuck's going on? What are you doing?' He didn't even believe me. I was trying to tell him I was making twenty, thirty thousand a month. Joe goes, 'Yeah, right. Twenty, thirty thousand a month, ridiculous.' It was unheard of. Even when I was making two thousand a week as a cold-caller, Joe would doubt me. He'd say, 'It's got to be a month to month you get paid.' I'd say, 'No, I'm telling you, every week.' He'd say, 'Bullshit!'

"When I first got the BMW, me and Stefanie went to this deli on Arthur Kill Road. My friends from Sea, Timmy and Joe, worked there as stock boys and were going to school. We made them come outside and see the car, and they freaked out. I beeped the horn, they came out, and they were like, 'Bullshit, it's not yours.' I showed them the lease. They wouldn't believe me. I tried talking Timmy and Joe into coming to work with me, but they weren't into that. But then when I got the BMW, they all wanted to come up to work.

"So then they started coming out with me. My friends from Staten Island would come out with me and I'd take like eight of them, and I'd pay for everybody. I didn't give a fuck. It cost me a thousand to go out with them, and it was nothing compared to going out with Benny. That cost three thousand. After a while Joe was like, 'Holy shit!'

"It was all around town. I was a legend. Everybody knew me."

CHAPTER THIRTEEN

The Bitch Boy was a perk Louis thought up himself. Most of the chop house brokers, even the very biggest, had no Bitch Boys, so Sally Leads was special.

Sally Leads was William Goldenberg, a seventeen-year-old Russian kid from Rego Park in Queens. He was about six feet one inch tall, blue-eyed and baby-faced, with light brown hair combed straight back. "He looked like a little boy. That was Leads. He had no story. No schooling, nothing," said Louis. When William first joined Louis's crew at Todd, Louis didn't give a fuck how Mr. and Mrs. Goldenberg had named their son. But after a while, the name had to go. Louis simply could not have a "William" in a crew of Petes and Bennys and Joeys. This was a chop house, after all.

"I said, 'I can't be calling you William. Horrible.' I said, 'Your nickname's Sal. I like it,'" says Louis.

Louis called him Leads because all Sal could do was "qualify" sales leads—asking them how much they made, whether they were in the stock market, etc. Elementary stuff. No selling involved. In other words, doing all the stuff that cold-callers were legally permitted to do. Sally could do that. But he simply didn't have what it took to go beyond that, to sell stock using Benny's name, to pitch clients, to break the law with flair and panache as Louis and Benny were doing.

So in recognition of his lack of larcenous talent, the name Sally Leads was born. It sounded nice. Sal didn't mind and it wasn't so terrible. At least Louis wasn't having Sal imitate a monkey, or read from *Green Eggs and Ham*. "It got so his own mother started calling him Sal," said Louis. "I'd call his house and say, 'Is Sal there?' And she'd call out to him, 'Sal!'"

Sal was a friend more than an employee, and gradually became a kind of surrogate younger brother. They hung out together, and Sally started sleeping on the sofa in Louis's new apartment. It was nice. Sally Leads was a good guy to have around.

He was Sally Leads, usually, or sometimes Sal or sometimes just Leads. But he knew his name. He would come when called. And if Sal or Sally Leads or Leads wasn't around, Mike Layden was always available to do stuff like park the car in a garage off Third Avenue.

But Louis didn't want to get too comfortable. Todd sucked.

It was a management issue. The chief executive officers of chop house firms—with a few exceptions like Jordan Belfort at Stratton Oakmont—were rarely actually in charge of the brokers who worked there. They hardly ever attempted to exert any authority. So they couldn't do much harm. But sometimes they got in the way. Sometimes they didn't do their job. Sometimes they had idiotic ethical concerns. They could be a pain in the ass.

As far as Louis was concerned, the president of Robert Todd was a problem. He was a guy named Robert Fallah. Fallah was no Roy Ageloff. He didn't have that magnetism. He wasn't a leader who could inspire the kids. Louis had to do his own inspiring. He ran the crew. And he didn't like it when anybody told him what to do. Particularly when they weren't doing what they were supposed to do, which was to give him "product"—stocks to sell.

Sure, he had autonomy at Todd. He was able to make more money at Todd than he could at Hanover. But there was no comparison between the two organizations. Robert Todd simply could not hold a candle to Hanover Sterling.

"Fallah didn't have involvement with the brokers. He had a big office but you couldn't even see him. He wasn't involved like Roy. Every once in a while he would hold a meeting, when there was an IPO. The brokers would go in his office and it wouldn't be an exciting meeting. It was serious," said Louis.

"This guy, Peter Cohen, he used to give the sales meetings and stuff like that. I wouldn't even listen. It was a joke. He reminded me of the guy from that movie *Glengarry Glen Ross*. He would talk about his Rolex. He was a good-dressed guy. You could see he was making some money. He would call the meetings in the afternoon, after four o'clock. I'm working, but four o'clock to five we'd take a break anyway. He was tall, six-one, slick-back hair. In his late twenties. He wore a Rolex but it was a two-tone Rolex, silver and gold. An Oyster, a Perpetual, not a Presidential. It was five grand. A Presidential cost twenty. He was sales manager or something, which was a bullshit title anyway, like he went around and promoted sales throughout the United States or something.

"He was just horrible. He would actually tell us how to sell. One meeting, after we started doing big money every month, he asked me to pitch. He used to do that. Somebody would pitch, or say their opening lines. He said, 'Louie, you want to help us out and give us your opening lines?' And I told him, 'No.' I wasn't going to tell everybody my opening lines.

"We had those meetings in the boardroom, but I would always sit way in the back. He would tell stories of how he made so much money, how he was such a success. 'I worked hard for this Rolex. I drive a nice car. I live in a nice house.' But this guy had no clue. Nice watch. I felt like telling him what a bullshit watch he had on. Probably living in not even a garage house in Long Island. He actually did drive a Mercedes but it wasn't the great Mercedes. It was like the E Class. Chris and Rocco, they had really serious money. This guy Cohen, he didn't have money, maybe two hundred a year. Which is good money. But not for that world. He didn't have commissions. Fallah paid him. So I'm just assuming he made that much. It probably wasn't even that much. He didn't have clients, the guy. He probably got a percentage of the brokers that he recruited, but anybody he recruited wasn't of any consequence."*

Todd just didn't have an adequate inventory of "house stocks" (chop stocks that were sold mainly at Todd). Todd was just like the Getty station after the credit-card guy stopped coming in. You can't make money when nobody is coming in with stolen credit cards, or stocks to sell.

"When we had an IPO there was no product. At Hanover you'd be able to get for clients maybe two or three million shares. But at Todd they'd say, 'We only got fifty thousand.' Fifty fucking thousand? Me and Benny used to buy it all in a second and nobody would get any of it."

That created resentment. Benny and Louis found themselves on the outs, not part of the "inner circle" of brokers usually found at all brokerages, chop houses and legit ones alike. Louis's fuck-you attitude didn't help. He was kind of an alternate-universe Massood Gilani—a guy who was unpopular because he was trying too hard to do his job, which in Louis's case was to separate investors from their money.

And even when there was a product, it was lackluster. Take Pacific Rim Entertainment. It was Louis's first IPO, and it was

---

*A few years later, while working at another chop house, Peter Cohen tried another way to move up to a better grade of Rolex. In 1999 he was indicted for insider trading involving advance copies of *Business Week*'s "Inside Wall Street" stock market column. He pleaded guilty to one felony count. In September 2002 he was sentenced to 30 days probation. The sales-maven-insider-trader Peter Cohen, by the way, should not be confused with the Peter Cohen who was chairman of Shearson in the 1980s.

a typical chop house IPO because it was a legitimate company. Generally speaking, companies that issued chop stocks were not dramatically different from a lot of other small companies. What made the chop stocks different were the premium prices they commanded and the special way they were sold— the zest, the enthusiasm (or the fraud, as regulators would say much later).

Pacific Rim went public on November 12, 1993, at a share price of $5. And members of the public who examined the prospectus, with the Robert Todd Financial Corporation logo at the bottom, would not have found any more than the usual red flags typical for any growing company. That's because Pacific Rim was not a fraud. It had never been tainted by scandal before or since the company went public, and in the years to come would not even get the usual shareholder suits that sometimes are slapped on even the most legit companies. Pacific Rim produced cartoons and operated an animated production facility in the city of Shenzhen in China. It even had a cute stock symbol, "TOON."

There was nothing fishy in the financial statements. True, the company was losing money, but it had a talented staff, six hundred workers in China, and a chairman who was a veteran of the entertainment business. This would have been great stuff for Louis's IPO pitch if he had cared. But he didn't. Only a moron would have pitched an IPO by talking about what the company did. Wasn't necessary. In fact, only the worst salesman in the world would need to *sell* an IPO, period. IPOs sold themselves in the early 1990s. Louis didn't have to read the prospectus, or even know if the company made cartoons or cigars or underarm deodorant, or nothing at all.

"My clients, I used to tease them. I'd call them up and I'd say to them, 'I got eye-pee-ohhhhhhhh!' And they'd say, 'I'm in.' These idiots, they thought this was the best thing since sliced bread. So they would send money and most of them would get five hundred shares, and they'd have to buy more in the aftermarket [after the company went public]. That's 'prepackaging a deal.'" Prepackaging a deal is mighty good for the brokerage selling the stock, as it keeps the share price up after the company goes public. But it screws anyone who happens to buy the stock, by artificially inflating the price. Or at least it is supposed to artificially inflate the price, when everything goes right.

Everything didn't go right with TOON. It never had much of a post-IPO run-up, despite the prepackaging, because Todd brokers just didn't have the buying power. The stock closed the first day of trading at $5.25, and after that it imitated a wet rag. By the end of 1994, TOON was eating dirt.

It was sad, and if Louis had noticed an item on TOON in the papers he might have read it. If he cared. Which he didn't.

CHAPTER FOURTEEN

DAH DAH—DAH DAH DAH—DAH DAH—DAH DAH
DAH! DAH DAH—DAH DAH DAH—DAH DAH DAH
DAH DAH! DAH DAH DAH DAH DAH DAH DAH DAH
DAH DAH DAH DAH DAH DAH!!!!!!!

Louis started every day with the soundtrack from *Rocky*.
Three times a day, like antibiotics. BANG. The kids, the cold-
callers, would BANG their fists, in rhythm with the music.
BANG. BANG. BANG.

It was that way at Robert Todd. And when Louis and
Benny left Robert Todd in July 1994, it was that way at their
next firm, A. T. Brod. It would be that way every day and at
every firm where they had cold-callers.

Louis would turn up the volume on the CD player and blast
the first cut from the *Rocky* CD, the one at the beginning of
the movie, every day starting at seven, when the cold-callers
started work. In the middle of the day he would play the training song. And then at the end—the victory song. Louis would
hold up the hand of the cold-caller who opened the most accounts and make him stand up. The champ. It was a good
thing for everybody to see.

Playing that music got the cold-callers pumped up. Movies
too. Louis would play them every chance he got on the VCR

in his office. But not just any movies. They had to be special. *Wall Street* pumped up the brokers. *Glengarry Glen Ross* did not. Some guy in a car begging for leads. Who'd want to be like that guy?

Louis got steamed when his cold-callers complained about the leads. They'd ask him for the "good leads." The *"Glengarry* leads." Sally Leads used to ask for them. He was fascinated with that movie. It made Louis hate *Glengarry* even more. The movie didn't understand salesmen.

"Guys don't get motivated by you talking to them about selling stock," said Louis. "I used to not motivate them like that. Motivating my guys was taking them to the bar at lunchtime and getting everybody fucked up. Wrecked. That was motivating my guys. Taking them to a strip joint and getting them all blow jobs. That motivated my guys. Playing the *Rocky* song in the morning, that would motivate my guys.

"That's how Roy did it. He'd come into the room and people would be psyched to see him. It would be good. Just his persona. A sick guy spending a lot of money. He's the motivator. 'Fuck, he's nuts!' You get psyched about that. You look at him and he's awesome. He don't give a fuck. He's making a million dollars a month, he's smacking people around, he's wearing pink suits. He's fucking nuts. He's out every night. He's got a limo driver waiting downstairs for him. That's motivating. That'll motivate you, in that type of business.

"Michael Milken—he ain't motivating to me. Bill Gates ain't motivating. I don't care he's the richest man in the world. He's not motivating. It's not fun to be Bill Gates because he don't live it up the way Roy does. In the chop houses you had kids from the streets. Their fathers probably sat at home and smoked cigars and had their feet up and fell asleep at nine o'clock. These kids meet guys who are going out, going to strip joints having crazy times, and making money, spending it, doing awesome things, going away. The cold-callers say, 'I want to do that. I want to be that guy.'"

Louis played the *Rocky* songs for the cold-callers but he could have been playing them for himself and for Benny. They were the Rockys of Wall Street. They were the lower-class bums who took on the Apollo Creeds of Wall Street and were beating them. Never mind that Rocky lost in the end. Benny and Louis were winning. They were mastering their craft, going to places like Scores where important people hung out. Making friends, establishing contacts, working hard. Raking it in.

Louis was pulling in over $100,000 a month. Not bad for a brokerage firm "assistant" who dropped out of community college. And that was still small potatoes compared to what some chop house brokers were getting.

At Brod the split wasn't 60–40 anymore. They were equal partners. They were back downtown now, just across the street from Battery Park at the tip of Manhattan. An old-fart building, but downstairs was the only amenity that really mattered—a bank where they could cash their checks.

At Brod, the checks came from a guy by the name of Jugal Kishore Taneja. "Jay" Taneja was fifty years old, of medium height, and stocky. He was a Cleveland financial exec with a clean record, a former engineer with a varied background. When he bought the firm in June 1993, in conjunction with a local brokerage firm official, it was noted with approval in *Crain's Cleveland Business*. "Mr. Taneja owns Bancapital Corp., a holding company in Independence for operations that range from a small intrastate brokerage house to oil and gas exploration companies," *Crain's* reported. The newspaper went on to say that the firm's Manhattan office will continue operating, "but its focus will grow to include the sale of stock to retail investors. . . . At present, A. T. Brod specializes in selling securities to institutional clients. Broadening its scope in New York will mean hiring more brokers there."

Louis and Benny flew out to Cleveland to meet their new boss.

"He took us out to dinner. It was nice, like in *Pretty Woman,* with the couch seats. Elegant. We didn't pay. He had a 500-class Mercedes, a huge house. We were psyched, 'cause we were going to work with somebody who had more money than us. Fallah might have had more money but he didn't spend it. This guy had a nice ring, nice watch. He was like a flashy little guy," said Louis.*

The *Crain's* story was on the mark. Brod was hiring brokers, and the firm's interest in the retail trade was amply borne out by the generosity of the deal with Louis and Benny. In a letter agreement with Benny, A. T. Brod—"Advisors to the Prudent Investor"—put the terms in writing, including a provision that "you are 'Team Players' and will do all in your power to comply with the regulations of the Firm, the NASD and the SEC, as well as the New York Stock Exchange."

Of course. Real team players. Particularly that unlicensed "Team Player," a twenty-year-old guy who wasn't old enough to sit at the bar of the private club upstairs from the Brod offices.

"We were the circle," said Louis. "We created our own circle. There were no other brokers there. We were the only guys. We went out there and took over the whole fucking place. It was awesome."

Comfortable too. They started out in cramped quarters on the twenty-first floor of the old-fart building, but after a few months Brod took over the entire twenty-sixth floor. Louis and Benny had the choicest real estate, a huge corner office looking to the west. They could see the bay out the window, the Statue of Liberty and Staten Island in the distance. "It was a slick office," said Louis. "We had the biggest office there. I remember Al Palagonia, the superbroker from D. H. Blair— he was a friend of Benny—he came up to Brod and said, 'Holy

---

*Years later, Taneja acknowledged meeting with Louis and Benny, and having them as guests at his home, but said he was rarely in New York and denied knowledge of any wrongdoing at the New York office of Brod.

shit! This is what they gave you?' It was huge. It had a couch and a love seat and a fucking thirty-six-inch TV with Sega, CNN, and cable. Two big monster black desks, with chairs in front of them, big black leather chairs in back. Then there was a glass window behind the couch that looked over all our cold-callers. It was awesome."

What a firm. Members of the New York Stock Exchange since 1958. Brod's founder could hold his head high anywhere on Wall Street. Albert T. Brod was eighty-one years old. He put his name on the door with pride, and stayed at the firm even though Taneja owned it now. Brod had a clean regulatory history. Not squeaky-clean, maybe—nobody's perfect— but pretty good overall for a firm that concentrated on investment banking for small companies.

Even its building was old Wall Street. Brod was at 17 Battery Place, the Whitehall Building, a carved-stone building of the kind more likely to be found in Chicago than in New York. It was in every postcard view of Lower Manhattan, just to the right of Battery Park City and smack in front of the World Trade Center.

Brod was the epitome of the Real Wall Street, the Wall Street of Brooks Brothers suits and private incomes and private clubs. Clubs like the Whitehall Lunch Club on the top floor. Al Brod was a member of the Whitehall Lunch Club. His record was unblemished. NASD records said he had even lived at the same address on Park Avenue since his birth in October 1913.

A. T. Brod was a class act. Old money. Tradition. Great reputation. All of the things Louis hated. But such things didn't matter. Old money could be taken. Tradition could be defied. Reputations destroyed.

Louis hated class. He liked cars. So he bought a Mercedes. He hated old stone buildings. He liked gleaming new ones. So at about the time Brod moved to the twenty-sixth floor, he moved from Staten Island to 200 Rector Place, due southwest of the proud and glorious Twin Towers. Not since Battery Park City was built on a mound of World Trade Center construction debris, back in the 1970s, had such a humongous and high-class building been erected there. Louis's new home was forty-six stories high. Louis was on the thirty-fourth floor, in the corner apartment facing southeast. On a clear day, with binoculars, he could look out of his office at Brod and see Sally Leads in his apartment.

Life was good and getting better. There was much to share. Louis was sharing with Stefanie, with Stefanie's parents, and with his own parents. Their trips to Atlantic City were becoming more frequent, more enjoyable. Louis loved playing blackjack. Sometimes he would go to Atlantic City with Sally Leads, or with Stefanie, or alone. He enjoyed it so much that sometimes he would come down from his hotel room in the middle of the night, back to the blackjack table. But even if he lost, it just meant sharing money, meaningless money, fuck-you money, with the casino. He could afford it. It was no problem. The money was coming in endlessly. Louis had the best job on the planet.

His job was great because his leads were awesome. Great selling required great leads. *Glengarry* leads. In the movie, the old man broke into the office and got caught. That's where the movie got it wrong. Nobody ever got caught. Not on Wall Street.

CHAPTER FIFTEEN

"They made it so easy for you to rob money. It was incredible. How could you not rob and steal? You want a broker license? Three grand. You need some leads to call, some people willing to get stolen from? Two grand. It was the easiest thing in the world.

"We had a guy, Ivan, who would go into the places and rob the leads for us. He was a black guy. He knew one of the guys who ran a crew at Brod. That's how we got the hook. Ivan was this nigger from Harlem, and he would just rob places. You know how many places used to get robbed on Wall Street? This guy would go in at night, break in, and rob the place.

"Ivan used to go to whatever the hottest place was at the time. For example, if First Hanover just did an IPO, this guy would come and say, 'I'm gonna go to First Hanover and rob the leads. You want first crack at them?' We paid a lot of money for leads. Sometimes nine, ten thousand for a few thousand leads. We'd pay sometimes two dollars a lead.

"Ivan broke into First Hanover while we were at A. T. Brod. He broke into A. S. Goldmen. This tough guy was running that place—we were afraid to use them right away. We waited a couple of months. At Brod we spent maybe twenty-five thousand dollars on leads. Ivan used to come to us first.

We were paying enough money that we would get the originals. He ran one copy for himself, one for us, and one for another broker. He was honest about that. He'd come to us after a year and say, 'Are you done beating up on those leads? I'll sell them to somebody else.'

"He would steal the client books. People would come in the next day, and the books were missing. Or he would copy them. He would actually spend time in the place copying them. Once he went to this place in New Jersey with one of my friends. They went in and stayed there for hours, copying leads. Then they put everything back. Ivan was smart. He made friends with the security guards—fellow black guys— and offered them money. He'd give them five hundred out of his pocket, go upstairs, break the window, go in, copy the leads, then leave.

"That happened to us once at Brod. Somebody came in and copied our book. We found out because people were calling our clients. We knew it was Ivan. One of my clients said he got called by somebody at some other firm.

"It was very funny, actually. He was a real project nigger. At first he acts like he's going to shake us down. 'That's what I do. I took the book.' Benny knew how to deal with them, because he used to sell blow to them. He's like, 'You got to be kidding me. You're gonna be dead.' Benny later tells me Ivan said he only sold it to two people, and he apologized. He was afraid somebody would kill him. Our crew was crazy. Everybody was a street guy, and they were fucking lunatics. They'd have beat this kid senseless."

CHAPTER SIXTEEN

It was a ritual now. A privilege of rank and earning power. Louis and Benny's office was in the power position at the far end of the twenty-sixth floor, farthest from the entrance. Every day Louis would saunter in at ten o'clock or later, stroll in with sunglasses on and hat down to his nose, past whatever sales meetings they might be having, past all of the kids working the phones, over to his corner office. The kids would stare at him, with his Rolex on his wrist and his custom-made shirt hanging out of his custom-tailored pants, and be envious. Which was okay.

He knew he was being watched. He used to be one of them. He used to watch as Chris Wolf slouched in late at Hanover. Chris Wolf, the Ferrari-driving rich guy. Now Louis was the rich guy, the Chris Wolf. It was a great feeling. And motivating to the kids, just as he was motivated watching Chris Wolf.

The money-disposal problem was worsening as summer gave way to fall of 1994 and A. T. Brod started to pay off for Louis, Benny, and their cold-callers. With $100,000 to $125,000 coming in every month, an ugly possibility reared its head. Louis might have to save some of it.

No way. His father used to save, and Louis did not want to be like his father, at least when it came to money. Louis's father worked and saved and struggled. If he were his father he might have put away some money for a rainy day. But he didn't know the meaning of a rainy day. Louis didn't even know what a cloud was. There were no clouds, let alone rain, in his life. If one appeared overhead, and it started raining, he might have thought someone had spilled a glass of water out of a window. He wasn't interested in buying a house or even a condo. What was he going to do with a house? You can live in a house, and a house like Roy's place in Richmondtown can be awesome, but houses aren't fun. All you do is live there.

The money was regular now. At Todd the money would come in as spurts—eighty or ninety grand one month, and next month maybe thirty. At Brod it was a hundred grand at least, every month. "The next month would come, we'd still have like seventy grand left over," said Louis. "It just started adding up and adding up. What to do with this money? It was ridiculous. George Donohue used to tell me, 'You know, it doesn't always come this easy.' But I thought it was never-ending, a never-ending saga. Because every month, we'd get sometimes three hundred grand. It was crazy. Twenty years old. I didn't know what to do with myself."

It was at about this time that Louis started getting manila envelopes from the IRS. He would throw them out without even opening them. Nick Pasciuto used to tell him that he would have to pay taxes someday. Bullshit. Louis was not ever paying taxes. "Once I had four or five hundred thousand dollars sitting in a fucking bank, and my accountant said, 'Send them a hundred thirty grand.' And I said, 'You don't understand. I'm not sending them any money. I'll get the cash out of the bank right now,'" said Louis. And he wasn't joking. He didn't like having his money in the bank. It was just sitting there, getting rat-shit interest, and all he would get for his cash would be receipts and account statements. Pieces of paper— just as he was taking money from his clients and giving them pieces of paper.

Louis was no fool. This paper-for-money shit would have to end. "I used to get paranoid to have it in the bank," said Louis. "Somebody's going to get it. I used to go to the bank, withdraw twenty, thirty thousand even though I didn't need it. I just didn't want it in there. I just felt not safe with it in the bank. I liked having it in my house—'Ah, there it is!' Ain't nobody taking it but me now.

"Used to take them an hour to count it up. I got so good at Marine Midland that I used to call the lady there in the morning and say, 'I'm coming at two o'clock. I'll need fifty thousand.' I'd go there, go to the back room, count the money, leave. I got it in hundreds. A couple of times I got twenty grand in twenties. It was tremendous.

'I put a safe in my apartment, in my walk-in closet, bolted to the floor. It was about three feet high, big, but I still didn't have room for all my shit. Me and Sally Leads were the only ones that had the combination. I used to have stacks of money in there—twenties, hundreds. I remember one time Frankie Balls [a cold-caller] asked me for like eight thousand and he thought I'd have to go to the bank and get it. I said, 'Nah, I'll give it to you. Come to the house.' I remember I looked in my safe and I said, 'I'll give it to him.' It didn't affect my stacks. I had like stacks of money. I didn't care about the eight thousand. I was just thinking about how I'd have to—I had a name for it—'load up.' I'd have to go load up again from the bank."

The money couldn't sit in a safe forever. Louis was no miser.

Nearly every weekend Louis and Stefanie went to South Beach in Miami, usually with Benny and his girlfriend Michelle. In the winters they had a rental at Hunter Mountain. When he wasn't on South Beach or Hunter Mountain, he was in Atlantic City. When he wasn't in one of those places or with Stefanie, he would be at another money funnel, Scores.

He would go there most weeknights, meeting important new people. Celebrities. Sports figures. The kind of people you meet in New York when you go to the right places and have a lot of money. And when you have a lot of money you have to look as if you have a lot of money. You don't buy suits off the rack and you don't wear a Seiko. Watches don't tell time. They tell something about you. They make a statement. He got his first Rolex right after he got to Todd, and it was on his wrist when he turned twenty. From then on he always had at least one Rolex, and by the time he got to Brod he had a bunch in his bedroom drawer.

Buying stuff was fun.

When he went to Tourneau on Madison Avenue for the Presidential, he came with a hat pulled over his nose and pajama-bottom-type pants. It was a thing to see. Coming into a store like Tourneau with Sally Leads, and being ignored, and going to the Rolex counter, and putting a stack of money on the counter. He got service. Good service.

"I went from wondering where I was going to get ten dollars to go back and forth from work, to buying stupid shit and not even thinking about it," said Louis. "It wouldn't bother me. I wouldn't think twice. I bought Louis Vuitton wallets. They're four hundred. I didn't care. I wouldn't think about it. People would go into a store and say, 'Ohhh . . .' I'd say, 'Nice wallet. How much? Three ninety-five? No big deal.' My mother got for Christmas a Hummel, my father got a Nautica jacket, Stefanie got all of Bloomingdale's. I would just go there and pick out the mannequins. I'd see a mannequin dressed in a girl's clothes and I'd tell the salesperson, 'That mannequin there.'

"I was always tan. I used to take time out of my day to go to the tanning salon. At lunchtime I'd leave, take a cab, go to the tanning salon, and come back. Facials. I'd get a face masque and stuff. Why not? Take the dirt out. Really deep-cleanse it. Barbershop once a week. I got my eyebrows waxed. Used to go to a salon, Hermitage. A men's salon. I'd go there and all in one day get a massage, manicure, facial, eyebrows, haircut. Never did that before.

"I used to get a massage up on 38th Street, and I'd have Sally Leads shoot up to Bloomingdale's and buy an outfit to wear to go out that night. This happened every other day. I wouldn't even wash the clothes. I was too lazy to take them to the wash. I didn't like them after a week. Didn't want to wear them no more. I'd buy new ones. It was irrational. Normal people would just take their clothes and wash them. But if I have to go home and wash them, I go, 'Nah, I don't want to do that. I need a new outfit. It's shit. Sucks. Fuck it.' Half the shit I bought I wouldn't wear."

"The money and the possessions were so important to him because they really did boost his self-esteem," said Stefanie. "He didn't have any. For him, I think, the money was self-worth. If he had no money, he was worth nothing. He wasn't a good enough person.

"He put too much of a value on the dollar. When he started work, he decided to become a big shot. All of a sudden all these people were coming out of the woodwork. Even the people he met. Who are these people? They weren't his friends. Two months ago he was nothing. Now we're treating them to dinner, buying them drinks. Taking them out. I would say to him, 'What happens when the money runs dry? Are they still going to be here? These aren't your friends. Your friends are the people you grew up with. If they're your friends they shouldn't be freeloading.' I think he didn't care as long as he had a lot of people who were interested in him, to hang out with him."

In the back of his mind, Louis knew that people were using him, maybe, just a little. But he didn't care. There was plenty of money to go around. Plenty for everybody, forever.

CHAPTER SEVENTEEN

When Benny brought a large, heavyset man named Frank Coppa up to A. T. Brod a few months after they started working there, it was a pain in the ass. Louis hated when strangers came by to visit.

Coppa met with Benny in the office alone. Louis was asked to leave. He hated it. There was nothing he hated more than being asked to leave somewhere.

So he went downstairs, down by Battery Park. He smoked for a while. Looked at the girls. Then he came back up and they were still talking. The door was closed. Frank was doing most of the talking. He was gesturing with his large, ham-sized hands. It went on for an hour and a half. Louis was sitting outside, in the boardroom, smoking. Excluded.

"It was so annoying," said Louis. "Then I called Benny on his extension and I said, 'Listen, what do you want me to do here? I got work to do, you know.' And he says, 'I don't know.'

"Frank was sitting in my chair. He was a big guy. About six-two, maybe two hundred and eighty pounds. Humongous. So he's sitting there, and they were talking about this great deal that Frank has and how we're going to raise lots of money. It was going to be the next fucking Mickey D's.

"At that time I didn't really know who he was. Benny didn't introduce me to him. Then, after he left, as he was walking out, he said, 'Louie, this is the guy who shook me down and took my 'Vette.'"

Frank sat in Louis's seat with comfort, regally, because he was at home. Frank had always been at home in brokerages, no matter where they were located—New Jersey, Long Island, or Manhattan. He was working with stocks and brokers as far back as the 1970s, and in 1979 he was convicted by the feds for his role in a stock deal involving a company called Tucker Drilling. Oil stocks were the dot.coms of the 1970s. People wanted to buy hot stocks. So Frank and his crew got oil company stock that was nearly worthless and gave brokers cash, under the table, to sell the stock to the public at high prices. "Cash deals."

Frank was back in the stock business by the late 1980s, only this time he was more careful and didn't get caught. When the feds sent him to prison in 1992 for tax evasion, it was for something entirely unrelated to Wall Street. In fact, it was such a bullshit thing that it got very little publicity at the time. He was accused of concealing income he got in the early 1980s from a school bus company that was controlled by members of his family. It was called My Three Sons, as in the 1960s TV series.

The name was more than a homage to Fred MacMurray. Frank actually had three sons. One became a doctor. The others, Frank Junior and Michael, stayed close to their father and went into business. The school bus business.

Frank got out of school buses after that and switched to chicken. Chicken restaurants. Chain restaurants, including a hot IPO called Boston Chicken, were serious stock plays at the time. That's why he had stopped by to see Benny. Chicken was the subject of conversation, a chain of fast-food chicken restaurants Frank's family ran called Chic-Chick. The way Frank talked about it that day at A. T. Brod, you'd think it was the greatest thing since God created the school bus leasing contract.

Frank Junior and Michael had both moved to Chic-Chick after they left their last line of work back in 1991. According to papers later filed by Chic-Chick with the New York secretary of state, Frank Junior had "owned and operated transit companies having bus contracts with the New York City Board of Education," and the same description applied to his older brother Michael, except for the ownership part.

It was not exactly a typical career transition—school buses to fried chicken—but there were commonalities. School-age children ride in school buses and eat fried chicken, no? Besides, management is management, and the Coppa name alone stood for something, particularly when stock was involved.

Frank wanted to take the company public, à la Boston Chicken, with Frank Junior slated to be the chairman and chief executive officer. The first thing he was going to do was to commence a "private placement" of Chic-Chick shares. That is a conventional and, usually, perfectly respectable capital-raising technique, used by thousands of companies. A private placement is a bit like an IPO, but without all the dumb SEC paperwork. In a private placement, wealthy investors—they have to be millionaires, by law—invest money in a company that is not yet public, often in the expectation that it will go public sometime down the road.

When a private placement works out okay, the investors can walk away very wealthy. If it goes wrong, they can lose every penny. The business can go bad, or—it happens—maybe the company doesn't exist at all. But that wasn't happening here. There were Chic-Chick restaurants. Six of them. None were owned by the company—all were owned and operated by outsiders, under franchise. But that was fine print and who gave a fuck about that?

For Frank Senior, the private placement was a way of

killing two pullets with one stone. He would raise money for
the company and, meanwhile, lay the groundwork for taking
the company public. That way everybody would make a bundle of money. Legally. Frank was enthusiastic—and hey, when
Frank wanted something, he usually got it. Whether it was a
private placement or Benny's 'Vette.

The 'Vette episode did not rankle Benny.

Guys always retain ties to their neighborhoods, and Frank
Coppa was no exception. He lived in New Jersey but, like a
salesman who knew the territory, he still had an exclusive
franchise over the vicinity of 86th Street at the eastern edge of
Bensonhurst by the elevated train line. As soon as you walked
onto the platform you were in Frank Coppa Country. It could
have been on the subway maps, for it was just as true as "86th
Street."

Frank's territory encompassed a low-income municipal
housing project called Marlboro Houses. By Benny's account,
the whole 'Vette business stemmed from the fact that Benny,
who lived in the vicinity, used to sell drugs at Marlboro back
in the 1980s and early 1990s, at the time when he was listed
on NASD records as "unemployed."

Frank was no neighborhood dope dealer, but Benny's enterprise fell under his jurisdiction, so Benny had to pay him
for the privilege, and he couldn't come up with the cash one
time. Frank got his 'Vette. He climbed into the 'Vette, somehow, and drove off with it.

Benny's drug dealing put him in contact with more than
just the honest, hardworking substance abusers of Marlboro
Houses. He got to know a guy in his mid-twenties, from
Queens originally, who had slicked-back blond hair and
looked a bit like Charlie Sheen. Al Palagonia was just starting
to make his name at D. H. Blair when he met Benny. And
when Hanover Sterling started up in 1992, Al introduced
Benny to his other friend, Roy Ageloff. Benny was genial and

smart, a hustler. Just the kind of fresh new blood Roy was looking for, a young kid uncontaminated by the Street.

In the years ahead, people on the outside, regulators and journalists, would have described Frank's visit to Brod as part of some kind of effort to "infiltrate" Brod. But the Frank-Benny-Brod relationship was a lot simpler than that. Frank was just bringing a business deal to an associate. And it was one hell of a deal.

It took a few months for the papers to be processed. Louis was not waiting with bated breath. Which was good. Because when Louis saw the Chic-Chick private placement memorandum, duly filed with the New York State Bureau of Investor Protection in February 1995, he almost gagged.

Louis was being asked to sell Chic-Chick "units" to his clients, and each of them cost $25,000. The units were in the form of a loan, at 10 percent, with some stock thrown in as a sweetener. But there was no way you could sugarcoat Chic-Chick. In 1994 the company had a financial statement that looked as if it was generated by a small-town church thrift shop—revenues of $163,581 and expenses of $158,568, with $59,736 in working capital. That was it. No 000s omitted.

True, Chic-Chick had "expansion" plans. Following this offering, the private placement memorandum said, "the Company intends to commence development of one (minimum) or two (maximum) Company owned restaurants." If the "casual atmosphere" didn't get them lining up outside the "one (minimum) or two (maximum)" Chic-Chick-owned and -operated restaurants, they might be enticed by the slogan, "Chicken with Good Taste."

"I used to say to Benny I had a pitch for Chic-Chick: 'Frank used to eat a lot of chicken when he was young, used to cook the chicken on the barbecue. And he told his son, "You should start a franchise chicken company."' I used to say they could put Frank in a chicken suit in front of the store, and that wouldn't sell the chicken. It wasn't even good chicken. The fries were rubbery. It was the stupidest fucking thing I ever saw in my life. They had the whole family working there. Frank Junior was really into it. I think that Frank Junior really wanted to make it go somewhere, but his father probably smacked him. 'Smarten up!'

"I used to pitch it by saying, 'Listen, I got something coming up. Chic-Chick. They got one franchise store and they're opening up nine more. Could be the next Kentucky Fried Chicken.' I felt like saying, 'Frank Coppa owns it. You know, the guy in the Mafia. They got his name right in the prospectus.' What else could you say about this company? It was fucking horrible. I couldn't sell it. These guys are putting on the pressure and I told Benny, 'Tell them I can't do it. I can sell a lady in white gloves an open jar of ketchup but I can't sell Chic-Chick.' Eventually I got about three hundred thousand dollars of it sold, I don't know how."

By now, New York State law prohibited smoking in most places of employment. Louis could always tell when Frank was arriving at Brod because he tended to disregard that particular statutory restriction. Frank was always smoking big cigars—"torpedoes"—and he didn't care much if anybody was gagging on the fumes. Louis observed that he always dressed well. Guys like him always wore stylish clothing, but a Guy like Frank was not a slave to conventions in men's clothing. Guys were fashion leaders, at least in their own circles.

"He always wore slacks, never jeans. Always grayish slacks, nice shoes. A button-down shirt. No tie. And a black, short mink coat. I mean, he wears a fur, mink jacket. Men don't wear mink jackets. Like how do you walk down Wall Street in a mink jacket and people not think that you're a gangster? He probably had it custom-made. You have to go to Fifth Avenue, to one of the fur stores there. These are the guys who wear a mink coat: Either John Gotti, or a black guy. Some pimp in Harlem.

"Frank wore a Rolex, but with style. Not gaudy. Not with diamonds. Not like mine. Mine had diamonds around the top, diamonds all over it. He just wore a gold Rolex, no diamonds, a bracelet, and a ring. Ring had a sick diamond on it. Then he had the cigar. It was about a foot long, I'm not kidding. But for him it was small. He was tremendous. All fat, but you don't tell him that. Like he ain't even a nice guy. Call him fat and he'd probably smack you around. He had big hands. Big Italian hands. Definitely a mean guy in his prime. You could tell."

Chic-Chick was an annoyance. But he had to pitch Chic-Chick. Benny made that clear. There was no choice. But Louis didn't care. He was building a business. And sometimes, when you build a business, you have to do people favors. That's how Wall Street works. Favors. Networking. Louis was learning that—learning to become a Wall Street guy.

CHAPTER EIGHTEEN

The chop house kids loved Howard Stern. His early morning radio show was as much a part of their lives as the pitches they read and the rips that were making them rich. The media called him a "shock jock," but that was the media for you—full of crap, as always. The press, and the yahoos and scrubs who tried to get him off the air, saw only the sensational stuff, the strippers, the butt bongo. To the chop house kids, Howard was just a guy from a blue-collar suburb who made good, who spoke his mind. He was a cool older guy. A Roy. Like Roy, Howard dressed as he wanted, didn't go in for the button-down life, told people in authority to go fuck themselves, didn't let the government cut off his balls. He had an entourage, just like Roy. He yelled at his people and gave them a hard time, just like Roy—and they still loved him. Just like Roy.

But it was the fight with the Federal Communications Commission, his constant running battle with the government, which was the most important common ground. Howard fought the FCC and won. The chop house kids were fighting the SEC and winning. And through it all—this was the part his detractors missed—Howard was always a family man. A private man, who lived on Long Island with his family and didn't cheat on his wife.

Louis wanted desperately to get Howard Stern as a client. It would be like getting God as a client. No, better than God, because there was no God. And there was a Howard Stern.

Louis began his campaign methodically. He decided to home in on the periphery, the entourage of on-air personalities who kept Howard fed with straight lines. One of the most popular was a former intern named John Melendez, "Stuttering John," who was noted for buttonholing celebrities at premieres and asking rude questions. Stuttering John was a young guy, only a bit older than Louis, and he was too young to have his own entourage.

It was Louis's idea to call Stuttering John, and he did it only a few weeks after he started working at Brod. John had talked on the air about how he was buying into IPOs, and Howard was goofing on him about it.

"Benny said, 'Yeah give him a call.' Benny would never do it because he has no balls. So I did it. I didn't give a shit. What was he going to say? Get off the phone, fuck you, hang up on me? That would be it. Dead issue.

"So I just called John out of the blue. I called the Howard Stern office and asked for John—'John Melendez, please.' He answered his own phone. I says, 'This is Ben Salmonese.' The first conversation was under Ben's name, because it was his license—if he looked into me, he'd have found I wasn't licensed. I used Benny's name, and made him some money. We sold him HOOP [Sure Shot] warrants. I told him, 'Listen, I'll buy you twenty thousand warrants. I'll buy them today, sell them in two days. If I don't do that, don't pay for them.' I was guaranteeing the money. So he said, 'Sure. Fuck it.' He didn't care."

Louis was selling a lot of warrants at Brod. He loved warrants. A warrant is a wager on the future price of a stock, and works about the same as a stock option. It gives you the right to get a stock at a certain price sometime in the future. War-rants can be a good investment if you think the underlying stock is going to really grow in value. If you spend a buck to buy a warrant that lets you get a hundred shares of a stock at $5 next year, and you think the stock is going to go up to $10 by then, that's pretty good, no?

But Louis never told his customers that. He said warrants were "trading vehicles." They were pieces of paper that, Louis insisted, were going to increase in price. What they repre-sented, what you could do with the warrant—he didn't get into that. He simply said warrants were a sure thing. Some-thing you buy at $1 and sell later at $2. Guaranteed.

What Louis told Stuttering John was pretty much the same pitch that Louis was giving a lot of clients—that the Sure Shot warrants were the next best thing to printing money. Louis was always amazed how it would work. They believed him! Sure Shot warrants were all pretty much controlled—"boxed"—by Louis and Benny and a few other Brod brokers, so Louis knew perfectly well who was going to make money and who wasn't.

Louis wasn't trying to rip off Stuttering John. He really wanted John to make money. He saw to that. He wanted Stut-tering John to be happy. He wanted John, the other Howard Stern people—and then Howard himself. The Holy butt-bongo-banging, stripper-ogling Grail.

"So we opened his account, and bought the warrants for John for about a dollar forty, and sold it for him for some-thing like three dollars in like two days. We made him thirty-five grand, something like that. I think he had only twenty grand he wanted to spend, so he wound up buying maybe six-teen thousand warrants. He was happy as anything. I called him back, and said, 'You got that sell confirmation?' He says, 'Yeah.' So I said, 'You can call up Kemper* and find out the

---

*Kemper Securities "cleared" trades for A. T. Brod—executing trades and issuing state-ments and other routine paperwork. Kemper also physically maintained the customer ac-counts.

balance in your account.' I'm sure he did, and found out he had like forty-something thousand in there. Then he sent the money."

Sure, Louis wanted referrals. But it was more than that. John was the real thing—a celebrity. Okay, a low-rent celebrity, not too well known outside the New York area or the Howard Stern orbit. But Howard was the King of All Media, and Stuttering John was an important part of the show. He had a band and was selling CDs. A great client. Any legit broker on the Real Wall Street could have told you that. And how many of them could have guaranteed him profits?

They had to meet.

"After he sends the check I call him and say maybe we should meet up. So I says Scores, 'cause we had a lot of pull there, not that he didn't. We met him at Scores. He was with a couple of his guys who worked at the station. When we shook his hand he kind of laughed. He was expecting a totally different situation. I was twenty years old, Benny had a leather motorcycle jacket on, a Michael Jackson jacket. We didn't really talk about business. We just told him we wanted referrals, and he was, like, laughing, and people were coming over to him and he was goofing on them. He was a goofball. He goofs on people.

"After a little while, that was it—he wanted to leave. He's a weird guy. One minute he's talking to you and the next minute he's out, done, goodbye. He wants to go. Gets annoyed fast. Strange dude. Gets very on the defensive. Somebody will say something in a light manner, and he'll answer it back, like, 'What do you mean?'"

Meeting John was great enough, but the next morning came Nirvana. He mentioned Louis and Benny on the air! "He said on the air how he thought he was going to meet a thirty-year-old man with a suit and tie, and how instead there's one guy wearing a motorcycle jacket and was the size of a frigging doorway. The other guy is going bald and looked like a frigging rat. Or something like that, he says—right on the air. He was talking about me and Benny."

Stuttering John was good with referrals too. One was Stern's producer and on-air regular, "Baba Booey," Gary Dell'Abate. Louis sold Gary Sure Shot International warrants for $2 to $2.25 each, and the warrants doubled to $4.50. For John, Louis also "worked the spreads." That was a simple way of making money for him. Louis had just found out about it, and had started to do it for himself.

The principle is simple. Every stock has two prices, a "bid" and an "ask." The bid is the price of the stock when a member of the public wants to sell a stock, and the ask is the price when a member of the public wants to buy a stock. The difference between the bid and the ask is the spread, which was huge for chop stocks. Ordinarily it is impossible for customers to buy stocks at the bid and sell at the ask. For a customer to do that, he had to have pull. John Melendez had pull. So Louis did the trades and made money for John, and John had no idea what was happening—only that he was making money. The spread for Sure Shot was something like 3 1/2 bid and 4 1/2 ask, so that was nice money. Louis did the trades at prices slightly different from the bids and asks, to avoid flagging the SEC.

Through John, Louis and Benny got two other Stern show regulars, Howard's sidekick Robin Quivers and his writer Jackie "the Jokeman" Martling. Both also profited from trades in Sure Shot warrants. For the Stern show people, this "Ben Salmonese" must have seemed awfully smart—a hot young broker with unusually good market timing. Sure Shot didn't seem to be a rigged stock. If they had access to even the most sophisticated trading machines, they could see that this was a legit company, that "Ben" worked for a legit, New York Stock Exchange–member brokerage house, and that everything was totally okay.

One of Stuttering John's referrals blew them away completely—a young executive at Atlantic Records named Craig Kallman. The hope was that Kallman would be able to give them still other referrals from the music world—who knows? Madonna, maybe. Metallica. Their heads were spinning. They had really reached the big time with Kallman. So Louis and Benny treated him right, making sure Kallman got $70,000 or so in profits, through trades in Sure Shot. Sure Shot was the number one A. T. Brod house stock, and for Louis and Benny it was terrific—like running a printing press cranking out hundred-dollar bills. They were running it off for themselves, so why not for guys like Stuttering John and Kallman who could help them out? Kallman "made it seem like he could get everyone in the world to get us money," said Louis.

Louis and Benny both started to fantasize, just a little, that maybe these guys, these legit people, could be their tickets to the Real Wall Street.

part three

LEGENDIZED

CHAPTER NINETEEN

The Real Wall Street didn't know they existed. They didn't have publicists planting stories about them in the financial press, and the media usually ignored their world. But that was okay. Louis and Benny were known among the people who counted. Their people. "We legendized ourselves on Wall Street. It was 'Benny and Louie.' We were known," says Louis. "Every firm was calling us to do business. L. T. Lawrence. First Hanover. They were calling us, making us offers. Sign-up bonuses. Fifty thousand. A hundred thousand."

They had to start thinking about the future. Well, not the future, exactly. They were actually thinking about thinking about the future. Louis and Benny never really planned, but they started to look ahead to the time when they would want to plan. They began to realize that with the referrals they were getting from Stuttering John, and hoped to get from Craig Kallman, maybe, just maybe, they could get clients for whom they could actually make money, who could enable them to cross that seemingly unbridgeable, unimaginably huge gulf that separated a former blow dealer and a community college dropout from that other Wall Street, Al Brod's Wall Street, A. T. Brod's Wall Street before they came to A. T. Brod and turned it into a chop house. Maybe they could start getting real commissions and sell real stocks. Maybe they could get into the world that was all around them, the Real Wall Street.

All they needed were enough big-bucks clients, clients with names, cool clients who would trust them with their money. No problem.

By the end of 1994 they were getting clients who would have been the envy of any brokerage firm on Wall Street. And not just more friends of Stuttering John, who was hanging out with them, and Brod broker Marco Fiore, more and more. They did it without connections, without referrals from John or Craig Kallman or Al Brod or the old fucks sipping tomato soup in the Whitehall Lunch Club, for that matter.

Louis and Benny were easing into the Real Wall Street in the classic way—by being in the right place at the right time and by working. Always working. Always be closing. They didn't go for that *Glengarry Glen Ross* crap in theory but they embodied it in practice. That was how Louis and Benny got Clifford Hicks, a punt returner for the New York Jets. No connections. Just old-fashioned balls, the kind of balls even the Real Wall Street would have admired. Going to a Jets game at the Meadowlands, and always working. Networking. Just as the white-shoe firms taught the recruits from Penn and Yale, only no white-bread fuck could have gotten Clifford Hicks as a client.

"We went to go see a Jets game and we had front-row seats so they could hear us. We were on the fifty-yard line right behind the Jets bench, so the players would notice us. Then afterward behind the stadium we went back to where the players leave, and we got Clifford Hicks's attention. He came over and started talking with us. We were just bullshitting about the game, we were being friends. We said we were brokers and we wanted a shot at making him some money. We guaranteed it to him. Told him we'd invest maybe five grand and make him twenty-five thousand. We were going to multiply his money. And he was interested, he said to give him a card or a number. Benny had a card on him. So we gave him the card. A couple of days later he called, left a message, and then I pitched him, and he sent five grand. We made him his twenty-five thousand or whatever and he started giving us referrals. He was our hook."

This was a lousy season for the Jets, but it was a great season for Louis and Benny, and now it was going to be a great season, financially, for Clifford Hicks and the players he started to refer. That was the plan. Everybody was going to make money—Louis, Benny, Clifford Hicks, his friends on the Jets, Stuttering John and his friends, Craig Kallman and his friends. Everybody. Everybody Louis and Benny wanted to make money.

"We made these guys great money. For Clifford Hicks of the Jets—we bought him the Sure Shot warrants, traded his account, took him in at the bid and out at the offer, made him money. Once I called him and I said, 'Hey, Cliff, I'm going to send you a check for twenty-five thousand.' And he says, 'Get the fuck out of here, man.' I say, 'I'm serious.' He says, 'Fucking great, man.' And I say, 'All I want you to do is introduce me to some of the boys.' He says, 'No doubt.' And he starts having them call. Alfred Oglesby called us. He says, 'Yeah, my boy Cliff, ya made some money. I wanna know how to get in on it.' That's how they talk to you. It's funny how they used to talk. Johnny Mitchell wasn't like that. He was an intelligent guy. An educated black man. He had big money. He used to make a million and a half a year."

Like the Stern people, the Jets players had business managers and accountants. But no private banker promised the kind of really great short-term trading profits that Louis and Benny were able to provide. Legitimately, for all the players knew. Benny had a clean record, and his name was on the confirmations. A. T. Brod was a clean firm, ignored by the press just as consistently as Hanover was ignored by the press. For all anybody could have known, these were two really great, hungry brokers, as terrific as traders as they were young and cool. Other brokers couldn't even attempt the awesome trades these guys were able to perform. Other brokers didn't promise big bucks and then deliver. But Louis and Benny weren't ordinary brokers. It was as if they were bookies who, somehow, had an uncanny ability to forecast the results of horse races. Who wouldn't want a bookie like that?

True, it wasn't as if *nobody* was going to be ripped off. The money had to come from somewhere, no?

Louis and Benny came up with a plan, beautiful in its symbiotic simplicity. They would have two types of clients—the Nobodies and the Celebrities. The idea was to get millions of dollars from the Celebrities, luring them in with the kinds of great, profitable trades that had made money for Stuttering John and the rest. They would put all those millions into solid New York Stock Exchange companies, mutual funds—real investments. Real Wall Street–type investments.

The Nobodies, the imbeciles at the other end of the cold-calls out in rural America, would pay the freight for the Celebrities. Their losses would subsidize the gains for the Celebrities, and they would be on the losing end of the trades that would be winners for the Celebrities. When Louis sold those Sure Shot warrants for the Celebrities like the Stern people, the Nobodies would be the buyers. And the Nobodies couldn't sell. Fuck 'em.

Having big accounts from Celebrities, accounts with real stocks and cash and so on, would serve another purpose vital for the operation of a chop house. Louis would be able to "park" stocks in the Celebrity accounts, on occasion, when it was necessary. Such as when a Nobody wanted to sell stock. If Louis couldn't talk him out of it, he might have to try to get the Nobody out of the stock just to keep the jerk from running to the NASD. Louis would have to get rid of the shares. That is where "parking" came in.

"You need time to sell a chop stock. You couldn't just sell it in the open market, you know. I figured I could put the chop stock in the Celebrity account for a couple of days, to give me time to unload it. I would give the Celebrity maybe thirty cents a share when I sold it. This way I wouldn't have to park the stock illegally while I was finding a buyer. You could park it legally with the money in the account. These sports guys wouldn't even ask what we were doing."

Besides, it was great hanging out with these guys. Clifford had all his teammates sign a football for Louis, and soon their signed jerseys, suitably framed, were on their office walls. They started hanging out. As friends, sort of. Louis and Benny were so close to the Jets' running back Brad Baxter that he called them once to pick up his dog at the airport and take it to his apartment. And they did it. They weren't his bitch boys, weren't Sally Leads. They were just doing what private bankers in the Real Wall Street did for their best clients.

They were legends, these guys. Clifford Hicks and Johnny Mitchell and Oglesby. Brad Baxter, who lived in Manhattan and also hung out at Scores. Then came the placekicker Nick Lowery and others. Referrals led to more referrals and soon they got five-time middleweight champ Vinnie Pazienza.

All great guys. All making money thanks to Louis and Benny.

Sure, the market was having tremors in the mid-1990s. IPOs were hot, and then cold, and then hot again. A smart broker didn't need to worry about the market all that much. A smart broker created his own bull market. In early 1995, when Louis and Benny saw their biggest paychecks at A. T. Brod, the dot.com, high-tech boom had not yet begun. But the best of the chop house kids had their own system for printing money, and Louis was becoming a master at it.

New clients would be generated by the cold-callers and Louis would "second trade" them—he'd zero in for the all-important sale of the chop stock or warrant. And once they got the chop stock he would do "crosses"—basically have the customers selling stock back and forth so that he could get more money out of them. Second trades and crosses. Second trades and crosses. It was the chop house mantra. It was that and it was more. A lot of paperwork and bullshit and dealing with the public. Dealing with the public was a bitch.

Their cold-callers might have had the impression that they were slouches, waltzing in late lots of the time, partying, leaving supervision of the cold-callers to Sally Leads and Chris Votas. But they couldn't see all the work involved, all the planning it took to get things humming.

When things were going good, Louis and Benny's well-oiled cold-calling machine operated so smoothly that they only needed to work for two weeks out of every month. But there was a lot going on behind the scenes. When customers complained and couldn't be shut up, the call had to go in to Shannon Johnson, an ex-Nasdaq official who worked at Hanover for a while and was the guy the chop house crews relied on to expedite license requests and placate customers. Shannon ran a consulting firm in Maryland, not far from Nasdaq headquarters. "Call Shannon"—that was the credo. Shannon was the Man. The cold-callers, seeing Louis come in late every day, not attending meetings, didn't know about Shannon and how important he was. They didn't know about boxing stocks—keeping them under control—or crosses and didn't care, because they didn't have to care.

Crosses were a bit complex, but the principle was simple—Louis had customers selling stocks to each other. For that to happen, about half of the clients had to be in one chop stock, and the other half were in another.

"I remember one time I had something like a hundred thousand shares of Sure Shot, and a hundred thousand shares of Sport Sciences 'in my book,' meaning they were owned by my clients. I think Sports Sciences was three dollars bid and three seventy-five ask. Sure Shot was three and a half bid and four ask. I wanted the clients to sell their Sports Sciences and buy the Sure Shot. The clients that owned the Sure Shot were going to sell that, to buy the Sports Sciences. That's crossing.

"I called up the people who owned Sports Sciences. 'Listen, Sports Sciences is at $3.00. It's not doing that well. I want you to buy Sure Shot. It's at four dollars a share. We'll sell your Sports Sciences and we're going to buy Sure Shot. All I need is a thousand bucks from you.' Easy sale.

"Then I called all the clients that owned Sure Shot, and told them I was swapping them Sure Shot for Sports Sciences. I can charge them the three seventy-five ask price for Sports Sciences, and I can add another twenty-five-cent markup legally.

"So the people who sell Sports Sciences were sending me a dollar a share to make up the price difference, which is a dollar a share for me—a hundred thousand dollars total from them. The people who swapped Sure Shot for Sports Sciences aren't paying me any money, but they're buying for four dollars—the stock that my other customers just sold for three. The whole hundred thousand that I raised, because of this cross, I kept. The whole fucking thing."

Pitching clients for the second trades and crosses was an art. The kind of stuff that came from within. It was like being a great football player, like being a Johnny Mitchell, or a great comedian like Jackie the Jokeman. It was talent. That was the word for it. Something you were born with. But talent needs to be practiced. Honed. Louis became an expert in investor psychology. He knew that people craved acceptance and hated rejection. He put that to work for him.

"Nobody in my book didn't have another trade. And if they didn't have another trade I'd fire them as a client. I'd literally yell at them. I'd say, 'You know what it is? I don't even want you as a client if you're not going to trade with me. You're fired. I'm sending your account out of here. I don't want you as a client.' And they'd take it to heart. They'd say,

'What do you mean?' I'd say, 'What do *you* mean, you don't want to do the trade? You know, I don't want to do no trades with you. You're fired. Take your account, get it out of here, give it to your other shit broker in fucking Texas. I don't want to do shit with you.'

"I'd hang up the phone on them. And they'd call back and say, 'I'm not fired! I'll send the money!'

"If they'd call up to sell I'd tell them to buy. Some guy would say, 'You know, Lou, I got to liquidate some funds. I'm buying a house.' I'd say, 'Let me call you right back. I'm in the middle of something.' I'd hang up the phone and call back like ten minutes later. I'd say, 'You wouldn't believe the opportunity that came across my desk. The stock that you're telling me to sell is about to go to seven. I need you to buy more.' He'd say, 'Keep what we got.' I'd totally reverse the situation.

"Some of these guys, ten thousand was all they had. I'd feel sorry for them. They were scrubs like. And they'd invest the whole thing. They'd tell you how much they had in their checking account. They'd say, 'I only got ninety-six hundred in there.' I'd say, 'What, you can't put another four hundred in your checking account? I need ten thousand.' He'd say, 'I get paid Thursday, so I can do it. I can put in another four hundred.' And they would send ten thousand to you. They'd wait for the paycheck, and try to cover the check. I used to think to myself, 'What is it with these guys? If all I had was forty thousand, maybe if I was dumb enough I'd invest like two. Not thirty-five.' Not all my money. They would throw in all their money. They really believed it. Like they were going to get a stock that was going to go from two to forty and they were going to be millionaires. I used to tell them, 'This stock will make you a millionaire.'

"If a client had like six hundred thousand with us, I said, 'You send me a couple of hundred thousand dollars, this stock will put you over the top. You'll be a million-dollar client. You'll be right in my A Book of million-dollar clients.' They

"We raised him up to be mannerable and respectful and all that."
Nick and the infant Louis on a Brooklyn street.

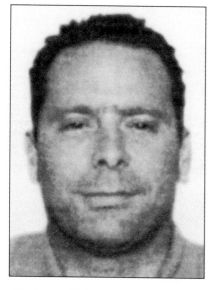

He dressed like a Guy and talked like a Guy and beat up people like a Guy. Roy Ageloff, boss of the brokers at Hanover Sterling & Co. *(Office of U.S. Attorney, Eastern District of New York)*

"Allie Shades" Malangone, Genovese skipper and reputed hidden power behind Hanover Sterling.

Superbroker Chris Wolf taught Louis about his special corner of Wall Street, where cash and chemistry were undisputed sovereigns. *(Office of U.S. Attorney, Eastern District of New York)*

Chris Wolf's partner Rocco Basile made stealing seem easy—but few knew, and fewer appreciated, that it was an art. *(Office of U.S. Attorney, Eastern District of New York)*

Louis and Stefanie in the BMW he acquired with his earnings from Robert Todd. *(Nicole Pasciuto)*

"Sally Leads" was a young cold-caller. He became Louis's friend and general factotum. *(Nicole Pasciuto)*

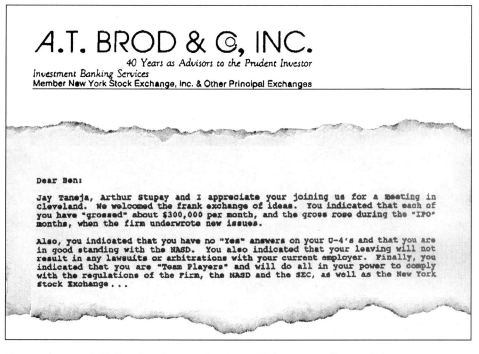

A.T. BROD & ©, INC.

40 Years as Advisors to the Prudent Investor
Investment Banking Services
Member New York Stock Exchange, Inc. & Other Principal Exchanges

Dear Ben:

Jay Taneja, Arthur Stupay and I appreciate your joining us for a meeting in Cleveland. We welcomed the frank exchange of ideas. You indicated that each of you have "grossed" about $300,000 per month, and the gross rose during the "IPO" months, when the firm underwrote new issues.

Also, you indicated that you have no "Yes" answers on your U-4's and that you are in good standing with the NASD. You also indicated that your leaving will not result in any lawsuits or arbitrations with your current employer. Finally, you indicated that you are "Team Players" and will do all in your power to comply with the regulations of the Firm, the NASD and the SEC, as well as the New York Stock Exchange . . .

Team players. A.T. Brod welcomes Louis and his partner Benny Salmonese, now on their honor to comply with securities regulations as they advise all those prudent investors.

Louis and Benny Salmonese took time out from A.T. Brod to relax in Jamaica, where they rang in the new year of 1995 and ran into a client from the recording industry. *(Stefanie Pasciuto)*

FBI TAMPA
6 22 99
990604

Wall Street's new breed of entrepreneur. DeCavalcante skipper Phil Abramo, ex-bagel-company consultant and drug dealer. Ran Sovereign Equity Management. *(FBI photo)*

Chris Wolf's not-so-silent partner Enrico Locascio teamed with "Black Dom" Dionisio to make sure that Vision Investment Group met its revenue targets. *(Office of U.S. Attorney, Eastern District of New York)*

Louis's pal Marco Fiore opened the New York office of Nationwide Securities, which began promisingly but didn't quite end that way. *(Nicole Pasciuto)*

Large man in mink. Bonanno skipper Frank Coppa. His chicken-restaurant private placement did not set Wall Street on fire.

I'll be his. . . . He'll be mine. Charlie Ricottone (second from right) with Louis at the wedding. The shiner was from somebody else. *(Nicole Pasciuto)*

Sonny Franzese in 1967, when he was a rising star in the Colombo family. By the mid-1990s he had a stock deal of his very own, but his power had ebbed.

Nationwide broker Tommy Deceglie (far left), who lost the Elmo sitdown, celebrates the Pasciuto nuptials. Fellow broker Dave Lavender is fourth from left and Sonny's man Howie Zelin is second from right. *(Nicole Pasciuto)*

Howard Stern radio sidekick "Stuttering John" Melendez was a friend and favored client—a Celebrity who unwittingly profited from trades that ripped off the Nobodies. *(Nicole Pasciuto)*

Louis on the deck of *CREAM*, named for the Wu-Tang Clan rap song "Cash Rules Everything Around Me."
(Nicole Pasciuto)

The Ferrari. *(Louis Pasciuto)*

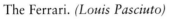

NOVEMBER 1997	WEEK 46

10 Monday (1500 RALPH) — Notes
500 Stef
2500 Charlie (30,510)
mk 500 (6,700)

11 Tuesday Veterans' Day (US) Remembrance Day (C)
Chal Lanna 7:30–9:30

12 Wednesday

NOVEMBER 1997	

Notes — 62,000 —

6 Thursday
1500 MIKE   13000 RALPH
6500 JOHN.
100 FRANKIE   300 DAVE (KILLER)   2,000 mis.
250 Oddie   500 JOHN-PK.
100 MYRON   100 MIKE RIG
500 Richie   1000 MIKE REBEL
500 JOHN.   1000 STEF

7 Friday
500 Charlie
900 JOEY (1000)
150 DAVE (KILLER)
500 JOHN PAL. (14,500)

8 Saturday   **9 Sunday**

By November 1997 the car and boat were gone, Stefanie was pregnant, and debts were piling up.

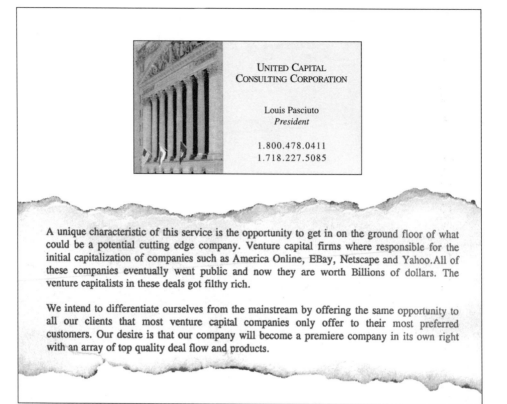

A unique characteristic of this service is the opportunity to get in on the ground floor of what could be a potential cutting edge company. Venture capital firms where responsible for the initial capitalization of companies such as America Online, EBay, Netscape and Yahoo. All of these companies eventually went public and now they are worth Billions of dollars. The venture capitalists in these deals got filthy rich.

We intend to differentiate ourselves from the mainstream by offering the same opportunity to all our clients that most venture capital companies only offer to their most preferred customers. Our desire is that our company will become a premiere company in its own right with an array of top quality deal flow and products.

United Capital's prospectus, 1999.

A message. Fran Pasciuto's car is torched, May 2000. *(Nicole Pasciuto)*

Louis in 2002.

used to hate being in my C book. 'You're in my C Book right now,' I used to tell them. 'Don't you want to get to the A Book?' 'Well, how do I get there?' They wanted to be your best guy. And I used to make them always feel like more important than the next guy. Meanwhile, there was no A, B, or C Book. I used to have the papers on the table. I used to have to search for their numbers. 'Where is this fuck?'

"Sometimes I used to feel bad for some of them. Because they really thought they were going to make money. But I would take their money. If you want to send me the money, send me the money, man. I've got cars and shit to buy. And after a while if I started to feel bad for somebody, I'd say to myself, 'You know what? If he's stupid enough to send it to me, fuck his ass. I'll steal his money.'"

CHAPTER TWENTY

Stefanie was beginning to talk about getting married, and Louis was okay with it.

Louis could find stability in his relationship with Stefanie and her family. Stability and—something else. Something that he had never had in his life, not since he was a baby. He didn't quite know what to call it. Boundaries? Limits? He wasn't sure what to call it.

His family didn't have much in the way of boundaries when he was a kid, and now that he was an adult he saw that Wall Street had no boundaries either. Louis had always set his own limits—by not having any. He did whatever the fuck he pleased. St. Joseph-by-the-Sea taught him that authority was dumb and could be ignored, and that society had no meaningful consequences for bad behavior. It prepared him for Wall Street.

George Donohue became a kind of second father. As Louis was growing up, Nick Pasciuto had become almost as much a buddy as he was a father. And when the money came in, when Louis moved to Manhattan, Nick, still burly and youthful in his mid-forties, started to hang out with him sometimes, and even stay over at the apartment. Fran came too, staying in the apartment with a friend of hers when Louis was out of town for a few days. Fran thought the apartment was beautiful, and she liked Stefanie, but she worried about her only son, her firstborn. She wondered if what he was doing, whatever that was, was going to hurt him. She remembered her days on Wall Street. She didn't like Wall Street.

George was different. George would gently question whether the money was going to come in forever, but he never lectured Louis, never nagged him, never sat in judgment. With George he could be an adult. With his parents he was always a kid.

Louis saw the way Stefanie acted toward her father. Their friends called the Donohues the Brady Bunch but there was a reason why they made movies and TV shows about the Brady Bunch and *My Three Sons* and, when Nick was a kid in the 1950s, that ultimate fantasy, *Father Knows Best*. People made fun of shows like that but there is something about that kind of pseudo-family that appeals to people, deep in the recesses of whatever value system or fantasy life they may possess.

In the Donohue household, father knew best. Louis saw that but could never quite understand it. George and Barbara taught Stefanie to—what was this? Work? Obey? Tell the truth? Louis saw it with his own two eyes and he didn't really know what to think about it. Her parents wouldn't even let her stay overnight at his apartment. Not that Louis was complaining.

There were other girls. Of course there were. Usually it didn't matter. He'd meet a girl and she was history before the bed dried. But when he met Deenie, it wasn't like that. Deenie was different. She was a dancer at Scores.

"At the time, a lot of people that were going to Scores were older businessmen. We were young kids with Benzes and lots of money and fancy watches, and not dressed in suit and ties, dressed in Calvin Klein casual wear. Dressed well. Always tan. So Deenie came over, she was talking, and you know what? I knew she wasn't like the regular girls there. You know, girls just looking to rob you for your money. They were always coming over to you, being all nice to you, because they're just trying to scam you for your money. They do what we do.

"Later on they talked about John Gotti, Jr., running the place but I never seen him there. I used to see actors in there all the time. I used to hang out with Stuttering John, hang out with the Jets. Brad Baxter and Johnny Mitchell used to come there a lot. I used to see, like, Ethan Hawke. Demi Moore I seen there one night. I was sitting right next to her. I was talking to her a little bit. She was hot, a good-looking girl. She was in there, learning for her movie *Striptease,* I think.

"So I went there a couple of times and Deenie comes over to me and says, 'What are you doing? How are you?' Blah blah blah. And she'd say, 'You want me to dance for you?' And I'd say, 'No, if you want to dance, dance for my friend.' I used to give her the money to dance with somebody else. I didn't want to dance with her. I kind of liked her a little bit and I didn't want her to dance. That ruins it. It ruins the relationship then. Then you just become another sucker on her list. So then I asked if she wanted to hang out one night. And she said, 'Yeah.' So I took her out, and that was it. We hit it off. She left that night, and then she came back a few days later and she stayed at my apartment almost every night since then.

"They were both great girls. Stefanie was a shy, innocent Irish girl. That innocent look. I'm very attracted to it. I don't like girls that wear makeup. Deenie was like that too. No makeup. That innocent look. I'm very attracted to it. The blond hair, the blue eyes, the pale skin. It drives me crazy."

CHAPTER TWENTY-ONE

When the stress of working on Wall Street got to be too much, it was time for a Mission.

They also called it a Bender. But "Mission" was a better word for what they did to relieve stress and overwork, because they were taking a little trip away from it all, a little trip to Blowland. They would take a vacation, right there in Battery Park City, in Louis's apartment. Louis even took a home video of one of his Missions. It was a vacation and you take a nice video of a great vacation so you can remember it fondly in the future.

"It was our break from the stress. It would be a Tuesday-Friday thing. I always knew when we were going to go on a Mission. You just knew. So I'd call Benny.

"'What do you want to do, Ben?'

"'I dunno. I don't want to go to work for a few days.'

"'Neither do I.'

"'Good. Want to go on a Mission?'

"'Yeah.'

"So we'd go on the Mission. We did a lot of cocaine and drank a lot of beers and fucked a lot of girls. We ordered them. We would get prostitutes sometimes because they were easy. Half the time we couldn't even fuck them because our dicks couldn't get hard because of the coke. So we'd have them just come around and walk around.

"We'd really bond, me and Benny, during these Missions. Once we had these whores come up to the apartment. These two girls we ordered from this prostitute service. One of them was this beautiful blond girl—she shouldn't have been a prostitute, this girl—and a girl that had multiple sclerosis or something like that. We're both fucked up. I say, 'Benny, I got the blonde.' And he must have not noticed. He says, 'Louie, I got the brunette. Look at her, she's dynamite.' Now, God forgive me, I don't mean to make fun, but her hands were all twisted. So I open the door, and Benny's on the floor, completely naked, and this girl was sucking his dick. And doing it all fucked up. But he didn't notice. So I said, 'Ben, what are you doing? The girl, Ben, she's fucked up.' He said, 'Louie, get out of here.'

"So we nicknamed her Handy Whore, like in the *Saturday Night Live* skit, Handy Man. And one of my other friends was there, and we were running around Benny, all high, and he was high, sitting on the floor getting his dick sucked by Handy Whore, and we're running around him, making fun of him, laughing. It was so funny. I guess you had to be there. I was laughing so hard, my ribs were aching. And I remember Benny getting up, naked, and was all high.

"We used to have black curtains on the windows. We couldn't have sunlight. I bought from Bed, Bath and Beyond a stack of like thirty black sheets, just for this purpose, to put them over the windows so no sunlight could get into the house. Because if we woke up in the morning—and we weren't sleeping; we were partying all night—and the sun came out, it was torture. It was the death of us. You have to be in that position to know what I mean. You're partying. You don't want the sun. You want gloomy, dead, morgue-looking territory. And you're paranoid, and the sun makes you more paranoid. If you do blow for a period of twenty-four hours or more, you get paranoid. I don't know why. If the phone rings—you get startled. Benny would be looking out the window, 'Who's coming?' I say, 'Who's coming? We're on the thirty-fourth fucking floor, Benny, who could be coming to the house?' He'd be looking out the window, so we'd have to cover up the windows with black curtains.

"So one time I took this video. I took the video prior, and the apartment is light and airy and beautiful. Floors all shiny. Then I took a video at the end—black curtains, beer all over, I'm talking about maybe twenty cases of beer. Cocaine all over every fucking possible flat surface. Girls and shit. When I was done I was done. And then I would realize. I'd walk around and I'd be like, 'What happened? What are we doing?'

"Benny used to have this thing about watching *The Lion King* after we did coke. I put in the video and he's crying, watching the fucking *Lion King*. This is the last day of the Mission, and it's over now. I would have to tell him it was over. He needed to be scolded into saying it's over.

"So he's on the couch, lying there, and I'm video-cameraing it, and he's got the beer, and I've got him drinking the beer at like nine in the morning and it smelled so bad, the apartment. You know that alcohol-coke mixed breath? It's just like this breath, it's so unique, and it stinks, it's this odor. So he's drinking the beer and he's like, 'Louie, what are you doing with that?' And he took a sip out of his beer, and he put it down, and I stayed on it with the video camera.

"You really bond with somebody when you're in these positions. You get to really know somebody's true colors."

Louis was learning a lot about himself too as he enjoyed the better things in life and spent money. He was learning what it was to be twenty-one and have access to an undepletable supply of money. He was learning that the more money he was getting, the more he was likely to get, and that it was never going to stop. He was learning that you didn't even have to think about money. That money was just there, and that he never had to worry about money again for the rest of his life. He could do what he needed to do to feel comfortable and relaxed. Like order a limo, for instance. But he would do more than just take one home late at night, the way most people on Wall Street might do, or use one to go back and forth from work.

"This was after my second or third big check at A. T. Brod. I got like a two-hundred-forty-thousand-dollar paycheck, and I just went berserk. Beserko. I took a hundred seventy in cash out of the bank. I went to Citibank and asked for it in cash. The fucking teller almost died. They had a security guard walk me to the door. I go, 'I'm fine, I'm fine. Don't worry. You ain't seen nothing yet. I'll be back for the rest tomorrow.' I just went home and I spent like sixty, seventy thousand in a week and a half.

"I was partying with Benny and we were doing coke and I was getting so paranoid that I wanted the limo running and downstairs in front of my building, because I was nervous, in case I had to make a breakaway. In case I had to make a getaway out of there. So I had the limo company send me a limo. Twenty-four hours a day. For a week. I used to look out my window. I told the guy, 'Park by the tree,' right downstairs, so I could spit on the car from my window. I'd look out my window and 'Okay, he's still there.' I'd have them change the limo drivers by my building.

"Then the limo driver left. I looked out the window and I went, 'Arggggh!' Fucking limo ain't there! 'Benny, the limo ain't there,' and he's a nervous wreck. Feeling his chest. I call the limo company and I go, 'Jerry. The limo's not here.' He says, 'The guy went to buy a pack of cigarettes. He had to get gas in the limo. You got him running the engine.'

"We paid a lot of money to do it, though. Ten thousand dollars for the limo to stay there for a week. Two thousand dollars a day. We didn't use it one time. We kept on telling the guy, 'Pull up to the front. We're coming down to go out.' We never made it downstairs to go out.'

"Then finally I went down with a girl, and we just went off. It was some chick, some friend of a Scores girl. I said, 'I want to go to Florida.' He says, 'Where you leaving from? Newark or LaGuardia?' I say, 'No, no. You don't understand. I want to take the limo to Florida. How much? I'll give you three grand.' He says, 'Done deal.' So he probably told the guy who ran the limo company he was driving me around in Jersey and New York for three or four days.

"I was so paranoid, I remember in the car. I didn't want to shower, and I wouldn't peek out the windows of the limo. I was fucked up. Fucked up bad. I don't know what it was. I was partying too much, really paranoid. The limo driver, he tells me on the way down there, the Carolinas or somewhere, he says he needed to take a shower. I says, 'Make sure you leave the car running.' He's yawning. He wanted to sleep at night in a hotel. I say, 'No, no. I'm staying in the limo.' I remember sitting there, biting my nails. Once he opened the partition and said he had to sleep, and I'm thinking, 'Oh, man, he's got to sleep. All right. We got to figure this out.' And I said, 'Listen, I'll give you an extra couple of hundred dollars to sleep in the limo.' So he slept in the front seat.

"I wouldn't even let the girl get out of the limo. I remember I wouldn't let her get out of the car. She'd say she had to go to the bathroom, and I'd go with her. Because I was afraid she was going to take off. 'I'm coming with you. There's no way I'm going to let you leave this limo.' I wouldn't even leave the limo. I'd have to go to the bathroom and I'd tell them to pull over to a deserted block. I didn't want nobody to see me. I don't know what it was. I was completely fucking paranoid. It took us two and a half days to get there and I didn't leave the limo for two and a half fucking days.

"So all week before this, while the limo was downstairs, I would call Stefanie. Ten-second conversations. 'Really busy.

Can't talk right now. 'Bye.' I would hope and pray that the machine would pick up so that I could just leave a machine message. Then when I went down to Florida I told her I had to go away on business.

"I was 'in Texas' for four days."

There were moments, not very many of them, but a few spare moments when he questioned what he was doing, when he started thinking that maybe he was making the wrong decision by getting involved—with Stefanie. He could relate to Deenie in a way that he couldn't relate to Stefanie. Deenie represented the new. Stefanie the old. It was hard to choose. There were things he could do with Deenie that he just couldn't do with Stefanie. Missions, for instance.

Deenie could deal with him being high. With Deenie there was a lot less lying, a lot less acting. He was who he was, who he had become. He could get high and he didn't have to hide that from her. He could never tell Stefanie that he got high. With Deenie he could be himself, who he really was.

Stefanie thought he was still the scrawny kid she met when they were seventeen, only now he was successful. A success on Wall Street.

But she wasn't supportive. She didn't understand him. She had stupid doubts, asinine questions.

So he didn't choose. During the week he had Deenie, the Manhattan girl. During the weekend, and during the week, he had Stefanie, the Staten Island girl. It was like working two jobs. Two shifts. But Louis was a hardworking guy.

"There ain't nobody who knows my life better than my doorman. You got to make him your best friend. I used to tip this guy like crazy, because he would know everything about me. If he wanted to give me up to either girl, it was easy. But I used to explain to him, 'Stefanie's my girl from Staten Island. She's my wife-to-be. Deenie's my sidekick girl.' I used to tell him my life because he knew anyway. He used to see me come in, leave, come in, leave. It was fucking nuts.

"So this is how my day went. I wake up in the morning, eight o'clock, eight-thirty. Sometimes seven. There's Deenie. 'Deenie, I'm going to work.' She says, 'Yeah, see you later.' She only had four hours of sleep. Me too. Then I go to work. Driven to work. Brod is right across West Street, but I don't give a fuck. I'm not walking. If Sally Leads is at the apartment he drives me to work. Otherwise I get the car, drive to work. Come back from work at lunchtime. Deenie's still in the apartment. Maybe have an afternoon sex session. If not, wake her up, so she can get on with her fucking day. She would sleep until six o'clock if not. So I'd wake her up. 'Come on, Deenie, you got to get your shit together.' She'd get up, get something to eat, fool around, whatever. And then I would go back to work. Now she would straighten up the apartment, she would clean up. She was a good girl.

"I come back to the apartment at four o'clock. She'd be there. Now mind you, Stefanie would think I'm working till seven or eight o'clock at night. I'm not. I'm working till four, four-thirty. If not, sometimes I'd stay at work till eleven o'clock. It depended. But I'd come home every day at four o'clock anyway. I would hang out with Deenie for a little while, go out and get something to eat. If not, she would leave. I'd drop her off at her apartment and she'd get ready to go to work.

"Then I would call Stefanie from my cell phone on the way back. This would be five-thirty, six o'clock. Sometimes I would have to go back to work and I wouldn't hang out with Stefanie. But if I wasn't working I'd call Stefanie and say, 'What are you doing? Do you want to come out here? Do you want me to come to Staten Island?' Most of the time she'd want to come out to the apartment. We'd go out to get something to eat, go back to the apartment, hang out, watch a movie, whatever, fool around. She'd go home at twelve o'clock. Now she'd be thinking I'm going to fucking bed at twelve o'clock. I'm not. I'm just starting.

"I would take a shower now, get dressed. Benny lives two blocks away in the 'projects' of Battery Park City, I used to call it. Gateway Plaza. Lowest buildings, shit buildings. Hallways stank. Horrible. So I'd call him at the projects down the block. 'What are you doing?' 'Nothing. Getting ready to go to Scores.' He was doing the same thing. He had Michelle, who would come over and hang out at the apartment, go home to Brooklyn, and he'd get ready, get dressed, go out with me. He was living the same fucking psycho lifestyle.

"He'd get dressed and pick me up, or I'd pick him up, and we'd go to Scores. He had his girl and I had my girl at Scores. He had all the girls at Scores, almost, Benny was a very good-looking kid. Puerto Rican-Italian. So we'd drink, party, do whatever we were doing for the night. Doing lines if we're doing blasts, whatever. We used to call it Scooby-Doo. That was our nickname for it. One of the kids that we got it from looked like Shaggy from Scooby-Doo.

"At four o'clock I'd be at Scores. Wait for Deenie to come out. We would go home. Maybe get a bite to eat at the twenty-four-hour McDonald's on Second Avenue. Go to Battery Park, park my car, go upstairs. She would take a shower. I used to make her take a shower because guys dance with her all night. So quick shower and we go to bed, do what we do, wake up, do it again. Call Stefanie in the morning during the day. 'Hey, babe. How's everything?'

"Sometimes in the morning I would do a blast just to get me through the day. How else was I going to live? I used to have to do a Valium just to get myself to sleep, because I was so overtired. I'd get, like, sixteen winds. I'd be on my third wind for the night. 'All right, I'm up again.' I'd take a Valium just to settle down and go to sleep. I mean, I was living two lives.

"I used to leave on Friday and not come back till Sunday,

and Deenie used to think I was hanging out with my friends. I would tell her that I promised my friends in Staten Island that on Friday nights after work I shut my beeper off and I have nothing to do with my New York life. And she believed it! So that was it. And she wouldn't ask no questions.

"My phone was picked up by neither girl. But one night I picked up the phone and Deenie was on the line and I said, 'Joe's not here.' Stefanie was right next to me. Deenie said what are you talking about and I said, 'Come on. Joe's not here.' Talk to you later.' Next day I said, 'Oh, Deenie, I was sleeping, you woke me up, I was dreaming.' I was good. I had my shit covered. Once Stefanie found a pair of panties. I just said it belonged to Sally Leads's girlfriend. He used to sleep over with her once in a while. She never questioned it."

The Missions poured coke-flavored honey over the knot that his life had become. And a new diversion was coming into use—Ecstasy. Not as dangerous as coke. Less likely to send you to the hospital. Safe, it seemed. Mellow. In the Chop House Wall Street of the 1990s, quaaludes and Ecstasy were so common that you'd think they were sold at the Duane Reade drugstores. Pills were popped like Vitamin C, and cocaine was scooped out like talcum in some old greaseball's barbershop. Coke wasn't used openly in the offices—except when it was absolutely necessary.

"Sometimes we'd have to. We were so fucking tired from partying that we'd do a fucking line or two just to get through the day. I sometimes would be fucked up, talking to clients. I mean, we were crazy. We were fucking maniacs. Man-i-acs.

"It wasn't as if we were drug addicts because we really weren't. I don't know why we did it. It wasn't as if we couldn't stop. If I didn't want to do it anymore, I just wouldn't do it. I had no fear that I was addicted to them at all. But we used to take it to the next level. I took Benny to the hospital twice, he almost thought he was going to have a heart attack. He was lying on the couch, 'Louie, please call the ambulance,' he says.

'I'm dying. I can't breathe. My heart's doing one-sixty. I'm about to fucking die.' He thought his heart was going to blow up.

"We went to South Beach one time. We stayed there like five days. We had a slew of drugs. Ecstasy, Valium, mushrooms, and cocaine. I never took mushrooms before in my life. They were these little things. They make you hallucinate. We were in a club and Benny handed me the bag, and he tells me to hold it. So I go, 'What do I do with it?' and he says, 'Eat 'em.' Now, I thought he told me to eat the whole bag. I ate the whole fucking bag. I was on a dance floor, and I lost control of my bowels.

"So I'm telling Benny I can't hold it in. I'm shitting. So he's dragging me into the bathroom, and there's a guy in the stall and he kicked the door open. And I remember the guy was sitting on the toilet bowl shitting and Benny grabbed him off the toilet bowl, threw him out of the way, and threw me in there. I couldn't control it. I was pissing and shitting. It was ridiculous. And then I had to leave the place with Benny's shirt tied around my waist, naked, because I had to leave my fucking jeans and underwear there. So I had to walk through this club. It was mad crowded, girls all over, and I had Benny's see-through Versace shirt, and my cock and my ass were hanging out. And Benny was around me, trying to cover it. It was ridiculous. It was like crazy. Fucking nuts.

"Another time, on another trip down there, they gave me all these fucking drugs, they gave me like Valium, Ecstasy, coke. They gave me them to hold. They said hold on to these, because they had to go back outside the club and get something. They were gone six, seven, eight hours. I couldn't find them. So I did all the drugs. I did them all. They came back and they found me, and my friend Mike Fusco said that I was on the sofa like fucking dead, and that he found me and that Benny was like, 'Where's the drugs?' And I said, 'I did them. I did them all.' And they said they had to carry me home. I don't even remember it."

When he was down in Miami—and he was there every week or two, with or without Stefanie—he would often run into his old friends, the two Chrises. Chris Wolf and Chris Paciello. Chris Wolf, the Hanover Sterling ace broker, had recovered nicely. Plastic surgery performs miracles. Now you could barely see the scar on his face from getting thrown through that plate-glass window on Broadway, during the harbor-toss and safe-stealing incident a couple of years before. Chris Paciello was from Staten Island and was known to Louis from the old days as a kind of street investment banker. His specialty was raising capital for himself by using a loaded gun. Somehow Chris Paciello wound up in South Beach, was operating a nightclub and showing up in the gossip columns, dating models.

Paciello was known to Louis as Chris Binge-a, or Binja—it wasn't set down in writing as a rule, so the spelling is approximate. That's Binge-a as in "binge." Chris Wolf and Chris Paciello had little in common except for substance usage and that both had changed their names—Chris Wolf to conceal Italian ancestry, and Chris Paciello (née Ludwigsen) to assume Italian ancestry. It was part of what one New York pol used to call the "gorgeous mosaic."

"We used to hang around with Chris Wolf and he was just nuts. He'd run around the Liquids club in South Beach, putting hits of Ecstasy in people's mouths. Me and Benny used to try to avoid him, because he'd want to stick 'em in your mouth. He'd say, 'Come on, let's fucking party!' He used to carry a bag—these pills were twenty-five dollars each—and he used to carry a bag of like a thousand of them and just give them to fucking everybody. He'd go, 'Here. Here. Here.' Just give them out.

"Liquids was Chris Binja's club, Chris Paciello. He would binge, just disappear for a month. He was nuts, that Chris too. He was nuts, we all were nuts. Chris Wolf was nuts because he would just OD like it was a fucking ritual. They were always taking him to the hospital. He was always foaming from the mouth somewhere in the corner. I mean, these are people—we'd go on the phone and get like a million dollars from investors and then we're laying on couches half dead, foaming from the mouth. Every once in a while it used to just hit me, imagine our clients seeing us now. Can't even talk."

That was a definite disadvantage of taking drugs. But there were social benefits to chemistry, apart from its self-medicating, stress-relief function. Just as Benny and Louis bonded during their Missions, drug use was a necessary social skill. Just as strip clubs like Scores were now assuming the same role as mahogany-paneled private clubs for previous generations, drugs were now supplanting alcohol to promote conviviality and good fellowship. In the 1960s, drugs were a counter-cultural phenomenon. Louis and Benny weren't part of any counterculture that they were aware of. They were, after all, members of the Establishment. Wall Streeters. Stockbrokers. Drugs were now apolitical, equal-opportunity mouth-foamers. They made bad times good. They made good times great. Sure, they could make great times bad, if you took too much. They had to watch that. They didn't.

Louis kept about $1,500 worth of coke in his safe at all times, right alongside the stacks, for easy access. It was important to have coke available at all times. But when Louis and Stefanie joined Benny and Michelle at the Sandals resort in Jamaica on New Year's Eve, Louis and Benny couldn't very well take the drugs with them on the plane. That threatened to deprive them of a necessary element in greeting the upcoming, outstanding year of 1995. But everything turned out okay. They found a Jamaican guy on the beach who had what they needed.

While they were in Jamaica they ran into Craig Kallman, who was staying at another resort and arranged to meet them.

They had mixed feelings about Kallman. He still hadn't come through with referrals. But Louis and Benny were still hoping that he would do what he had promised. They had made good money for him, after all. It was the least he could do. In their new life they would have to get used to running into big shots like Kallman when they were on vacation. He was a cool youngish guy, in his thirties. But he was—they couldn't put their finger on it—maybe a little standoffish.

They still had hopes the Real Wall Street was in their future. But right now, the Chop House Wall Street was too much fun to leave. Life was drugs and sex and money and money and money and money. So much money that some of it had to be, almost literally, flushed down the toilet.

CHAPTER TWENTY-TWO

One of the nice things about having money is that you can buy off your guilt.

As the piles in his safe multiplied like horny cockroaches, Louis slowly began to realize that he would have so much to confess, if he confessed, that the penance would set a new record in the Vatican or St. Patrick's Cathedral or wherever. There would be no Hail Marys doled out by the priest or the Pope or whomever. He would be, maybe, nailed to a cross right in the middle of Battery Park City. He would hang from the cross and Stefanie and Deenie and his customers—everybody—would be jeering.

Sure he was guilty. He knew it. He ignored what the priests taught him, he thought it was a lot of crap, but some of that bullshit seeped into his brain. He couldn't help it. If he could have taken out his brain and tossed it in the dishwasher, he would have done it. But he couldn't, so he did the next best thing. He bought off his guilt. Expiated it. Cleansed the money. Lost it.

There was no better guilt-relief mechanism than the ability to take money—this precious thing that was the focus of his life—and lose it.

Gambling wasn't recreation anymore. It was money exorcism.

By 1995, the stock market had become a gambling outlet for many people. But Louis wouldn't have been caught dead playing the market. He could have day-traded or traded options, but screw that. Louis didn't buy stocks he couldn't control. That was for scrubs. But gambling was cool, and he was gambling on football and baseball and basketball and blackjack even though he tended to lose whatever he gambled. But it didn't matter because the more he lost the more he bet, and the more he bet the more he lost, and then he would bet and lose and it would go on and on.

Sometimes he would drive down to Atlantic City on weeknights, just for the night, with Sally Leads or a friend from Staten Island named Danny. They wouldn't book a room. They'd book a chair at the tables. Then they'd do an all-nighter playing blackjack. That was his game. He'd sometimes play a little craps, but he stayed with blackjack because it gave you a chance. It wasn't for scrubs, like the slots. Louis was no scrub. He'd do a little card counting. Counting tens and aces. After all, he wasn't trying to lose. Quite the contrary.

If you watch for the tens and the picture cards, if you concentrate, you have an edge over the house. That is a mathematical fact. With an edge, you win in the long run. You can see the cards on the table and figure out what is coming.

And people can see you.

"I used to get a crowd of people watching me. Fifteen hundred a hand. Two thousand a hand. I'd double down on twelve, which was unheard-of. People used to watch because they had to announce it. 'Double down on twelve!' It was a big thing. You never double down on twelve in blackjack. That's insane. If you get a ten, you lose. But I used to see tons of tens come out and I say, 'No way a ten is coming out.' I'd double down. I'd get like a seven and I'd win. People would cheer.

"I was the Man. It felt good. They'd give me a room. Two, three Jacuzzis, wet bar, stocked bar, fucking kitchen, living room, two bedrooms, four bathrooms. Free dinners. They used to send bottles of Cristal and fruit baskets up to the fucking room. They picked me up in Staten Island in a limo one time. They gave me Knicks tickets. I used to go to the back room, see the pit bosses.

"'Hey, Lou, how's everything? Got your lucky hat on?'

"'Yeah, I'm ready to play.'

"Everybody out there is playing twenty, ten dollars a hand. I'd sit down with thirty thousand. I'd make a scene. I used to like to make a scene. Sometimes I'd go in there with sunglasses on, a bandanna, checkered sweatsuit on, and start betting three thousand a hand. People used to say, 'Who the fuck is this guy?' I used to hear them. I'd make a fucking show.

"I used to see a lot of rich people in that place. Ted Turner sat right next to me at blackjack. He was playing fifty, a hundred thousand a hand. Special chips. Ten thousand dollars a chip.

"Stefanie hated to watch me. I used to say, 'Come on, babe, sit next to me.' But she used to hate me when I was down there. I'd turn into somebody else. She couldn't talk to me when I was gambling. There was no talking to me. I wasn't laughing. I used to sit there with the chips, flipping them in and out. My dad sat next to me a couple of times. He was shitting in his pants—I'm gambling half his yearly salary in one hand. I remember I gave him a thousand to gamble. He took the money. He goes, 'I lost it.' It was so funny."

When he couldn't go down to Atlantic City there would be the football games on Sundays. First $500 a game. Then $1,000. Then $5,000. Louis began betting with several bookies, because he bet more than any single bookie could handle.

Louis began to see what it meant to be a Whale—a loser. A pampered loser, taken in a limo to a place to lose money. Except that he didn't care. He was losing fuck-you money. It was making him feel good. Stefanie didn't like it. Fuck her. She didn't understand him. It was starting to become an issue— the money. She was benefiting. He was buying her stuff. Why didn't she appreciate it?

She was acting as if he were doing something wrong, and that sucked.

STEFANIE: "It was a fantasy world. At the time it seemed like unreal. Even though it was happening, it was like, 'My God! How can this be my life? This is what I do?' Spend my winter going skiing every weekend, or go to Miami. Every year it was something else. It just didn't feel real.

"It was exciting, but I was always worried. I don't know if it's just my nature. I'd say to him, 'You can afford this?' He'd say, 'Yeah, I can. No problem. No problem.' He'd be working all these hours. I'd say, 'What kind of place is this? You don't get a salary?' 'I work on commissions.' It just didn't make any sense to me.

"His response to me questioning him about it was that I was not supportive. That's all he ever said to me, 'You don't believe in me?' 'No, it's not that I don't believe in you. It's just that I question it because it doesn't seem right. It just doesn't seem like it's legal. It just doesn't seem like this is the way it works, that you can get these people to invest this money, they lose all their money and you're making money. I don't know.'

"The stocks were always shit stocks. He got these people to invest in them and all these complaints are coming in. Maybe after the second or third time he switched jobs. I started to feel it wasn't so kosher, it just didn't seem to make sense for this to be a legal profession. I said, 'I can't imagine this is legal.' And he used to say, 'Oh, you don't know what you're talking about. You don't believe in me.'"

CHAPTER TWENTY-THREE

Times were so great that it barely made a ripple in Louis's world when Hanover Sterling, his beloved alma mater, went out of business.

It happened early in 1995, not long after Louis got back from the Caribbean. First came whispers, picked up by financial columnist Dan Dorfman, that Hanover was under SEC investigation. Then all hell broke loose. The Hanover house stocks collapsed, and so did Hanover. Roy had a box on those stocks, but somebody had busted the box, just smashed it on the floor. It wasn't supposed to happen. Louis went over to Pine Street to see for himself. Roy, his mentor, was saying goodbye. It was sad. Louis went back to Brod. "I didn't want to be there because I left him like two years ago so I felt funny. He was standing at the door, while everybody had to leave with their shit, because Nasdaq was coming over. They came over with video cameras," said Louis.

From what Louis had heard, Roy was simply overwhelmed by something that wasn't supposed to be a factor, not even remotely, at Hanover—the market. Yep, the free market in stocks, the Real Wall Street, had profited at Hanover's expense. Hanover was shorted, and Roy miscalculated—he fought the short-sellers. They profit by selling stocks they don't own, in the hope of eventually buying back the stocks at a lower price. For chop houses, whose rips depend on keeping prices high, short-selling can be a calamity. It means that somebody is flooding the market with shares, driving down the price. Roy kept on buying, to keep the price from dropping. It didn't work. "His balls were bigger than his pockets," said Louis. "The shorts just kept on shorting and shorting and shorting. Roy probably figured he'd keep the price up for a few days and they'd have to cover [buy the shares they had sold short] and fuck them. But those short-sellers ripped [the Hanover stocks] to shreds. They have a lot of money, those guys. A. T. Brod shorted the shit out of them too. Everybody started shorting Hanover stocks once they started going down. Roy probably ticked off somebody and they crushed him. I felt bad."

Sure, the shorts had swarmed over Hanover like vultures on carrion. But the only reason they were able to do that was because Hanover was selling house stocks—chop stocks. Stocks that Hanover controlled, that were really not worth very much, but had been driven upward by all the ways Louis was using at Brod—ways that he had learned at Hanover. You can't have a rip unless the stock is worth very little to begin with, and then is sold for a hell of a lot more than it is worth.

The shorts cut the prices and destroyed the rips—and that sank Hanover, and even brought down the firm that had cleared trades for Hanover. Adler Coleman was the name, and like Brod it was owned by respectable people and was a member of the New York Stock Exchange.

In late February, Hanover was shut by the NASD because its capital had been depleted by Roy's face-off with the shorts, and Adler Coleman filed for bankruptcy. As the shorts came in for the kill, the press finally began to show a little interest in Hanover, mainly because of Adler Coleman's failure. And also because of other things. Oddities. Dorfman complained to *Business Week* that he had received death threats, as did a

New York Post reporter who interviewed some Hanover people at a local bar. But generally, the press portrayed Hanover as a victim of the shorts. Lowell Schatzer was quoted as saying the firm was a victim of a "bear raid."

Not a word appeared in the press at the time—except for those death threats—even hinting that Hanover was anything but a legit firm that had been torpedoed by the shorts. That story went swiftly into the press clips and databases and became the commonly accepted explanation for the biggest chop house collapse of the era. One reason was that the bankruptcy court trustee for Adler Coleman, Edwin Mishkin, publicly blamed the shorts. In a statement to the press in March 1995, Mishkin said, "Based upon his preliminary investigation to date, [Mishkin] believes that questionable short-selling in these securities [the Hanover chop stocks] led to the demise of Hanover Sterling."

The "Hanover victim" canard became an instant part of the folklore of Wall Street, a major chunk of the little that appeared in the press about chop houses in 1995. The press swallowed that bullshit so readily that Louis wasn't surprised when nobody noticed that he put A. T. Brod out of business.

It happened just a month after Hanover collapsed. For the first time since he came to Wall Street two and a half years before, Louis was experiencing something vaguely resembling failure. It was not a pleasant sensation.

He experienced that feeling for the first time in his life in the office of Jay Taneja. Louis was owed "commission" money—that is, money from the rips. Jay wasn't paying. He had reasons. Good reasons. He explained them. Louis wasn't listening. He sat there quietly while Jay Taneja was talking. He sat and heard the words and looked at him, and what he was thinking would have made Jay Taneja turn pale. He was thinking, I will put you out of business. Louis sat there and thought and decided, that very moment in Jay Taneja's office, to put down A. T. Brod, to flush it down the toilet as if it were a hamster that had started to smell. He had built A. T. Brod and now he could take it down. He took it down.

It was March of 1995. Spring. Fuck spring. Nothing was going right. Louis was owed money. Period. He didn't want to hear excuses. Jay Taneja was giving him excuses.

It was a market thing, pretty much the same thing that had happened to Hanover—only this time there was nothing in the papers. Kemper Securities was holding on to Brod's money, including their commissions, including Taneja's own money. Louis didn't know, and if he knew, he wouldn't have cared. He wanted his money.

"We were supposed to get paid a lot of money for the gross that we did the month before. We were supposed to be paid three hundred grand. Jay Taneja calls us into the office. He says, 'I can't pay you the money unless you clean the inventory.' There was too much stock in inventory. People were selling stock outside the firm, and he kept buying it. It was actually shorts, though we didn't know that. They were selling stock.

"He ran out of his own trading money, so he decided to use the money that was in the commission account, to cover the buys. He should have come to us and said, 'Listen, guys, I got stock hitting the desk. I need to either go down [in price] or give me some buys. 'Cause I can't afford it no more. I'm running out of money.' Instead he took it upon himself to use our commission money." Now all the stock was in inventory and he wanted it cleaned out. "So when he told me and Benny that, I was thinking like, 'What, are you kidding? You can't pay me now, and you want me to clean up your inventory to get paid?'"

Louis did what he had to do. No problem, he told Jay Taneja. Louis went back to his office and closed the door. He then wrote up buy orders for his customers—phony orders he knew they would quickly cancel: "wooden tickets."

"We handed them in to trading and the inventory was cleaned out," said Louis. "The next day we got paid a hundred and twenty grand from the commissions we were owed. The day after that the trades were canceled. He was fucked. The next day the firm went out of business. Fuck him. It served him right. I didn't give a fuck. I had plenty of places to go. We had plenty of money. We could be out of work for six months and it wouldn't matter.

"It was chaotic. It was ridiculous what was going on. People were freaking the fuck out. One of Marco's cold-callers had one of Jay's guys by the throat. Because they wouldn't pay. That's the worst thing you can do to a broker. A guy works all month to get paid. He scams, robs, steals. You got to pay. What's the sense of robbing and stealing and defrauding people if you're not going to be paid for it?"

It was all over. Brod was history. Louis was at the office when it happened, and he reacted by piling his things on his chair. It had wheels, which was good.

"Benny said, 'That's it?'

"I said, 'What are we going to do, stay here, wait until the rent runs out? I'm going home. I'm taking a break. Who cares?'

"He says, 'You don't care, Louie?'

"I said, 'I don't care, Ben. I just don't fucking care.' I didn't give a fuck about the firm. I just cared that I lost money. But I just shrugged it off and said, 'Ehh, what are you going to do? Came easy, goes easy.'

"I wheeled my big leather chair, with my two client books, my Play Station, I wheeled it out on the street. I walked along West Street up toward the World Trade Center. I waited for the cars to go, crossed the street, took it into my building, went upstairs, and put it in my spare bedroom. And that was it. I started calling clients from home. I said, 'Yeah, I'm leaving the firm. It went out of business. The bums. I'll send you out a transfer form.'"

In the end, it was the regulators who, technically, put Brod out of its misery. All those wooden tickets had kept share prices rising for a day or so, but then they collapsed when the trades were canceled. The firm's capital had now fallen below NYSE and SEC levels. The NYSE performed the coup de grâce on March 28, when it stopped the firm from trading.

For the second time in little more than a month, a brokerage firm had gone out of business because its stocks suddenly weren't worth anything. What did it mean? The significance simply didn't reach too far into the psyches of either the press or the regulators.

The wire services ran brief items that were mainly picked up in Ohio and especially in Cleveland, where Jay Taneja was portrayed as a local businessman who had tried hard and run into a string of bad luck. "Though its 85-year-old chairman and founder Albert T. Brod begged for its life, the A. T. Brod & Co. stock brokerage was put to death last week," *Crain's Cleveland Business* reported on April 3. "According to Mr. Taneja, A. T. Brod was killed by short-sellers, its own poor management and a 'ruthless' executive at Kemper Securities Group in Chicago," said *Crain's*. The story went on to say that Jay had met with Kemper on March 29, a day after the NYSE pulled the plug. Kemper had called the meeting, the newspaper said, because Brod owed it nearly $7 million for stock bought by Kemper on Brod's behalf. That was all the stock Louis and Benny were supposed to have unloaded, in return for their commissions.

JAY TANEJA: "I took a big loss. Four, five million dollars. I was not from the Wall Street. I did not know. I got into it by mistake. People took a lot of advantage. . . . It was a nightmare for me. I did not know anybody. . . . If you ask me, was I running the business, I say no. I didn't have any knowledge. I went through a complete New York Stock Exchange inquiry, and they did not find a single thing on me. Why? Because they called me, 'You are so dumb. Everybody thought you would have made a lot of money.' And I lost a lot of money because I did not know the business.*

"I did not [hold back commission money]. I got money released from Kemper by putting my money, personal money, as a collateral, to get that money released. All that money was released. They were claiming more money on the wooden tickets. . . . The problem was money was not owed to them. But I got money released.

"I started a book myself. *Wall Street Mafia.* I wrote three chapters, and I withdraw myself. Because it was so scary."

Louis kept his word when he said he was going to take it easy. Brod had been a grind. The constant stress was no good. It was great money, but it was beginning to seem that the more money he made, the more it meant trouble. He and Benny relaxed for a month or so, and started to give some thought to their next move. In the Wall Street of mid-1995 there were plenty of opportunities for two ambitious young brokers who had a proven track record of success.

The brokers were everything. The firms were nothing. That was the lesson of A. T. Brod. But Louis also saw that, powerful as brokers were, they could still be fucked. When Jay Taneja said he wasn't going to pay them their commissions, there wasn't anything Louis and Benny could do to get the money. It was a problem. It added to the stress of the situation.

---

*The NYSE and other regulators did not implicate Taneja in any wrongdoing. But Brod didn't exactly get any medals from the NYSE. In a disciplinary action announced two years after Brod went out of business, the NYSE permanently banned Brod from the exchange. (Brod was long defunct, so this was a largely symbolic act.) The NYSE found that Brod had committed multiple violations of exchange rules. Among other things, the NYSE disciplinary panel made note of the wooden tickets Louis wrote in March 1995, said that "unauthorized staff had the ability to enter the trading room during the relevant period," and that "firm procedures were inadequate to detect or prevent misconduct in connection with execution of orders." The decision was silent on whether or not the brokers were owed any money by Brod.

Overall, the good of the system outweighed the bad—the stress, and the occasional snippets of crummy press. Stories about hard-driving stockbrokers were beginning to creep into the papers. But the thousands of tattooed, shaved-headed, Armani-clad, unregistered kids rarely got any kind of attention from anybody. That's how well the system was working, with all its flaws. The regulators were still wonderful in 1995. They could cause problems but they didn't, because they didn't get it.

By the mid 1990s the NASD was under competent leadership, run by an ambitious former brokerage exec and government official named Frank Zarb. Another veteran Wall Street guy was in charge at the SEC—Arthur Levitt, a publicity-conscious former chairman of the American Stock Exchange. These were good, solid guys. Not that it meant anything. When it came to the chop houses, nothing much had changed since the days when Massood Gilani was being told to mind his own business.

At Brod, the NASD would do periodic examinations. The accountants would come by in their polyester suits and go through trade tickets and try to see if there were any red flags—while they were right in the bullring and the red flag was being waved in their faces, and they didn't see it because they weren't looking for it. It didn't matter if they cared about their jobs, as Gilani did when he blew the whistle on Hanover, or if they didn't give a shit. They didn't understand how the firms worked, or how the brokers made money. They were looking for regular commissions, not rips concealed as trading profits, so they never found them. It was as if they were doctors looking in the throat to find out if some guy had hemorrhoids.

It was a splendid ignorance, and it was not confined to the regulators. Sometimes the managements of large, well-established brokerages had no idea what was going on under their noses. They were not ashamed of it. On the contrary, ignorance was sometimes embraced—so long as it did not cross over into the legally troublesome area of "failure to supervise."

Louis read the *Wall Street Journal* every day now, at least the front page. He read about how a guy named Joseph Jett was able to convince a whole bunch of people at Kidder Peabody that he was the greatest bond trader in the history of mankind. He used complex strategies. They were so complex that nobody understood them. Eventually the SEC charged that Jett had been playing games with the accounting system and using his employers' ignorance against them. Jett denied the charges. No, he said, his bosses weren't ignorant. They knew what he was doing. Yes, Kidder Peabody said, its management was ignorant. But not criminally or civilly-liable ignorant. Only Jett was truly guilty, they said.

Were the Kidder people criminals or just stupid? It was a question being seriously debated at the time. It was a close question.

Louis had no opinion on that issue. He thought most people were stupid. He also thought Wall Street was crooked. In fact, he held that opinion so firmly that he decided the time had come. He was going to get himself a license and become a genuine, bona fide stockbroker.

CHAPTER TWENTY-FOUR

Louis decided to become Louis—officially. He had been Benny long enough. With a brokerage license, he would be able to call people on the phone and say that he was Louis Pasciuto.

It had to happen eventually—even if Benny wasn't pretty damn sick and tired of Louis using his name. Getting a license was okay with Louis. After all, here he was—twenty-one years old, a veteran of three major chop houses. He had run crews of cold-callers at two of the firms and was raking in over $100,000 a month. He had clients in show business and the world of sports. He had personally driven one of his three employers out of business. He had done all of this without being a licensed broker.

Louis filed the paperwork to take the test for the NASD broker license, the Series 7, about a month after leaving Brod. By that time, he and Benny had started work at a little firm with an office in the World Trade Center. Its name was Sovereign Equity Management.

Louis took the Series 7 when he was at Hanover. He had better things to do with his time than study, so he got 40 percent. Louis figured that if he really applied himself he could definitely ace the test. Only one problem: He still had better things to do with his time then memorizing a lot of bullshit sales-practice rules that everybody knew were a crock. It was a dilemma, but easily solvable.

Louis made up his mind. He decided to pass the test. Or to put it more accurately, he decided that the test would be passed. In order to become Louise Pasciuto, officially, someone else would have to become Louis Pasciuto, officially.

For the chop house kids, Series 7 tests were like any other lame formality that could be overcome with a little cash. Ever since he was at Robert Todd, Louis had heard that people were paying kids, mainly Russians, to take the tests for them. He was dubious.

"I was nervous to do it when I first heard about it at Robert Todd, because I said to myself this was going to catch up with me. There was no way that these people were going to get away with it. You had people getting licensed that hadn't finished high school and couldn't read a book. So I figure I had to be smarter than that. I wasn't going to ask some Russian I didn't know to take the test for me, give him three grand. It wouldn't work."

Louis approached a former cold-caller to take the test for him. He was a bright kid—his father was a heart surgeon on Long Island. He agreed to do it for $10,000.

"I paid more than other guys were paying because I wanted it done right," said Louis. "I wanted to be sure he shut his mouth and everything was done perfect. I paid twenty-five hundred just for the IDs alone, on top of that. You had to show a driver's license. I went to a printer who was a friend of my father's and I got the ID. I got a perfect driver's license with the watermark and everything. A cop could have played with it and he wouldn't have known. It was laminated perfect. It actually felt rubbery like the actual license."

The NASD—no fools, they—required two forms of ID, so Louis got a gym card made along with the license. Just to be on the safe side, Louis gave the kid his wallet, in case he had to show even more ID. Louis even gave him one of his shirts and ties, the actual clothing of Louis Pasciuto. It was brilliant.

With the surgeon's kid taking the test, Louis got an overall grade of 88 percent. There were separate grades for every subject area covered by the test. His highest grade in any single subject area was 100 percent—a perfect score. The subject was "regulation." That made sense. The actual Louis Pasciuto was a self-regulating entity. Nobody told him what to do except Louis Pasciuto, and in that sense he was a true Wall Street guy.

At Sovereign, the newly licensed Louis was going to be equal partners with Benny for the clients they already had, and Louis was going to start getting his own client book, under his own name for the first time. He was paid a small sign-up bonus. To get it, Louis had to meet Phil.

Phil was at 90 Broad Street, which was where Sovereign was planning to move in a few weeks. The offices were empty. But Phil was there.

Phil was standing by the window, hands clasped behind his back. Looking out. He was a quiet guy. Louis had never heard of him. In fact, nobody had ever heard of Phil. And Phil liked it that way just fine.

Philip C. Abramo was just a few weeks shy of fifty. His hair, once jet-black, had become a kind of tarnished-quarter silver. But Phil kept in shape and when he smiled the years melted away. He had a broad, infectious grin. Guys like Phil weren't known for their smiles. They were known for a kind of blank stare, and for a certain look in their eyes. It was an important look, a revenue-generating look in much the same way as Louis had a revenue-generating way of firing clients and getting people to be frightened that they may not get a chance to give Louis money that he would not give back. That is how Louis made a living. Phil made a living by that stare.

Phil had that look, but he didn't use it very often, because he didn't have to, not when you learned that he was Phil Abramo. And once you learned that he was Phil Abramo, that was sufficient and his look would be blank, his eyes a kind of spoiled-salami brown. Phil didn't talk unnecessarily. He didn't have to talk. Talking was for idiots. John Gotti talked. He talked so much that he was living in a six-by-eight-foot cell in Marion, Indiana.

Phil had visited Gotti at the Ravenite Social Club before Gotti went to Marion, in the days when Gotti thought it was great to force Guys to come and talk with him at the Ravenite, right in the middle of a heavily traveled district of Manhattan where the FBI and New York City police could look and watch and listen.

Phil went. He had to. No choice. He had his own club, around the corner on Mott Street, one the cops weren't watching. But it didn't matter. He went back and forth to the Ravenite, the club that was practically in the guidebooks it was so well known, and the cops watched Phil as he met John Gotti. They counted his visits. Twenty-five times.

Phil Abramo made his living by being Phil Abramo, just as John Gotti made his living by being John Gotti and Frank Coppa made his living by being Frank Coppa. He made his living by seeing to it that people paid him money for two broad categories of reasons:

1. They paid Phil Abramo to remove obstacles to their livelihoods or lives.
2. They paid Phil Abramo because he was a potential obstacle to their livelihoods or lives.

This was how Guys like Phil Abramo made their living. It was not a growth business in the early mid-nineties. Phil could thank John Gotti for that. By keeping a high profile at the Ravenite and in the tabloids, by mouthing off in front of FBI microphones, by forcing other Guys to meet him at the

Ravenite where they could be watched and counted, he made the world of Guys into an uncomfortably public world. How does a Guy make money under such circumstances?

Phil Abramo always found a way, which was to quietly tend to business. He lived in a blue-collar district of Saddle Brook, a little town in northern New Jersey where outsiders rarely ventured, except to visit the Jewish cemeteries on the outskirts. While Gotti was flashy and violent and stupid, Phil was educated—four years of college—and he kept his name out of the papers. The newspapers, that is. He was in other papers. SEC files.

Phil Abramo was in a whole bunch of SEC files—but not because the SEC had him under surveillance or anything like that. No, Phil Abramo was in the SEC's files because he did the filing. He had to. It was the law. He had to obey the law. He was a CEO.

In the late eighties and early nineties, Phil Abramo headed a series of "blind pools"—basically companies set up for the purpose of making investments and buying other companies. Blind pools have a sorry history, because in the eighties they were often used by penny stock promoters as a way of packaging cruddy companies that were then sold off to the public the way Louis was selling chop stocks in the nineties. But Abramo's blind pools never got off the ground. All he basically did was file papers with the SEC, thereby supplying anyone who looked with a full biography of Philip C. Abramo.

Phil's SEC filings skipped over his early career.

As a young man in the early 1970s he was involved in general merchandising (possession of stolen property) and purchase and sale of pharmaceuticals (conspiracy to sell heroin). Some years later, Phil confided to a friend that his incarceration from the latter episode put him in touch with Gambino-affiliated Guys, who saw to it that his career moved forward.

In the 1980s he had found himself a mentor, a man by the name of Thomas Quinn. Quinn was a lawyer and a very prominent penny stock promoter, back in the days when chop stocks went by the name of "penny stocks," though the game—the rip—was essentially the same. One of the stocks Quinn brought public was a company called Bagel Nosh. Phil was on the books as a "consultant" to Bagel Nosh back in the early 1980s, not long after it went public.

The Quinn-Abramo friendship never wavered as the years went on. When authorities in France nabbed Quinn on charges of securities fraud in 1988, Phil's unlisted phone number was in his notebook. When the SEC questioned Phil about Quinn, he decided to invoke his Fifth Amendment privilege against self-incrimination. But not everyone in Phil's life was quite so reticent. He learned that the next time he popped into the feds' gun sights. In 1994, he was indicted by a federal grand jury in Newark for running a scam preying on poor people who couldn't get credit. In return for paying him money, he would arrange for them to get loans.

So they would pay him money—and he wouldn't arrange for them to get loans. It was a terrific scam—simple, low-maintenance. People sent money. Phil took it. Christmas every day.

According to court records, one day in 1991 Phil had a conversation with an associate in the scam, a man by the name of John Forte. "We had a lengthy discussion," Forte later testified, "and it was terminated by Phil saying if—this is his company. He was going to run it the way he saw fit. It's not that much money. He would throw it out on the street and send me home in little pieces."

Forte gave this testimony at a bail-revocation hearing. The judge decided not to revoke Phil's bail. Forte decided that one session in the witness chair, staring into those spoiled-salami eyes, was enough. He wasn't testifying at any trial of Phil Abramo. Phil wound up pleading to lesser charges—and getting less jail time than Forte did. None of this got any publicity at the time, and when Phil was sent away for a year in prison, there was no press conference announcing the conviction of a major "organized crime figure."

Phil was wrestling with the loan-scam charges at the time he got Sovereign up and running in '95. All the while he kept in touch with his old pal Quinn, who was now back from France. In the mid-1990s Quinn was still a subject of SEC suits seeking to seize his assets to satisfy unpaid civil penalties dating back to the penny stock days. But despite all the litigating and scrutiny, Quinn's dealings with an ex-dope-dealer-bagel-consultant-construction-company-operator-economic-consultant from New Jersey just didn't raise much of a fuss among the feds. Phil continued to operate on the Street, without anyone paying particularly close attention.

It's not very likely that anyone in a position of authority was aware that Phil was standing at a window on the fourteenth floor of 90 Broad Street, staring out at Manhattan and giving one of his guys $5,000 to give to Louis.

Louis had never heard of Phil before, and was not familiar with his history, but that information wasn't necessary. The way he stood at the window was enough.

"The quiet ones are the bad ones. They're the bad guys. He just wouldn't talk much. When I was up there, the place was empty and he just stood by the window, hands behind his back, looking out. It was nerve-wracking. You understand? Phil's standing by the window. Walking around, looking out windows.

"I knew that he was, like, a Guy. I heard about it. But it wasn't like somebody said, 'We got a firm starting up. We got one of the gangsters from Jersey. He's a skipper. If you don't come to work he'll probably kill you.' Nobody said anything like that.

"Besides, Phil would have had you fooled a little bit. If you looked at his face, when he's cleaned up he really doesn't look like a fucking gangster. As soon as he opens his mouth, the way he talks, his mannerisms, is a dead giveaway. He's just a very nonchalant guy. There's certain mannerisms a gangster has. A Guy that knows that you're never going to get over on him. There's a certain mannerism about him, like when he talks to you. They just look at you, and there's this gray in their eye, and you just know. He knows. Somebody like Phil or Frank Coppa, he'd say, 'It's your choice.' Just make the right choice, but it's your choice. That's more scary than him smacking you or beating the shit out of you."

Louis never really thought about why Phil—a Guy like Phil—was at Sovereign. He just seemed to belong. After all, Phil was there because it was his money. It was the same with Frank Coppa. He came to Brod to watch his money. Louis had seen a lot of Frank at Brod, mainly talking to Benny. Benny was cutting in Frank on warrants, making nice short-term profits for him. But when all was said and done, Frank was just a visitor at Brod. A client, more or less.

This was different. Phil was Sovereign.

After Louis saw Phil and got his $5,000 he put a desk in his office at 90 Broad. "I sat down in my office for a few days, with nothing to do. Every day product was coming, was coming, was coming. There was never any product. Then finally they had product, and I wasn't gonna do it," said Louis.

The problem was that Sovereign was a ripoff. Not a ripoff of the clients. That was a given. Sovereign was out to rip off the brokers. No way. "They got some stock, and the rips were like nothing. It was bullshit. A ripoff. I'm not doing it. So I told Benny I'm not doing it. I gave them back their five grand. I had no choice about that," said Louis.

What Louis wanted, what he had just started hearing about, were cash deals. You sold stock, you were paid your rip right away, in cash. That's where the real money was. Frank's guys did them back in the 1980s, and got sent to jail for them, in one of the few criminal prosecutions that came out of the penny stock era. Louis heard about this marvelous new method of compensation from Chris Wolf.

"Wall Street's a small world, especially in Battery Park City. We all lived in Battery Park City. So after A. T. Brod was over, Chris one night was really drunk at the Tunnel and he gave me money to buy a drink. I didn't want the money—I had plenty of money—but he's drunk. So he gives me the money and he's got all this cash. He's got cash coming out of all his pockets, stuck in his pants. Everyplace. Bulging out all over. Must have been about fifty thousand. He was so loaded he gave me a thousand for a four-dollar drink, and says I should keep the change. I say, 'Where'd you get this fucking cash?' He says, 'A new type of business.' He says, 'You get paid under the table for stock.'"

Louis always liked Chris Wolf, and seeing Chris with all the cash made him like Chris even more. Chris and Rocco were at a new firm, also one he could see out his window at Battery Park City. Greenway Capital Corporation was on the nineteenth floor of 45 Broadway. It was a brand-new building just a couple of doors down from Morgan Williams, that great bar where Roy and Louis bonded on the night of the boat-ride due dilly that left Chris with the scar, fading now.

Greenway overlooked the bull statue at Bowling Green park. It was so close they could have stuck their heads out the windows and spit on the bull. The kids at Greenway never did that but it would have made sense. They didn't need the bull market to make money. The bull market was for losers.

CHAPTER TWENTY-FIVE

Greenway was like coming home, if home was a combination social club, parochial-school yard, and lunatic asylum. It was a bit like Hanover, only without the Roy-imposed order and corporal punishment.

Louis had a huge office that looked all the way up Broadway. The offices seemed to have been thrown together at random from IKEA and the Salvation Army Thrift Store. But that was okay. Everybody was having fun.

"It was a zoo. They would run in the water fountains downstairs. Joe Temp did a half million, pulled his pants down, ran through the fountain. They were crazy psychopaths. There were no rules at Greenway. We came and went as we pleased. We had parties up there, we got high. We had everything. We got a Wiffle ball bat and played Wiffle ball."

Rocco and Chris had their own crew, about thirty-five or forty kids in all. Benny had stayed at Sovereign, and Louis went to Greenway with about eighteen cold-callers. The crews were separated from each other, as they were at Hanover. Louis had his own boardroom. "I didn't like my guys associating with anybody else," said Louis. "Cancer. That's what I used to call it. Other people have a different work ethic. They cause your guys to have cancer, like. It rubs off on them. These guys work like this, your guys start to work like that. I used to train my guys my own way, according to my rules. They start seeing other people's rules, they get different ideas."

Being around guys like Chris and Rocco, guys who really knew how to sell stock, was important because selling stock wasn't getting any easier. The public was starting to get wise to chop stocks. It was a gradual thing. People wanted to hear about the companies. Were they legitimate? It was a concern now, and a lot of customers were wondering if the stocks they were pitched were phonies. Clients were getting wise to big spreads (big differences between the bid and ask prices). Chop stocks had huge spreads. They could find out that kind of stuff easily. The Internet was just beginning, but there were plenty of ways to get quotes and corporate info. People were getting smarter. But not so smart that they weren't going to buy stocks over the phone.

But the change in public attitudes was gradual, and Louis and the others didn't think about it too much. They had more important things on their minds. Mentoring, for instance. Now that he actually had a license, Louis decided to share it with one of the underprivileged cold-callers who was not so blessed. A kid named John was showing promise on the phone, so Louis let him run his own book of clients as a kind of junior partner, using Louis's name just as Louis had used Benny's name. In a warmhearted moment he had even cut the kid in on a deal. John borrowed $11,000 to sink into a deal involving warrants in a company called Zanart. John was promised a share of the profits in return.

Louis had his doubts about Greenway, but the money was good. For every $100,000 in stock he sold, Louis got $25,000 in cash, which was put in a paper bag and provided to him promptly on, usually, Tuesdays. The cash came from a guy Louis knew only as Bobby.

"Bobby Cash Deals, I used to call him. He used to drive a

Rolls-Royce and park it right in front of Greenway. Some cold-caller would go sit in the car. Bobby would give him a hundred bucks, while Bobby came upstairs. He was old, about fifty years old. Gray hair. Cowboy-looking guy. About six feet three inches tall. Always had a cast on his arm, for some damn reason, this guy. And he had an associate with him, who also was named Bobby. They used to come up with the suitcase. We knew, when we seen them walk through the door, it was payday. They were the suitcase guys. They'd come up to Greenway and bring the money."

It was a good life, at least for Louis. But it wasn't such a great life for Chris. His two partners were at Greenway almost constantly. They didn't own Greenway. They didn't have to. They owned Chris.

They were Dom and Rico—Black Dom Dionisio and Enrico Locascio, who had come up to Hanover, armed with submachine guns, during the safe-stealing incident. Now they kept their guns out of sight but were at Greenway almost every day.

Louis started to hear that Black Dom and Rico were always in Chris's face, making his life miserable. There were lurid rumors. He didn't know whether to believe them or not. But it was clear that they were at Greenway all the time to watch their investment—Chris Wolf.

Dom was as humongous as Louis remembered him from Hanover, and he now got to know Rico, whose snarl could melt ice cream across the room.

Louis saw the Guys at Greenway and said hello to them and that was that. They were none of his business.

His business was making money. The money was good. But Louis wasn't happy at Greenway despite the cash and the conviviality. He felt tense. A little jealous, maybe. With all the big earners there, he was always going to be a small fish in a large (and smelly) pond. It wasn't long before Louis started to get restless.

What he really wanted was his own firm, and his old friend
Marco Fiore was offering just that, more or less. Marco was
opening the New York branch office of a Fort Worth–based
brokerage firm called Nationwide Securities. Benny was ditch-
ing Sovereign and going to the offices that Marco was leasing
for Nationwide at 5 Hanover Square, in the same space occu-
pied by Hanover Sterling when it was just starting up, before
moving to 88 Pine. Hanover Square was down by the tip of
Manhattan, where the streets are crooked and narrow. Lots of
chop houses were setting up shop down in the tall stone buildings that overlooked those crooked streets.

Louis and Benny, partners again, were going to run the
firm. At Greenway he could never be part of the inner circle
and get the real dough. Goddamn politics. The curse of Wall
Street. To overcome politics, and make the most money, you
must be the boss. He was learning that.

Louis had to be in control. It was more than just the money.
He had to do things his way. He had to be in charge. At Na-
tionwide he could be in control. And in the same place where
Roy started Hanover! It was terrific. Everybody was psyched.

Louis brought his cold-callers with him. Even John, the
promising kid he had cut in on the Zanart warrant deal. Being
a mentor wasn't all it was cracked up to be. Louis felt that
John didn't work hard enough for his share of the warrant
profits. He decided to hold back some of the money. That
would serve him right.

John didn't like it. Tough.

In September 1995, Louis and a few of his cold-callers
made the move to Nationwide at Hanover Square. A mover
transported his beautiful new mahogany desk and leather
chair a few blocks to the new building, with its great history
and even better promise. The plan was to move to even bigger
and better offices at 100 Wall Street in a couple of months.
And 100 Wall was just around the corner from 88 Pine, where

Louis got his start at Hanover. They were in the footsteps of greatness. And the name—Nationwide—sounded so patriotic.

Everything was terrific as Louis got his stuff moved into his new office, even though John was still ragging on him for the money. Blow me, Louis told him. But John kept it up.

"He kept on asking for it, asking for it, but I wasn't giving it to him," said Louis. "I says, 'You're not getting it.' And he says, 'You know what? I'm going to tell my cousin.' And I go, 'I don't give a fuck. Tell your cousin. Tell him to come see me.'"

part four

A GUY LIKE ME

CHAPTER TWENTY-SIX

"I walk into my office at Nationwide, late in the morning. Nobody was there, because we were just moving in. There's this guy in my office. Tan guy. He's sitting at my desk, my chair. I walked in.

"'Do you know who I am?'

"'No.'

"'I'm Charlie. I'm John's cousin.'

"'Okay.'

"'Sit down.'

"Now I'm a little scared. I'm kind of shaken up. I don't know what's going to happen.

"'You owe my cousin some money.'

"I says, 'Well, I gave him five thousand, what I thought he deserves.'

"He says, 'It's not about who deserves what. You made an agreement. You're going to pay him the twenty thousand.' He explains, if I don't pay the money—in a roundabout way he doesn't say he's going to beat my face in, he doesn't talk like that, he says, the $20,000 is not worth the consequences, the repercussions of not paying.

"Then I says, 'I don't think it's fair for me to pay him the twenty thousand.'

"He says, 'What do you think is fair? I'm going to be fair now.' I say fifteen. And he says, 'Okay, I want it tomorrow. No later than tomorrow.'"

Charlie was burly, a little pudgy, moon-faced, about Louis's height. He seemed to be in his late thirties. His hair was combed straight back. He dressed nicely. But Louis couldn't concentrate on what he was wearing at the moment, even though that was the first thing he usually noticed about a person.

Nobody had ever talked to Louis like that before, except his father maybe, or George Donohue sometimes, or the priests at Sea, or the cops who'd pull him over for speeding. But Louis never listened to his father, and George was a friend. Easygoing. Charlie wasn't easygoing. Neither were the cops, but he didn't give a shit about the cops and the priests. He'd take the ticket or show George's PBA badge and not get a ticket, and keep on speeding. There was something about this guy Louis couldn't put his finger on, so he asked Benny, when Benny got into the office that day. "Benny says, 'Pay him the money.' I say, 'Why?' and Benny says, 'He's nobody to mess with, he's going to get you if you don't pay him the money. Pay him the money.' I asked Marco, he tells me the same thing—the guy is very respected, has a great reputation, pay him the money."

But that wasn't a good enough reason. Louis had the $15,000, it was in the stacks in his safe at home, and he wasn't going to pay it. He just decided to do what he usually did when people wanted money, or a stock sold, or whatever people wanted him to do that he wasn't going to do. He just didn't pay it any attention.

"So now, taking lightly the subject, I avoid him. He beeps me the next day. I don't call him. Beeps me the day after that. I don't call him. I decide to call like four days later. Charlie tells me, 'Louis, you think you're going to make a fucking jerk out of me? Meet me in Brooklyn, right now. A half hour you got.' He gives me the address of a pizzeria on West First and Kings Highway.

"So I go to the pizzeria. A guy there says Charlie's at an auto body shop across the street. I get there, I get out of the car, it's my Mercedes four-door. I'm very head down, like puppy-dog scared, and he says, 'Come with me.' I didn't want to go, you know. But I go. He takes me downstairs to this basement-type situation, it's all dark, and he smacks me.

"He tells me, 'You going to make a fucking jerk out of me? You brought the money, right?' And I don't tell him no, because I only brought seventy-five hundred with me, so I don't tell him I don't got it all, right downstairs in the basement, because I figure if I told him I didn't have it all, I was probably going to stay in the basement.

"I says, 'Yeah, I got it, it's up in the car.' So we get up to the car, I give him the seventy-five hundred, and he says, 'You've got the balls to bring me seventy-five hundred fucking dollars. You owe me fifteen thousand. Do you know who I am? Do you have any idea?' He says, 'You're not taking your car. Leave your car.'"

"Leave your car?" This guy wanted to take his car? Wanted to keep his car? Steal his car? Or hold it until he got paid? It wasn't clear. Louis could have told him to go fuck himself. Louis was in good shape. He could have taken on this Charlie. Maybe. But something told him that maybe that wouldn't be a good idea.

"'How am I going to get home?' He says, 'I don't give a fuck. Give me the keys to your car.'

"So he makes me give him the keys. I start to walk away and he makes me come back. He says, 'I don't want your fucking shit in the trunk. Take it out of there.' So I take all the car stuff out of the trunk and I give him my key and I leave my car there. I got to get on the train.

"About twenty minutes later he beeps me. I was on the elevated train at McDonald Avenue. I had gone a few stops.

When he beeped me I was on the train. I got off the train, called him from the pay phone, and he says 'Come back here right now.' I went to the opposite platform, got on the train going back, mind you with my fucking bin, a crate of oil, all my car shit. So it takes me a half hour.

"I get back to the place and he says, 'If you don't come to-morrow with the other seventy-five hundred, don't come. I'll find you.' This is when he tells me, 'You're with me now.' He gives me the car back and I give him the seventy-five hundred the next day."

"So I bring over the other seventy-five hundred and he ac-tually takes me out to dinner that night. He played bad guy. Now it's good guy, because he probably sees, look at this kid, 500-series Mercedes, brought me fifteen thousand without even sweating it. At the time I was thinking, maybe this is a good thing. I need a gangster, I'm making a hundred thousand dollars a month. People are always trying to beat me out of what I'm owed."

Louis met Charlie at 101, a sleek new restaurant on Fourth Avenue in Fort Hamilton, a pleasant middle-class neighbor-hood in the shadow of the Verrazano-Narrows Bridge.

"I was very impressed with this guy. We walked in. It was crowded but we sat right down. Everybody knew him. About a hundred people come over to him while we're eating, kiss-ing him hello, how are you doing. Two people sent over a bot-tle of wine.

"With me, he was very friendly. Not saying, 'You have no choice, you're giving me ten thousand warrants a deal, and that's that.' Very friendly and nonchalant. He tells me, 'Sorry we had to meet on these terms. I think we could do a lot to-gether. How's Wall Street treating you? Any up-and-coming deals?' he asks me. He says, 'I don't want a free ride. I don't expect nothing for free. I want to invest money. So the deal you got coming around, count me in—I want to invest.'

"I think this is a great thing. I'm thinking, wow, I'll invest this guy's money. Look at him. He knows everybody. He's definitely—he's out there. Everybody knew him. Kissing him hello. Charlie is very tan. Always tan. Dead-of-winter-tan. No-matter-what-tan. But he denies that he ever goes to a tanning salon. Slicked-back hair. Kind of receding hairline. Good-looking guy. Very distinguished guy. Stocky. A little muscle behind him. And you would not mistake him for who he is. If you put a picture of him in your mind, that's what he looks like. He just looks like that typical Brooklyn gangster.

"He wears black mockneck shirts. Not a high turtleneck. Low. Silk black turtleneck, mockneck shirts. That's what he wears. He'll wear a sports jacket, slacks, and, like, snakeskin shoes. Really flashy shoes. Gold watch—Rolex. No chains or anything around his neck. Nothing like that. Ring, Rolex. That's it. Very sharp-dressed. Very sharp. Always a different-color sports jacket. So if he was wearing all black it would be a printed sports jacket. A sharp dresser. Dressed very well."

Impressed as he was with how Charlie dressed, Louis could see that Charlie was only vaguely familiar with Wall Street, as if maybe he learned about it by watching the Charlie Sheen movie. But that was okay. The people out there, members of the public, often have only a slight understanding of how the Street works. But Charlie had one insight into the Street that the general public, as well as the regulators and the press, just didn't have at the time. He knew that kids from his neighborhood were on Wall Street, cold-calling people, and making money. That was all he needed to know. He knew that and he knew he was entitled. He didn't know much else. He didn't know what an IPO was, even though IPOs were getting a lot of press at the time. That was okay too. Louis read the *News* and *Post* but didn't get to the business section most days.

Louis told him about the hot new IPO that was due out in a couple of months, Gaylord Companies. It made specialty cookware, and the lead underwriter was a firm called RAS Securities, which didn't have the army of brokers that Nationwide could bring to the table. But they didn't discuss the product line or the underwriter or anything like that. What they discussed was that it was a great deal, and that Charlie could make a lot of money. It seemed like the kind of thing to say at the time—that Charlie could make a lot of money, and that Louis could make it for him. Louis said that. Said how much he could make. Mentioned specific numbers. It seemed like the thing to do, there at 101, with people coming over and with Charlie looking so good.

Charlie was definitely interested. He definitely wanted to do business. He wanted to invest. He said that. He would invest. A new client. Like Craig Kallman, who was not coming through with referrals, or the Jets guys, who were becoming a pain in the ass, or Baba Booey and Stuttering John, who were more trouble than they were worth. Howard Stern as a client? It wasn't happening. Stuttering John didn't even try.

Louis had to think of the future. Not plan. He never planned. But he was getting married. He was going to start a family. Maybe Charlie could be good for him. Maybe Charlie could help.

At Brod, Louis got beat out of the money he was owed. At Greenway and now Nationwide, he was doing cash deals. What if Bobby Cash Deals had decided not to pay? What could Louis have done? Sue? Not for cash deals. They were handshake deals. Deals that he knew were illegal—"undisclosed compensation," the lawyers would call it. What could he do if there was a beef over the cash? Go up against Black Dom and Rico? The kid John had done the right thing. He felt strongly about the $20,000 so he went to his cousin.

Charlie knew he could be useful. He said so. But he did it in a nice way, a funny way. "Kind of made me laugh, Charlie," said Louis. "He was very blunt the way he would talk. He wouldn't hold anything back. He was that kind of gangster. He wasn't a quiet guy. He says, 'You're taking down big money over there. All you little pricks think you're going to run around, make big money, and not share with us Guys.' He says, 'One day you're going to need a Guy like me.'"

Charlie was older than Louis and had done a lot of living. Charlie didn't talk about it at first, but nothing had come easy for him. Charlie was from a blue-collar neighborhood and he was a blue-collar guy. He had never gone to college. Nothing was given to him. Everything he had, all that he had achieved in life, he took with his own two hands.

CHAPTER TWENTY-SEVEN

It was a chilly spring morning, April 16, 1981. Lee Polanski was driving his sky-blue Cadillac convertible down a street in Merrick, Long Island, when he saw the three guys, walking. Lee was heading north on Frankel Boulevard, taking his wife Jessica to the train station. The three guys were on the sidewalk, walking south. He saw them. They didn't see him.

Lee knew one of them. He didn't know him well enough to wave at him, but just enough to say to himself—not even to his wife, just to himself—hey, I know that guy. And it was not a bad memory at all. A memory of a nice guy, a young guy, a guy who liked kids.

It was Charlie. Charlie Ricottone. It was a pleasant memory.

Lee was a young guy himself, in his early thirties, and he was from Brooklyn originally. Now he was manager of a supermarket. He and his wife were starting a family, and after they were married in the early 1970s they had moved out to a bedroom community in Nassau County, as had generations of upwardly mobile Brooklyn couples over the years. That's what happens in New York. An outer-borough tradition, almost. Bronx people move to Westchester. Brooklyn people move to Long Island or Staten Island. So Lee moved to Long

Island and by the summer of 1979 they had a two-year-old daughter, Annie. Jessica Polanski was pregnant with their second child, and they were adding a room to the house. It was a last-minute, hurried kind of thing, because Mrs. Polanski was due in August, so the crew worked hard to get it finished on time. Charlie was part of the crew and he was at the house, working, all summer.

Charlie stood out in Lee's memory of that hectic but joyous summer. He was more than just another guy in the crew, hauling and cutting lumber and painting the freshly installed plasterboard. He was a nice guy. A jovial guy. Lee was home during much of July, and he got to know Charlie very, very well. Jessica would make lunch for the guys on the construction project, and they would relax and talk. Charlie was a personable, young guy, just twenty-one at the time. He was hardworking, a go-getter. He and the rest of the guys on the construction crew worked capably to finish the addition, which they did on the day Jessica gave birth to Jennie, on August 3, 1979.

Lee liked Charlie so much, and was so pleased with his diligence and good nature, that he had Charlie come back and do some more painting, once the extra room was finished. When Lee threw a birthday party for Jennie a year later, Charlie was invited. It was only natural. He was such a nice guy. And it was a great party. Charlie stayed till late that night, drinking and joking and posing for pictures with the rest of the gang and having a great time.

Now, driving to drop off his wife at the station, it was seven months later, and Charlie and two other guys were walking south. Toward his house. The thought didn't really jell in Lee's mind. He was in a hurry to get his wife to the Long Island Railroad station for her train. He dropped her off at the station and went home. His two daughters were home. His housekeeper was home.

Lee drove into the driveway, got out of the car, and opened

the front door to his house. He had one foot inside when he saw the gun. A man with a gun was standing to his right, behind the door, wearing a stocking mask.

The man with the gun said, "We have your kids upstairs. Come into the house—" but he wasn't able to finish what he was saying because Lee turned around and ran outside yelling, "Help!" As he got to the end of the driveway, he stumbled and fell, gashing his hands.

The man with the gun and the stocking mask, and a man without a gun but with a stocking mask, walked over to Lee on the ground. "Don't do that," the man with the gun told Lee. "Don't be stupid," he told him.

Lee came inside. A voice from upstairs said, "Rip that chain off his neck." He knew about the chain, even though he was upstairs and out of sight. Lee took the chain off and gave the man with the gun his chain, his other jewelry, and the money in his pockets.

The voice again: "Where's your wife? Where's her ring?" Lee replied that she wasn't there, that he had just driven her to the railroad station.

The voice was angry, impatient.

"You're lying," said the voice.

"I'm not lying," said Lee. "You know, it's obvious she's not here." It was obvious. She wasn't there. And she was wearing her ring.

"Where's the jewelry boxes?" the voice asked. Still upstairs.

"I have no jewelry boxes," said Lee.

The voice knew about them too. Lee used to have jewelry boxes in his closet. But he had a burglary. So he took them out.

The voice upstairs kept asking about the wife, and the ring, and kept getting the same answer. Not there.

The two men with stocking masks led Lee down to the basement. The voice continued to ask about the wife and jewelry and the ring. As if asking would make them appear.

A knife ripped the shirt up his back. An order was given. He removed his pants. Another order. He removed his underpants. He put his hands behind his back and they were bound with duct tape. His hands hurt. They were still bleeding from the fall, but there wasn't anything he could do about that.

The voice said, "Is that all you have? I thought it was a lot of money." It was a lot of money—$1,500. Lee's store was open late the night before and he hadn't had a chance to deposit all the cash. But the voice expected more. The voice wanted more and the voice was threatening.

The voice told him that if he didn't do everything he was told, he would take the children. The voice told him that if he loved the children, he would not do anything stupid.

The men with the stocking masks left. The voice stopped talking. The housekeeper came downstairs and untied Lee. The police came.

Lee was reluctant to tell the Nassau County detectives that the voice belonged to his friend, the nice young guy he got to know a couple of years before, who came to his kid's party. He was reluctant to show them the pictures that he took on the deck, the ones showing Charlie. He was reluctant to tell the detectives that he knew where they could find Charlie. He was afraid that, maybe, Charlie might come back.

But the detective in charge of the case knew just what to say. He had heard that kind of thing before. Charlie might come back anyway, he told Lee. Better that he be in jail.

Lee told him what he knew. By the end of the day, the three men who came to his house were in custody and were arranging bail. There was Charlie, his sister's boyfriend Anthony Cella, and a third man they both knew.

While he was in police custody, Cella gave a statement to Nassau County detectives implicating Charlie. He described the weapons. He described the split. About enough to buy each of them a nice 27-inch color television set.

Charlie pleaded guilty to one count of robbery in the first

degree, and on May 21, 1982, he appeared for sentencing in Nassau County Court. He was accompanied by his lawyer, Thomas Davenport.

"I have just had occasion to read the probation report," said Davenport. "It is one of the most scathing reports I have ever read, I must confess.

"The one aspect that concerns me the most that I [have] personal knowledge on is the lack of Charles Ricottone's remorse. I think, unfortunately, Mr. Ricottone gives the appearance of a sense of swagger. I think that is done to mask and not to betray his feelings.

"I have a deep sense that he is remorseful not just that he was caught. I think he did a foolish thing and he recognizes it and he violated a trust and a friendship and he recognizes that."

Apparently the judge recognized that too. Charlie was sentenced to six to ten years in prison, which was the least severe sentence he could have received. While serving his time at the Clinton correctional facility in Dannemora, Charlie tried to appeal his conviction. A lawyer was appointed by the Appellate Division of the New York State Supreme Court. After investigating the case and interviewing Charlie, whose charm and loquaciousness impressed him, the lawyer asked to be relieved on the grounds that there was no basis for appeal. The request was granted.

Charlie was released from Mid-Orange Correctional Center on February 12, 1988.

The prison experience molded Charlie's psyche, and his career. By the time he was in his mid-thirties, he was well on his way to achieving his goal of becoming a Guy.

A little over four years later, Charlie and a friend had dinner at a restaurant on a pier jutting into Jamaica Bay, in the Canarsie section of Brooklyn. They climbed into a car. Charlie's friend was behind the wheel. It was about eight-thirty in the evening of April 23, 1992.

The restaurant was on U.S. government property—the Gateway National Recreation Area. Charlie and his friend might not have known that. A lot of Brooklynites don't know that much of Jamaica Bay is a national park. Property of the U.S. government.

A National Park Service policeman, Paul Dorogoff, observed the vehicle traveling at approximately ten miles per hour in a five-mile-per-hour zone. Dorogoff motioned for the car to stop. Charlie's friend, not identified in court records, was civil and consented to administration of a sobriety test. Charlie was not civil. While his friend was being administered the test, Charlie "exited the vehicle and repeatedly approached your deponent and interfered with the sobriety test," Dorogoff stated in an affidavit in support of the arrest of Charles Ricottone for assaulting a federal officer. Dorogoff's affidavit continued:

> While your deponent was writing the summons, the defendant repeatedly threatened your deponent, for instance by saying that he was "going to hit that scumbag with a two-by-four in his fucking face," and that he was going to "open that motherfucker's head."
>
> Subsequently, a number of other Park Police officers arrived on the scene and attempted to place the defendant under arrest. The defendant forcibly resisted arrest by struggling with the Park Police officers and with New York City police officers who were attempting to assist. . . . The defendant refused to identify himself but instead claimed that his name was "John Doe."

One of the cops wound up with a sprained thumb. It was no big deal. And if the Canarsie pier brawl had been adjudicated in the city's criminal justice system, Charlie would have wound up getting a short jail term at the most, or maybe nothing at all. But now prosecutors were making, literally, a federal case out of it. And when Charlie was released on $50,000 bond, the U.S. Attorney's Office insisted on "special conditions" not ordinarily found in most bail documents. Charlie, who gave his address as Oceanside, Long Island, agreed not to enter Brooklyn or to communicate with thirty-nine individuals. The list included just about every Guy of consequence who was allied with a Colombo family honcho named Victor Orena in his war with another faction of the Colombos, headed by Alphonse Persico. Apart from Orena himself and various Orena relatives, the list included "Wild Bill" Cutolo, the Colombo skipper who was Black Dom's uncle and a close associate of Orena.

On June 8, 1992, Charlie was arrested again. He was in Brooklyn, in violation of a condition of his release. The car he was using was stolen. FBI agents were following him at the time, and prosecutors said the FBI men suspected that Charlie and the other people in the car were up to no good, apart from being in a car that didn't belong to them. In fact, the FBI men were following them because they thought the people in the car were part of a "hit team" and were going to kill somebody.

The Brooklyn incident was a troublesome issue when Charlie came up for sentencing on November 13, 1992, before U.S. District Court Judge Reena Raggi. Charlie had been caught red-handed violating the bail conditions. He had every reason to expect Raggi would throw the book at him. The judge had a presentence report in front of her that detailed the FBI's concerns, including Charlie's alleged status as a Colombo family associate. Assistant U.S. Attorney Karen Popp told the judge that when he was arrested in Brooklyn for the stolen car thing, "he indicated to an FBI agent that he hated me. I was a pain in the ass. And he would like to kill me."

Popp asked for forfeiture of the entire $50,000 bond, and a maximum ten-month sentence for the Canarsie pier brawl.

Popp believed Charlie could afford the forfeiture because "the defendant's illegal occupation of being a part of a hit team is very lucrative."

James DiPietro, Charlie's lawyer, conceded that some of the things Charlie had done weren't particularly nice. The threat against Popp, for instance. A very bad joke, he insisted. He conceded that his client had been in Brooklyn, where he was not supposed to be.

DiPietro complained that seeing Charlie "lose fifty thousand dollars for the indiscretion that brings him before the court would be a little harsh." He went on to say that Charlie was a diabetic, but working hard despite his handicap, and helping out his father, who wasn't well either, in the family window business. "He's working with his father and helping support the family," said the lawyer.

Popp countered by saying that the "indiscretion" in Brooklyn was preceded by tossing of guns out the window, and that towels that could have been used as silencers were found in the car at the time.

Federal defendants are given an opportunity to personally plead their case before sentencing. Charlie addressed the judge:

"What I want to say is mostly that I'm very sorry for the incident that happened because the incident in question is just about me having an argument with a federal officer that got out of hand and I used abusive language.

"As far as assaulting an officer, Your Honor, I mean I understand you have to go by what you read. You weren't there. I can only tell you, I never assaulted, picked up my hands. I was surrounded by fifteen or so police officers asking me to lay on the floor. You're under arrest. And I was saying, well, what am I being arrested for?

"They just kept on telling me, get on the floor. You are under arrest. I was intoxicated. I did not get on the floor. With that, they surrounded me with German shepherd dogs that for some reason was left out of all the papers and they subdued me to the floor.

"I have never raised my hand to an officer. I'm very sorry for this incident. It snowballed into all these things and I just am very sorry for the incident that happened this night because it's costing me very dearly."

Judge Raggi accepted Charlie's apology.

She refused to buy the "hit team" argument, and told prosecutors to put up or shut up—prosecute him if they thought he was out to kill somebody. Even though he was caught red-handed violating the conditions of his release, Raggi forfeited just $15,000 of his $50,000 bond. She shrugged off the threat against Popp. She called it "less than funny" and said, "It does give me pause about whether or not you understand the responsibility of every citizen to obey the law."

Raggi didn't pause very long. She rejected the government's plea for a maximum ten-month sentence and sentenced Charlie to the lowest term of incarceration allowed under the guidelines: four months in prison plus one year of supervised release. He went to prison just after the turn of the year 1993, and served his four months.

Not long after returning to society, Charlie again found himself running afoul of the criminal justice system. The charges were filed on Valentine's Day, 1994. The offense: violating the terms of his supervised release. The particulars: Charlie changed his address without telling his probation officer, lied about his address on papers that he filed with the Probation Department, and failed to let a probation officer into his residence as required by law.

Charlie pleaded guilty and was sentenced to six months in prison. On June 6, 1994, Charlie surrendered to the federal prison at White Deer, Pennsylvania, to begin serving his term of imprisonment.

Despite Judge Raggi's bend-over-backward-till-the-vertebrae-crack leniency, that brawl at the Canarsie pier cost Charlie ten months of his life, $15,000 from the forfeited bond, and probably a nice hunk of change in legal fees.

All this may sound a bit weird, or even sick, to the average person. But Guys aren't average people. Guys don't play by the rules. They couldn't care less about the legal consequences of their actions. It's not crazy at all. It's what being a Guy is all about.

The incident in Canarsie, and its aftermath, says more about the durability of Guys than a whole shelf-full of criminology texts, with their insistence that Guys have a role in society by providing services not otherwise available. Guys are here because we want them, supposedly. Sure we do. We like home-invasion robberies. We want to buy worthless stocks.

"There is no reason why La Cosa Nostra should not be relegated to history within a few years," former Attorney General Ramsey Clark wrote in his book *Crime in America,* back in 1970. "It is on the ropes now. The question is why we have endured it so long."

That isn't the question at all.

"We" don't endure Guys. Guys endure prison. It's the price they pay for being Guys. In return they get status, power, freedom—and the money they get from the guys who steal.

CHAPTER TWENTY-EIGHT

Charlie changed things.

It was like being a parent for the first time, and realizing that the bundle of joy in your bassinet is going to change your life forever. It was the same with having a Guy in your life. Having a Guy in your life changed things forever. Before he met Charlie, Louis didn't know what it would be like to have a Guy like Charlie. But now that he had Charlie, now that he had a Guy, he couldn't imagine life without Charlie.

In the immediate afterglow of the dinner with Charlie—well, he couldn't have felt better. He was moving up in the world. A guy with a Guy. "It was a great dinner. I felt good about myself at the time. At the time I felt, 'Wow, this is cool,'" said Louis.

Life with Charlie was different but better, definitely better. Louis was convinced of that. Sure, if Louis thought real hard about his initial interactions with Charlie, he might have seen that it was Charlie who was benefiting, at least financially—even if what Charlie said was true about Louis needing him. And Charlie didn't make it easy for Louis to deal with him. He was not particularly polite. His phone manners, at times, lacked civility. Louis couldn't con him, couldn't put him off. That point he raised about Louis needing him was not a debatable proposition. Charlie was not offering his services to Louis. He was not selling himself. That wasn't the point at all.

"It's not like I could say, 'Maybe I'll just never talk to him again.' That just wasn't going to happen. But it's also not like I decided to pick up the phone and call the guy. It's not like I called the guy in a couple of days and said, 'Hey, Charlie, how you doing? I made ten grand. Would you like some of it?' He called me."

The calls began a couple of days after their meeting in 101. It was a pleasant call, inquiring about a pending IPO. A client call. No problem.

Louis waited a few hours before calling him back the first time he saw Charlie's phone number on his pager. It was a mistake.

"He said, 'What the fuck. You don't call me. I just want to let you know, you call me back when I beep you.' He goes, 'I beep you from a pay phone. I don't want to be waiting around until you fucking call me.'"

They met again a few weeks later. Another pleasant business meeting, this time to talk about the Gaylord IPO. Charlie wanted to invest. And like any investor, he was worried about his exposure to downside market risk. "He says 'I'm not going to lose money, right? How much am I going to make?'"

Louis figured Charlie could make about $30,000 if he put up $10,000. He said so. It was a good-faith guess. Not the guarantee he had given to Stuttering John.

Louis wasn't really sure what his relationship with Charlie was supposed to be. It wasn't something they taught you in preparation for the Series 7, even if he had actually studied for the test. What do you do when a Guy comes into your life? He was afraid to ask his father. He knew what his father would say. He knew how Nick Pasciuto felt about Guys—you stay away from them.

No way he was asking George Donohue.

One thing you do, when a Guy comes into your life, is eat.

Louis had already begun to put on the pounds at Brod. It was the sedentary habits and eating out all the time, in restaurants such as Angelo's in Little Italy, where his favorite waiter, Bruno, always knew to bring over a plate of calamari in red sauce over spaghetti. The skinny kid was getting a bull neck. Charlie made Louis's bull neck widen, and helped him develop a growing pot belly, by introducing him to the better Guy Italian restaurants in Brooklyn like Zio's and Mezzanote in Bay Ridge.

Over meals, with Louis not having to fight too hard for the check, they were getting to know each other. Becoming, almost, friends. "He'd talk about some of his war stories that he had, like the time that he threw a glass in some bar and smashed the guy. Then he brought up that he did a lot of time in prison for something that was really scary. It happened out in Nassau County.

"From what he told me, he had a guy held hostage on Long Island. He told me he went into a house, the people were supposed to be away, they weren't, and he had a hostage situation. He says he didn't get out and the police arrested him right there. He made it seem like it was a bad scene, with hostage negotiators and everything, helicopters flying over the house. After that, whenever I watched a movie about a hostage situation, I thought about Charlie."

Louis tried to bring his new almost-friend up to speed on how money was made on Wall Street. He explained it as simply as he could, because Charlie did not have a particularly good grasp of the principles of finance.

"I tried to explain it to him, but he had trouble with it. Finally I say, 'Look, you're buying it for a penny, and you're selling it for two dollars.' Like with warrants I didn't explain to him what exactly it was, or he had an option to buy stock, or anything like that. It was just, 'Give me the money. I'll give you thirty grand.' Because there was no point. Even if I explained it to him, he wouldn't understand. I knew he was a simple-fucking-minded guy, but he's definitely shrewd."

Charlie made it clear from the start that he was going to be more than a friend, and more than a client, though Louis had a hard time figuring out just what he would be. This much was sure, though: Charlie was going to be around—physically. He was never going to stray too far from his money, or from his new money generator.

"When he came up to my office to see me at Nationwide, it was a surprise out of nowhere. 'How you doing, Louie. Let me open my account.' That's what he was coming up there to do. Open his account. He opened it under his girlfriend's name. I opened the account, and he sent a ten-thousand-dollar check. He did like he said he would. He actually bought stock on the first deal, Gaylord. It was amazing."

The money in Charlie's account was set aside for two thousand shares of Gaylord common stock, and Louis was throwing in five thousand warrants. He was going to make a bundle—$30,000 on a $10,000 investment. That is what he told Charlie. He was going to make some good money for Charlie, his new Guy friend.

But things weren't going as planned. Louis was annoyed at the way he and his partners were going to split up the warrants from the Gaylord deal. So Louis decided to quit.

Chris Wolf was through with Greenway and now he had set up shop just down the street, at 63 Wall—Vision Investment Group. They were going to be selling stock in a company called Auxer Enterprises—AUXI—from Vision. Louis liked AUXI. He liked Vision—good name. He liked Chris. Chris would treat him fairly. Bobby Cash Deals was at Vision. Vision would have to be better. He was sure of that.

So he went to Vision, taking Sally Leads and nobody else.

In comparison to Vision, Greenway could have been the Main Reading Room of the New York Public Library.

"Vision was just completely fucking insane. It looked like a rave. Like a fucking underground club. Real shithole office. You walked in, there were three offices. That was it. Dozens of guys on drugs, hanging out in the office. All punks working up there."

The Chris-Rocco team was over. Rocco Basile had gone to another firm, State Capital Markets, and now there was a new team—Chris-Dom-Rico. It was the same arrangement as at Greenway, except that Dom and Rico were now running the place. And the stories about Chris and his two keepers weren't rumors anymore. Louis saw for himself how Black Dom and Rico bullied Chris and shook him down, driving his cars and, in the case of Rico, even living in his apartment. Chris wasn't a willing roommate: "Rico forced his fucking way in there. 'I'm taking the second bedroom. Fuck you.'"

Vision was a nightmare. And not just because of the occasional bloody nose, as was doled out at Hanover. Brokers who crossed Rico and Dom were getting beaten senseless. "Dom and Rico beat the shit out of my friend Armando, hung him out the window. Armando told me. What happened was, he pitched some client, the client reneged on the trade. He and his friend went to the client's house and robbed the guy. They took coins from the guy. And then he left his card there. He was fucking nuts, Armando. Then the guy called the firm and talked to the manager, which was Dom. So he made Armando return the coins, and then they beat the shit out of him. They made him walk through the fucking 'train' under everybody's legs. Dom had everybody in the firm make a circle, and then Armando had to crawl in the circle and everybody would hit him in the back of his ass with a fucking newspaper. He'd walk to the end and then Dom would be there with a Whiffle ball bat. Bam!"

Louis never fell afoul of the Vision style of employee discipline. Charlie saw to that. Charlie went up to Vision as soon as Louis started working there, and told Black Dom to leave him alone. It was nice. It was as if Charlie had become his big brother, telling the schoolyard bully to lay off. "Charlie said, 'He's with me,'" said Louis. "If Dom had a problem, he was supposed to call Charlie."

It was great to be protected from physical violence. At least Charlie could do that much. It made it easier to pay Charlie. And it was good that it was easier because Charlie was expecting to be paid.

Charlie never came out and said it in so many words, but he was anticipating a regular flow of money from Louis. Louis's earnings from Vision were pretty good, about $150,000. Charlie didn't know that, because he wasn't there. But he could always ask around. "I said to myself, if he talks to Black Dom, God forbid word gets out that I just made a hundred fifty grand. The fucking guy is going to lose his wig. I figured that if I give him money, he'll never go around asking."

But how much to give? This wasn't like tipping the building superintendent at Christmas, but there were similarities. The same question is involved: How much will make him happy?

Charlie was never very happy with having to write out a check for $10,000 to buy Gaylord warrants. It seemed to Charlie that Louis was asking him to take a risk, and Guys don't take risks. Guys agree with half of the concept of risk-taking—the "taking" part.

Charlie kept asking about his $10,000. Was he going to get stuck for that money?

So Louis decided, what the fuck. It was fuck-you money anyway. He opened the safe in his apartment, pulled $10,000 out of the stacks, drove to the pizzeria at West First and Kings Highway, and gave the money to Charlie.

He had earned it, in a way. What the fuck.

Even with Charlie's protection keeping Dom and Rico off his back, after about seven weeks at Vision Louis decided that he had had enough. He couldn't take that kind of scene any-

more. He was too old. He was about to turn twenty-two. So
when Benny offered to give Louis a better deal, Louis came
back to Nationwide. He picked up where he left off. His office, his cold-callers, his clients. Everything. Bygones were bygones.

Gaylord had just gone public and there was a lot of work
to be done. Nationwide's traders, who were at the home office in Texas, made a mess of the warrant trades. They all
wound up making a pretty good profit, despite the screwup.

Charlie made about $27,000 off the Gaylord deal, $3,000
less than Louis had expected, because of the screwup in Texas.
Still, it was a pretty good return on investment—almost 200
percent. Not bad, considering that he had gotten the $10,000
back, making the $27,000 more of a gift than a return on in-
vested capital.

But Charlie made it clear that he had expectations from
Louis, and that they were high. "Almost" a 200 percent return on his investment—even when his investment was re-
funded—was not good enough. If 200 percent was promised
it had to be *exactly* 200 percent that was delivered.

One of his expectations, one that Louis was not used to,
was that Louis had to do everything he said he was going to
do. That was always a problem for Louis. At Sea, the priests
made a big fuss about that. His father and mother were always pissed that Louis didn't keep his promises, and it was
starting to become an issue for Stefanie as well.

Charlie felt strongly about the subject of keeping promises
as well. As a matter of fact, Charlie took a very broad view of
what a promise was—basically any expression of intent, any
forecast of things to come. It became an obligation, an expectation. A deal.

And Louis was learning that there was a final arbiter in any
dispute or difference of opinion that might arise between
Louis and Charlie. His name was Charlie. He invariably ruled
in favor of Charlie. This Gaylord IPO provided Louis with his

very first experience with Charlie's concept of contractual obligations as they relate to broker-client relations.

Louis had indicated an expectation that Charlie was going to get back $30,000 if he put up $10,000. So that is what Charlie wanted—$30,000—even though he got back the $10,000. It was a deal. As Charlie put it, "I thought we were looking at thirty grand."

Louis made his point as best he could, describing how the traders in Texas screwed up for everybody, but Charlie did not feel his arguments were persuasive. Louis appealed to his sense of fair play and common sense, to no avail. Charlie had made a decision. It was a final ruling, it was in favor of Charlie, and there was no appeal.

So Louis did the only thing that he could do under the circumstances. He went to his apartment, pulled $3,000 out of the stacks, drove to the pizzeria, and gave the money to Charlie.

Louis didn't like it, but he figured he could afford it. Besides, Charlie was a necessity. Things were starting to get nasty. A confrontation with Rico and Black Dom, shortly after he left Vision, proved that.

Louis had gotten paid from Vision about $80,000 from the sale of AUXI stock to a particular client. This client later transferred the stock out of Vision and sold it. That was no good. Once a chop stock is sold to a client and the broker gets the commission, it is supposed to disappear. The chop house doesn't want to see it again.

If the client transfers the stock to another firm and sells it, the stock—in this case AUXI—winds up coming back to the chop house, in this case Vision. That's because Vision was the only firm that dealt in the stock on the Street. If someone out there was selling, Vision had to be the buyer. And that wasn't the idea. Vision wanted to sell that piece of shit, not buy it.

So Louis had a problem. Rico and Dom wanted the commission paid back to them.

"Rico was trying to get in touch with me, and I was avoiding him. So Black Dom came to find me and he wanted the money back. And he says, 'I don't care about Charlie. I don't care about anybody. If I see you on the street, you're dead.' So I knew he didn't care. This kid didn't care about nobody. They would beat people up and not care if they were around anybody. They didn't care. They'd worry about the consequences afterwards."

Charlie had to call his own Guy to intervene. Charlie had a Guy of his own. All of the Guys had Guys of their own. Sometimes Charlie said his Guy was Barry, a Genovese out on Coney Island. Sometimes Charlie said his Guy was Little Benji, a Colombo skipper. So Louis figured Charlie had two Guys. Charlie never clarified the matter.

This time, according to Charlie, he called Barry. Barry was a respected Coney Island gangster. Never convicted, rarely arrested. That was why he was so respected. "Nothing happens in Coney Island without him knowing it," says one ex-detective who used to work the organized crime beat. "He's a stone killer," says this ex-cop. Well, Coney Island is a tough neighborhood.

"Charlie had to call Barry up. Barry's a made Guy with the Genoveses, an old-timer. You don't hear his name that much. Barry called up Wild Bill to tell Dom to chill out, I'm going to pay the money. I had to pay the money. And I couldn't even pay it to Charlie. I had to pay it right to Dom. That's the way it worked out. Charlie told me, 'Louie, you got yourself in a fucking mess.' Dom was Wild Bill's nephew. Bill was a very strong gangster, very feared and strong." The problem was resolved by Louis getting the stock into someone else's account. Everything went very smoothly.

Louis needed a Charlie to deal with a Dom. That's the way it was on Wall Street. That's how bad it was getting. At least Charlie was rational, in his own way. With Charlie, only one thing mattered—money. But at least he was consistent about it. Nothing else was consistent in Louis's life.

At the same time that his life on the Street was getting more complicated and violent, his private life was going nuts.

Sure, the lies were still working. He was juggling Deenie and Stefanie, and they were both in the air, and he wasn't dropping either of them. But Stefanie had set a wedding date: April 27, 1996. The clock was ticking. He was getting married and he had to figure out what to do with Deenie—or Stefanie. It was getting so he wasn't in control over what was going on under his own roof. It wasn't any good.

"If Stefanie would come to my house surprisingly, I would be aggravated. A couple of times she came to the house without telling me and I would say, 'What the fuck are you doing here?'

"That's what happened on my twenty-second birthday, November 1995. Deenie was in my apartment, sleeping. I got up, went to work, as usual. I had plans with Stefanie that evening. I called Stefanie's house at about eleven-thirty and her mother says, 'She's on her way to New York.' I thought to myself, 'Oh, shit.' On her way to fucking New York. Got to be kidding me. I say to her mother, 'Oh, thanks. 'Bye!'

"I ran home to my apartment. I didn't even get into my car—my car was in the garage. Stefanie didn't have a key, but the doorman would let her in. I told the doorman this is my wife-to-be. I couldn't have Stefanie saying she couldn't get in there. She wanted a key and I postponed it—didn't make a copy of it. Never made a fucking copy. Took me like years to make a copy.

"So she was on her way to my apartment in the city. And I had to go home and tell Deenie to get out. So I say, 'Get out.' She says, 'What are you talking about?' I say, 'My father is on his way here. He's fucking nuts right now.' It was chaos. She says, 'What do you mean?' She's sleeping. I'm picking her up.

I say, 'Come on, you've got to get the fuck out. He's going fucking crazy. You know my father.' She did know my father. She had met him and she knew my father was a maniac.

"So I threw her out. I put her in a cab. I walked her downstairs. I said, 'Sorry, babe. I love you. 'Bye.' Literally not thirty seconds after I get into my apartment, Stefanie walks through the door. I'm like, 'Holy shit.' I was probably pale white. I was on the couch, panting. I was casual. I say, 'Oh, what are you doing here?' I didn't get mad at her at that time. It was my birthday, she was surprising me, she had balloons. It was so sweet. She was going to come clean the apartment, when I got home she was going to have the dinner ready and have the apartment really cleaned. She said, 'Can you please go back to work so I can surprise you like I was going to?' I say, 'Okay.'

"They were like my clients. I was lying to them like I was lying to my clients."

It didn't feel good. But he was with Charlie now, and Charlie was protecting him, and it made him feel better about everything. Nobody else would have been able to help him with Dom—not the cops, not the Pope, not Bill Clinton, not God. Only Charlie. As he got to know Charlie through the tail end of 1995, he began to realize that Charlie was a power greater than anything he had ever seen before.

He didn't want to get rid of Charlie, even if he had a chance. If he could have pushed a button and gotten rid of Charlie, he would not have pushed that button.

Even his doorman could see that his life was chaotic, and even his doorman could have told him that Charlie could bring some order to his life. He started saying that to himself, saying it from the moment he realized he couldn't get rid of Charlie, no matter what.

Charlie could end the chaos, maybe. He kept on saying that to himself, over and over again, when the pressure began to build.

*   *   *

By the time he got to Nationwide, gambling and losing was a part of his life that just wasn't going away. Like Charlie. Nobody knew how his gambling was becoming a problem. Certainly not his mother, and she didn't like him gambling even when he was winning. What else was new? Louis never could please his mother. And he sure wasn't pleasing her now, no matter much money he made on the Street. She always had an issue. Now it was the way he lived his life.

"The whole lifestyle—she was just against it. I was turning into my father. 'Be careful—you'll wind up just like your father.' I didn't want to hear it. And my father would come to my house and I'd have to hear my mother telling me, 'Don't let him in the house!' What am I supposed to do? He rings the doorbell, I let him in. She didn't like it because he would stay, go partying and not go home. I'm not going to say no. I'm not his father. He's my father.

"We'd go out to dinner with Stefanie and her parents on a Friday night, and then we'd leave for Atlantic City right from dinner. It was fucking ridiculous. Nuts. Everybody thought it was okay. Nobody ever said anything. Her father never said to me, 'What are you doing? Why are you going to Atlantic City at eleven o'clock?'

"One time when we were in Atlantic City I snuck downstairs at like six in the morning, while Stefanie was sleeping. She woke up. She came downstairs and she found me at the table. I was drinking. She goes, 'What the fuck are you doing?' I was down to like three grand, from the forty thousand. And the pit boss is like, 'Get him out of here. He's fucking nuts.' I had a marker for like thirty grand.

"I went back to the room and threw up."

CHAPTER TWENTY-NINE

Charlie liked Louis, and Louis had to admit that he was starting to like Charlie. No, he was not the kind of guy Louis
would want to hang out with under ordinary circumstances.
But he didn't mind being around the guy. And besides, having
a Guy was making more and more good solid business sense
at Nationwide. That's because Louis saw that he was going to
have to deal with gangsters whether he liked it or not.

Frank Coppa was coming up to Nationwide frequently
now to get his cut from the IPOs, but mainly to be sure the
brokers were pushing Chic-Chick. Frank felt very strongly
about the company. His sons were officers of Chic-Chick.
Frank Junior was going to be CEO. There was just no arguing with Frank on the subject. The company's selling points,
or lack thereof, were simply not a topic for debate at 100 Wall
Street when Frank was around.

"When he came up to Nationwide everybody was always
nervous. You always had to watch what you said with him.
Like he could kid you. But then, you couldn't kid back at all.
Because then he'd be, like, annoyed. So there was no kidding
with Frank. He could bust your balls. He'd say, 'Why don't
you wear a suit or something, you look like shit,' and then if
you even remotely try to say it back to him, 'You're fat and

fucking ugly,' you'd be dead. So you just laugh. 'Ha ha, great. . . .' So everybody was always nervous when he was there. 'Frank's in the office.' You got to watch what you say, blah blah blah.

"'Are you going to do it, Lou?'

"'I'm going to do it, Frank.'"

"He'd be like that when I had to cross him out of a stock. Because he started realizing that Benny didn't do the buying of the stock, in the crosses. You got to get somebody to buy the stock, and I'd do that. So he started asking me:

"'Do you have buying for my stock?'

"'Yeah, I do, Frank.'

"'Are you going to do it?'

"'Yeah. Yes, I'm going to do it.'

"'You're sure you're going to do it?'

"'Yes. It'll be done.'

"And I'd do it, like, instantaneously. I wouldn't even wait to do it. Because I knew he'd be back there the next day looking for his confirmation. He'd come up and look to see his tickets. Like when he wanted a stock sold, there was no getting around it. Marco, Benny, everybody just frantically tried to get rid of his stock. It was a major fucking issue.

"'Frank's on the phone. Wants to sell his stock.'

"'Arghhhhhhh.'

"He's a very scary guy, very intimidating-looking guy. More intimidating-looking than Charlie. He's just quiet. He don't say anything. He just sits there, two hundred and eighty pounds, in his mink coat."

Frank Junior would come with his father to Nationwide at times, to tell the brokers of the great things going on at Chic-Chick and to find out how the private placement was selling. Frank Junior was five years older than Louis, and grew up on Staten Island in a huge house near St. Joseph-by-the-Sea. A nice guy, basically. But sometimes Frank Senior would come up to the office with a guy who wasn't nice at all, a mean-looking guy named Gene Lombardo. Gene was big—bigger even than Frank—and he had a kind of craggy face that reminded Louis of the actor Tom Berenger. Alone or accompanied, Frank would meet with Benny or Louis or their Nationwide partner Marco Fiore. Marco was now sharing an apartment with Stuttering John, and he had new pals—the Coppas. Frank, Frank Junior, and Marco were forging a relationship.

"Marco started hanging out with Frank Junior. Like an idiot. I remember him walking around. 'Ooh, Frank Junior's my friend.' Yeah, right. They had him. Once I heard him yelling at Marco. Frank was up there with him, and Gene was there too. Gene was taken there to really intimidate Marco. Marco opened his mouth, agreed to do some Chic-Chick, and then he couldn't do it. And then boom. 'No, no, you got to do Chic-Chick.' That was the meeting. They were yelling at him about Chic-Chick. 'You got to do it.' You said you were going to do it and it's like gold. 'You said you were going to raise a couple of hundred thousand for Chic-Chick. Where is it?' We all had to do some, no matter what we thought of it."

Marco liked the idea of being friendly with Frank Junior. Frank Junior liked it too, and so did Frank Senior. That was the idea—friendship. Obligation. They had to sell Chic-Chick. It was a promise. A promise is a promise. People can't go around breaking promises. But it's not as if they were robbing anybody, or shaking them down.

That was the way it was with Frank, in the way he dealt with Benny and Marco, and that was the way it was with Charlie, in the way he was dealing with Louis during those first few months when he was at Nationwide. It was probably that way with Guys since the first Guy emerged from the primordial muck. Louis was seeing this, and learning this, and understanding what it meant and why it worked even though he wasn't able to do anything about it. He wasn't able to do anything about it because it worked. He had a Guy now, and when he thought that maybe it wasn't right, that maybe he shouldn't have to give Charlie money or sell that crappy chicken private placement, he wouldn't do anything because Frank and Charlie had planted second thoughts.

That was the whole trick to being a Guy.

It was something the movies didn't show, when they portrayed gangsters, because it is hard to show somebody having a second thought. Second thoughts aren't glamorous. There are no guns involved, usually, with planting a second thought. It happens all in the mind. It means that you do what a Guy wants because he has gotten in your head, and he has a relationship with you. You think twice about not doing what he wants, or getting pissed and saying no.

It was a little bit like the way Louis got his clients to send him money, over the phone, without even meeting him. With his clients, Louis's objective was to get in their heads, to establish a relationship with them, manipulate them. Pick up a pen, he'd say. Pick up a pen. "Don't you want to get in my A Book?" To get people to really want to be in your A Book or to pick up a pen, you have got to be in their heads. So now, for Louis and Benny and Marco, the Guys were in their heads, planting the second thoughts that kept them saying yes and saying no problem.

"They didn't come in and say, 'You're giving me stock and warrants. That's it. I'm in the stir now. It's over.' Everybody knew who Frank was. We knew he had the power. He could easily have come in, sat in the chair and said, 'You're going to give me three thousand in cash a month, and I'm getting IPO warrants and you're going to cross me out. I'm making fifty grand a month off this firm.' And we would have been like, 'Okay.' There would've been nothing to do. But he didn't do that.

"Frank comes in as your friend. 'Heyyy, guys. What's going on? Let's make some money.' When you start to hate him you second-guess yourself. 'He's all right. He's my friend.' They got you second-guessing. They put a second thought in your head. They almost make themselves like they're your girlfriend. The way Charlie used to beep me and I'm not calling him back, I used to say, 'What, am I making this guy come or something?' Almost like you're married to the guy. It's just fascinating how they get in there, into your head."

Louis wasn't reading the papers much, which was just as well, because if he did, he would know that what he was seeing at Nationwide surely had to be a figment of his imagination. There shouldn't have been any Guys at Nationwide. They shouldn't have been anywhere at all. According to all the papers, Guys were on the run. They were through. John Gotti had been put in prison for the rest of his life, and the Commission trial was also a big victory for the government. Louis didn't read books, so he didn't read how the FBI was winning the war against Guys. Yet here they were, real as life, at Hanover and Sovereign and Greenway and Brod and Vision and now Nationwide. And people were as scared of them as ever. They could do whatever they wanted and Louis and Benny and Marco had nothing to say about it.

As he got better acquainted with Charlie, he began to learn how Charlie got to be a Guy. Louis knew from Charlie's "war stories" that he had been a "shooter" a few years before, when a Colombo family skipper named Victor Orena and his pals were trying to take over the family, then headed by the imprisoned Carmine Persico and his son Alphonse. Charlie used to report to a skipper named Lenny Dello, who was aligned with Orena. Once he pulled open his shirt and showed Louis a scar on his chest—a bullet scar, Charlie said. A war wound. Charlie kept the jacket with the bullet hole, a bomber jacket, and would talk about how a veterinarian extracted the bullet from his chest.

Charlie was lucky. *Daily News* columnist Jerry Capeci did a body count when the smoke cleared and found that twelve people died in the Orena-Persico conflict, including a kid who worked in a Bensonhurst bagel shop and happened to be in the wrong place at the wrong time.

Louis always counted himself lucky. Not as a gambler, but in life. Lucky that good fortune had put him in touch with the right people. He was lucky meeting Roy, lucky meeting Stefanie, lucky meeting Benny, lucky meeting Charlie.

CHAPTER THIRTY

As the latest Nationwide deal approached, involving the IPO of a company called Thermo-Mizer, Charlie stopped hinting and began talking about the kind of money he wanted from the deal. Without getting specific about amounts or percentages, he made it clear he expected a bigger piece than he had gotten from Gaylord.

"I don't know who he knew up there, or how he knew, but he knew exactly how much money I was making, and what I was making and how I was making it. What, when, where, how. For some reason this guy knew everything. Somebody must have been telling him. Maybe his cousin John was telling him. Then he comes to me and says, 'I know you took down a lot more than you shared with me on that deal. Next time that won't happen.'"

How could Louis argue? He wouldn't have had a leg to stand on. Charlie was earning his money. Louis and Benny were now using Charlie to do things for them. "We sent him to a client who wouldn't pay. Guy's name was Michael. He was from Queens. Bought a hundred thousand dollars' worth of Gaylord warrants and reneged. Cost me thirty thousand. Charlie went there and got the money. I don't know what he did, but two days later I got a check from the fucking guy. That's all I know."

The collection proved that Charlie could be a useful Guy to have around. They might have benefited, all of them, even more if Charlie was "made"—initiated into full-time membership. But that wasn't happening. Charlie was on the shelf. And as he told it, it wasn't because of anything wrong that he might have done—maybe being too much of a hothead, even for a Guy, or because of any other kind of blot on his record. By his account, it was because he tried to do the right thing, and got blackballed as a result. It happened right after the Colombo wars, which ended with Persico victorious.

"I used to ask him when are you going to get your thing, your button. I used to tell him if you get your thing, then I can just rob everybody. I used to go like that—push the side of my nose. Meaning get straightened out. When is he going to get straightened out. At first he didn't tell me about it, but then as we got to be more friends he was more open about it.

"Supposedly Charlie and his friend Joe Botch, and this guy Lenny Dello, did a score. It was $300,000 or something like that. He didn't say what it was, but I think it was a robbery. Lenny Dello's father was a skipper in the Colombo family, also named Lenny, and his son Lenny Dello, Jr., was Charlie's partner.

"They do the score. Lenny and Charlie get the money and they're going to get Joe a piece. But Lenny wanted to give Joe only like fifty grand. So Charlie, maybe he gets a vision of some type of morals. He told Joe he was going to split it three ways, and he wanted to give Joe a hundred grand. So that's what Charlie did. He gave Joe the hundred. And he had a big beef with Lenny over that. Lenny's father told him no, you're going to give Joe fifty and you're going to bring the rest here, and we're going to split it up. And Charlie didn't listen to that. He gave Joe a hundred.

"So this is the story he told me. There was a big blowup

with Lenny's father, a fistfight with his son, and they shelfed him. They were going to make him. He was going to get made, Charlie. And they shelfed him. That was it. He was banned. Lenny was best friends with him since they were little, since they were eighteen, seventeen years old. Didn't talk to him no more. Nothing. To this day he hasn't talked to him."

That, at least, was the story as Charlie told it. As far as Louis knew, it was as much the gospel truth as the story of the hostage situation on Long Island.

There was no question that Charlie had a lot of status, a lot of respect in Brooklyn. Louis could see that himself, as he visited Charlie at his apartment, and hung out with him at Scores and in the bars and restaurants in Bay Ridge and Bensonhurst where Guys could be comfortable and unwind.

Louis saw how Charlie was treated with fear and, almost, reverence. And he also saw what Charlie was like when he let his guard down. "He could be a right guy if he wanted to be," said Louis. "A lot of times I'd go out with him and get drunk with him and stuff. He used to get wrecked. He used to drink martinis. He'd get an Absolut martini or a Belvedere martini, or a Grey Goose martini, all the good vodkas. 'In and out with the vermouth.' And then he'd say it again, more forceful like. 'In and out with the vermouth.' Like really dry. Hardly any vermouth. Almost straight vodka with an olive."

Charlie had his quirks, as do most people. Well, maybe a bit more. Something—the prison experience, maybe—had done something to Charlie's method of housekeeping. Charlie believed in order. So did Louis, but Charlie took it to another level.

"We would go over to his apartment sometimes, when we were changing to go out. His apartment was immaculately clean. It was a bullshit apartment, only a one-bedroom apartment, but it was nicely furnished. He had a nice sectional in his living room. Nice TV. His dining room table was big, like wood. Nice. He had expensive furniture. His clothing closet was like he was still in jail. That's probably why—he was in jail so long he was institutionalized. Probably all he could do in jail was clean stuff. He was a fanatic about it. Your shoes had to be off. 'Take your shoes off!' He acted like I was dirty. Dirty? I got a fucking seven-hundred-dollar suit on. What 'dirty'? I'd eat a fucking Oreo cookie and he'd literally follow me around with a Dustbuster. 'You're fucking eating an Oreo cookie—eat 'em outside.' He spent too much time in a shit-hole.

"His pants were so perfectly creased it was ridiculous. Not even a bend all the way down to the cuff. We'd get into the car, and he'd take this foam thing and brush his shoes.

"His refrigerator was a psycho refrigerator. Shit was facing front, lined up. His suits were color-coordinated in the closets, with fucking slacks on the bottom and suits on the top, everything perfect. He had eight-hundred-dollar shoes. Snakeskin shoes.

"When we were getting ready to go he was never fucking ready. He was doing his hair. He'd spray it, because he had a bald spot, so he'd spray it with this black shit. *Shhhhhhhhhh.* He'd go outside his house into the fucking hallway, and spray it and come back in. Never in the house. Are you kidding? I took a shower in his house one time, and it was fucking the end of the world. Because he was like, 'Don't drip any fucking water.' I couldn't drip water anywhere. He was annoyed when I had to take a shit in his bathroom. 'Can you go in the pizzeria and take a shit in there? You got to shit in my fucking toilet?' And then he'd use that shit against me. 'I let you shit in my toilet, shower in my fucking bathroom.'

"Charlie used to have a lot of locks on the door, and he had one of those police locks, with the bar that went in the floor. He used to roll up the money and keep it in this three-inch pipe, which was threaded, and screw it right into this standpipe in his bedroom. It looked like part of the pipe. It was brilliant."

It was clear that Charlie was one of the more prominent citizens of his little part of Brooklyn, the section of Kings Highway just west of the elevated train on McDonald Avenue. To the east was Roy Ageloff's old neighborhood—and George Donohue's old beat—Midwood—and to the south and west was Frank Coppa's turf, Bensonhurst. Charlie's neighborhood was still mostly Italian though outsiders, Russians and Asians, were moving in. But the area still had more than its share of pizzerias. The pizzeria at West First and Kings Highway was just down the street from Charlie's apartment. He used an area in the back, by the kitchen, for meetings and to take cash after Louis had made a trip to the stacks. Charlie acted as if he owned the place. He didn't, not that it mattered. The pizzeria was in the neighborhood. Charlie's neighborhood. And that still meant something, even though this was the late 1990s and Guys were supposed to be on the way out.

"I used to be there early, because Charlie used to have me meet him sometimes eight o'clock in the morning. He was up at like six-thirty in the morning. I think he used to run or something. Every morning at nine-thirty somebody would bring him coffee. This kid Louie. He was a retarded, a slow kid. He used to run around and do Charlie's errands. Come in the morning with coffee, move his car for him, for the alternate-side-of-the-street parking. 'Move my car!'

"He'd be dressed and ready, dressed in like a full uniform, by nine o'clock in the morning. Maybe he wanted to feel like he had a job. Sometimes he'd sleep late. He had everybody in the neighborhood doing favors for him. Everybody would say hello to him as he's walking down the block. He used to get his nails done on the corner. Sometimes I'd meet him while he was getting his nails done. He had this other place he'd go for espresso, and they had a table where nobody else would sit. Every time I went in there, nobody was sitting at his table. He used to park his car in other people's driveways. They would just call him on the phone when he had to move the car.

"He had four Louies in his life. There was me, the guy who owned the pizzeria, and his friend Louie owned the building that he lived in. I remember a couple of times people were making noise in the hallway, and he says, 'Pipe down, there!' They go, 'Sorry, Charlie.'"

By the time of the Thermo-Mizer deal, Charlie pulled as much weight at Nationwide as he did in his neighborhood. Everybody was getting big money from Thermo-Mizer, and Charlie made sure he got a nice piece of the deal himself. Louis gave him thirty thousand Thermo-Mizer warrants, which meant $60,000 in profits, once the company went public at the end of February 1996.

Shortly after the Thermo-Mizer deal came out, Charlie provided Louis with further proof that he was earning his keep and not just robbing Louis. Somebody out there was shorting Thermo-Mizer, and it had to be stopped. If the shorting continued, the price of the stock and warrants was going to drop. There was too much money at stake.

"Charlie and one of his goons went to go see somebody. It was a small firm—I forget the name. This was the story he told us later: He went in, and the trader had the door locked. So Charlie was knocking on the door. Trader opened the door. Charlie put his foot into it and the guy was scared shit. Wouldn't open the door, and Charlie kind of like cracked him through the door. The guy didn't short the stock no more. Charlie's very good. He got it done."

The other product going out to customers, at about the same time as Thermo-Mizer, was the stock of a company called Spectratek. It was a cash deal, which was great. But this particular cash deal came with its own Guy. Louis saw him come up to Nationwide.

"The first day he comes up there I don't think anything about it. It's some old man, looks like he needs a cane and a wheelchair to get around. He's got this huge black guy with him. So he's in there talking with Glenn [Benussi]. But then, after he left, Benny comes to me and says, 'What are we getting ourselves involved in here? It's fucking Sonny Franzese!'"

Louis shrugged. He had never heard of Sonny Franzese.

CHAPTER THIRTY-ONE

"John 'Sonny' Franzese was, among many other things, a chameleon," his son, Michael Franzese, wrote in a 1992 book called *Quiting the Mob*. "He could change his colors so fast, over such a wide range of personalities, that he could have fooled any dozen psychiatrists into thinking he was certifiable." The description was apt, not just for Sonny but for all the leading Guys of his generation. They were in control—in every sense of the word. They weren't frightened by jail and they didn't become "cooperators."

In the 1960s, Guys like Sonny served their time, even if it meant fifty years in jail—the sentence imposed on Sonny for a bank robbery conviction. He served it until he was paroled, and kept his mouth shut. Years later, other Guys cooperated in the face of far less jail time.

Sonny was such a legend that his son, a self-described Colombo skipper, shimmered in his reflected glory and wrote an autobiography in which he lingered at length on his dad's career. Until the bank robbery conviction—his son insisted it was a frame-up—Sonny had done it all. He had risen to skipper on the strength of sheer guts and moneymaking prowess. He had the makings of becoming the John Gotti of his generation, had he not been nabbed for that bank robbery. He kept a low profile and, unlike Gotti, he didn't sneer at legitimate business. He owned a piece of the classic porn movie *Deep Throat,* and was involved in the record business. He was such a notable Guy that in 1968 he was the subject of a massive article in the old *Life* magazine on that scary new phenomenon known as organized crime. In page after page, the article described how Sonny had beaten a murder rap, in a lengthy trial in which his legal team had wiped up the floor with prosecutors in Queens. Guys were at their peak. It must have been glorious—right up to the moment he was sent to prison for fifty years for that bank robbery.

By the end of his career, Sonny could have written a book himself—*When Bad Things Happen to Bad People.* Sonny's reward for his loyalty was betrayal. He was forced to step down as a skipper. But even though treated shabbily, he always remained a Guy, true to the code of being a Guy. After serving ten years of his fifty-year sentence, he was released on parole in 1979. But he was sent back for two years in 1982 for accidentally running into a Gambino skipper named Carmine Lombardozzi. It was an accident, his son insisted. Could have happened to anyone. (Don't you just hate it when you run into Carmine Lombardozzi?) Sonny got another eight years in prison in 1986, again for consorting with a known criminal. Ten years for bank robbery. Ten years for violating parole. It is a thing that Guys do, even when they are past seventy.*

In 1996 Sonny was out of jail and became involved, somehow, in pushing the Spectratek stock. Benny was totally bummed out.

"Benny says, 'Don't do no Spectratek.' But how could you not do it? It was thirty percent cash. So we did Spectratek. I didn't know who this Sonny was. I didn't know about the

---

*Sonny was sent back to jail in 1998, again for parole violation, and again for associating with Guys. One of them was Lenny Dello, Sr., Charlie's former skipper. Small world.

book. I just heard Sonny was a major old-timer, a very crazy old-timer. And I couldn't believe that he was up in our office. I says, 'What is he doing up here?' I never really talked to the guy. It was just, 'Hello.' I had my own Guy, so I wasn't looking at any other gangster. I was happy with my gangster. Besides, Sonny was just a dirty-looking old man, a broken-down old man. A broken-down valise. That's Charlie's words. That's what he'd call a washed-up wiseguy."

A Guy organizational chart at Nationwide would have been simple and linear. Charlie's role was limited at Nationwide to taking Louis's money. "Charlie didn't have much to do with the firm, because Frank was up there," said Louis. "The only person he could get money from was me. He couldn't corral anyone else, because Frank was involved, and he wasn't going to step on Frank's toes. He wouldn't dare do that."

Family "territories" didn't mean anything on Wall Street. Though nobody ever used terms like "open city" that used to describe Las Vegas and Miami, Wall Street firms pretty much fit that definition, which used to describe areas not in the territory of any particular family. The only thing that mattered on Wall Street was personal relationships—which Guy had a connection with which broker. Somehow, Sonny had formed a relationship with Glenn Benussi and Howie Zelin. How, or why, Louis didn't know.

Sonny was sharing in the Thermo-Mizer warrants, but his main interest at Nationwide was in pushing the Spectratek deal. It was his Chic-Chick. He felt very strongly about it. Louis discovered that the hard way when one of his customers tried to sell the stock. When Louis refused, the customer "back-doored" the stock—had it transferred out of Nationwide, and then sold it. It was the same thing that led to the beef with Black Dom. It was happening more often, and it was annoying. Clients were learning that they could get rid of stock, when a chop house broker wouldn't sell it, by just transferring it to another firm and selling it there. Any fair person could see that it wasn't Louis's fault.

"Marco and Glenn call me in. Sonny's not there, but his black guy is there. Marco's telling me to buy the stock back and get the stock sold to somebody else. I got to buy it back today? I wasn't doing it. Suddenly this black guy comes at me out of nowhere. He's tremendi. Six-foot-six. Huge. Grabs me by the throat. 'Buy it back today. You know what I'm saying?' I'm going, 'Arghhhhhhh.' He's choking the life out of me. Marco pulled him off me and I fell on the floor."

Before long, Louis had the last laugh. Sonny simply didn't have clout anymore. He might have been able to outsmart those Queens prosecutors in 1967, but in 1996 Wall Street he was just another Guy in a world where there were plenty of Guys. It didn't matter that his kid wrote his memoirs. Sonny was washed up. Louis saw that with his own two eyes when the Thermo-Mizer deal was completed.

"Marco started having a problem with Glenn and Howie over a lot of political crap—the Thermo-Mizer warrants, dividing up the money from the branch office. Shit like that. Marco did most of the politics shit for us. Me and Benny just worked and raised money. We could have given two fucks about anything except running the trading.

"The main problem was the warrants from Thermo-Mizer. Howie wanted to give Sonny some warrants off the top, and then we split the rest. He wanted to pay their Guy off the top, while we had to pay our Guys out of our share. So it was a big problem. Frank and Sonny had a meeting downstairs, in a restaurant across the street, and that was it. Frank won. We had discretion. We gave out the warrants to the brokers. Howie wanted to do all that. But he got cut out. Glenn and Howie got their hundred and twenty thousand warrants each, and that was it. Frank just took control of the whole situation."

Frank's price for serving as their advocate was $50,000, or

just under $17,000 each for Louis, Benny, and Marco. Louis figured it was well worth the price. It was great having control of the New York office, great winning against Sonny. But the exhilaration was short-lived. Victory was followed by stupidity. If Louis had any faith in mankind, he would have lost it.

CHAPTER THIRTY-TWO

This was getting to be ridiculous. Hanover, then Brod, and now Nationwide experiencing the same cancer—the malignant phenomenon known as the free market.

Some fuck-heads outside the firm were selling Nationwide's chop stocks. And the owners of Nationwide, down in Fort Worth, wanted to hold back commissions from the brokers to pay for the stock. It was as if they and Jay Taneja were reading the same *How to Run a Chop House* instruction manual. Louis, Benny, Marco, and their Guys had already made a bundle from trading the warrants. So they weren't hurting. These commissions were mainly owed to their cold-callers and brokers.

They had to act fast. The brokers were counting on that money. "Once three days go by and the brokers don't get paid, they get pissed off," said Louis. "They don't come to work, the firm goes out of business. Without the brokers, what kind of firm have you got?"

The guys who ran these chop houses never learned. Jay Taneja didn't learn, and now Kevin Williams, the president of Nationwide, was going to have to learn that you just don't treat people this way. Louis and his pals were going to have to take a trip down to Fort Worth, to visit Kevin. They were going to face him down. It was a selfless thing. Chivalrous, almost. Going to bat for their guys, their cold-callers. People did stuff like that out West. Louis had seen in the western movies that when guys had a dispute, they just went out to the person who owed them money and looked them straight in the eye with a steely gaze. Sometimes the guys in the movies brought along a gunslinger.

"These were the guys who went down to Texas: Me, Marco, Dave Lavender, Pete Restivo, Carl Banks, and Charlie. The money was owed to all of us, and we decided to take Charlie with us so we could intimidate the guy. We'd give Charlie, whatever, ten thousand dollars for that. So we flew down there. We got to Dallas, rented a car, drove out to Fort Worth, to the offices down some dirt road in the middle of nowhere next to a motel.

"The cops were waiting for us. Somebody from the firm, I think it was Howie Zelin, called there to probably get on Kevin's good side, and told him we were coming down. The cops stayed outside while Charlie went inside with Marco. They were talking with Kevin. Kevin started being, like, loud and boisterous, and screaming and hollering, and the cops came in and said to Marco, 'You guys are better off going back to New York.' We left. We would have got arrested.

"When I saw the cops I just walked the other way. I didn't want to have anything to do with it. Just hung out with Dave and we smoked cigarettes until they came out. We didn't want to get arrested in Texas. That would be the worst. Charlie said, 'I don't want to get incarcerated in Texas.'

"It was a wasted trip. We flew to Texas that day and went home that night. We drove back to the airport, got back on the plane, and went back. The whole way back in the plane, Charlie's telling me, 'You fucking guys wasted my fucking time. This fucking shit.' I wanted to kill myself. All squeezed in there with Charlie next to me. We were flying coach. He was practically on my lap. He wanted to sit next to me so he could torture me. I say, 'Don't tell me. I didn't want you to come. Marco did.'"

It was crazy taking Charlie to Texas. What was going to happen if they had gotten paid? Would Charlie have been satisfied with $10,000? Of course not.

But that was a moot point. After they got back from their wasted trip to Texas, Nationwide was finished. No wooden tickets this time. Louis had already gotten paid most of what he was owed, so he didn't care anymore. Louis knew he was in demand, that he could get a job anywhere on the Street— his corner of the Street. Chop House Wall Street. No more illusions. No more dreams about moving over to the Real Wall Street. Louis and Benny had given up the idea that they could ever be legitimate, ever sell real stock to real clients. They were with Charlie and Frank and Sonny now. It wasn't all that bad. Louis saw the way Charlie was treated. He saw the awe Frank inspired. What was wrong with that?

By the time Louis picked up his client book and left Nationwide's offices at 100 Wall Street, he had already gotten rid of his big-name customers. Craig Kallman, the sports guys, the Howard Stern people were all gone. Stuttering John, now sharing an apartment with their partner Marco Fiore, was still a good friend. But as investors these guys were more trouble than they were worth.

Poor Johnny Mitchell, the Jets player—his son died, and they had to cash him out of his stock right away. Guys like him believed Louis and Benny were real brokers. It was ridiculous. Sure, the signed Jets jerseys were cool. But the novelty had worn off by the time Johnny Mitchell called to get out of his stock. Louis did it, crossing him out of the stock as a favor, because of his kid. Benny wanted to keep the name clients but Louis was firm. That was it. No more name clients. No more clients they couldn't rip off, except, of course, for the Guys.

Benny required some convincing. He still had Celebrity-Nobody dreams. Not Louis. "I said, 'You don't understand,

Ben. Win, lose, or draw, it don't matter. We're the ones who should be making the money. They're not going to send us any more money. And if they do, we can't beat them anyway.' Lots of time I'm crossing them out of three, four hundred thousand dollars' worth of stock, while I could be crossing myself out. I used to not like it after a while. I felt like I was giving these people free money. Enough of this referral shit. Fuck that shit.

"I loved Stuttering John. But I said, 'We made him eighty grand one time, and that's it. What are we going to do, keep making him eighty grand every six months? Fuck him.' He wants to invest ten thousand, make a few thousand. I said we shouldn't even invest his money, we should just send him a couple of thousand each month and make him happy. For real. Because it was just too much of a hassle. John would call every day. 'Where's my money?' I used to see him because I used to hang out with him, and he'd ask about his 'investments.' After a while we just sent him back his money.

"I didn't want to deal with Craig Kallman anymore. He used to give us the dream. 'You're going to have Metallica and Madonna as clients.' Benny would get all excited, but after a while I was like, 'We're going to make him two hundred thousand and he's going to laugh at us and not give us any clients.' Yeah, it would be great if he could give us these clients. But that wasn't happening. I wanted to rob as much money as I possibly can as fast as I can, and that was it."

At the same time that he was getting the big names out of his client book, Louis had another cleanup operation under way. He had do something on the Deenie-Stefanie front. He had decided which one to dump. He just couldn't continue with things as they were. Not with Stefanie planning a wedding. The confusion, the effort involved, the complications were all too much. Guilt, the stink of it, was oppressive. His conscience was coming out of its stupor, like one of those near-stiffs he saw in the TV movies, lying in a coma, barely in existence, but still with a tiny bit of life and maybe even capable of hearing sounds. He was gambling more and more and more, which somehow made him feel better, so his conscience was behaving itself, lying there, half dead, or, better still, ignored.

Louis dropped Deenie. He didn't have much choice. One weekend a friend of his, Frankie Balls, ratted him out. "I said to him, 'What, were you trying to get her in the sack?' She didn't have proof or anything. If she had asked me, I would have said, 'What? Fuck you. Get the hell out of here.' But that was it. It just started to fall apart after that. And I made, like, a decision. I decided to go with Stefanie."

Stefanie was the kind of woman who could be the mother of his children—a wife. Stefanie wasn't flashy but she represented stability, honesty. All the qualities he didn't have. When they got engaged he gave her a beautiful ring, with a 3.1-carat almost-flawless diamond as big as a hunk of popcorn. And as far as Stefanie knew, he was a faithful, if not always available, fiancé who worked hard, had a lot of guy friends, and had to be away a lot.

Now he would try, really hard, to put the lies behind him too. He had to admit, they were good lies. He was an excellent liar. So great a liar that he was starting to hate it. Lying to clients was one thing. That was business. That was Wall Street. Everybody lied on Wall Street. But lying to Stefanie was different. More complicated.

"It was annoying after a while. 'What am I going to tell her now? What story am I going to fucking come up with?' I was supposed to be home at eight at night. It's fucking seven in the morning. I didn't call. What am I going to say? 'What happened?' 'Benny got into a car accident. He almost died. Lost a leg. They sewed it back on.' There was a cockamamie story every time. One time I said we went to go see Benny's father in the cemetery and I couldn't get him to leave. Benny was fucked up. He said, 'Louie, as my friend take me to the cemetery.' I couldn't get him to leave. There was no phone. The battery on my phone died. Benny was hysterical crying. He wanted to sleep on the grave. I couldn't leave the guy there!

"Then my friend Ronnie's father got sick in jail and I had to go visit him. 'You going to come home and change first?' 'No.' I couldn't come home and change because I was with seventy-five girls in Benny's apartment. I wasn't even seeing Ronnie.

"I ran out of gas. You know how many times I ran out of gas? All I did was run out of gas. One time I told her some guy cut me off, and I followed him all the way to Connecticut. 'I wanted to kill the guy. I was trying to follow him and catch up with him. I couldn't catch up with him. I wind up going over the Triborough Bridge. I'm in fucking Connecticut. Got lost. Had to come back. It was a mess.' Followed the guy all the way to Connecticut. I started believing this shit myself. I'd wake up in the morning and I'd say, 'I can't believe I followed that asshole to Connecticut.'"

Louis knew he had to stop complicating his life, that he had to put his relationship with Stefanie on a new footing. But the secrets could not end, not entirely. Louis let Stefanie know about Charlie, but just that he was a friend who had joined him in some business venture. He couldn't let her know exactly the kind of relationship that he had with Charlie. He would have had difficulty putting it into words anyway. He wasn't sure what it was. Besides, his relationship with Charlie was changing—and not for the better. They were becoming more intimate, in the sense that Louis began to realize that he was being fucked.

The honeymoon was over by the time Nationwide was out of his life, and now Louis and Charlie were like any normal married couple. They knew each other very well. And one of the things that Louis learned by now was that Charlie wasn't a fair guy, not a square shooter, not even with Cousin John.

John told Louis that he got only $2,500 of the $15,000

Charlie collected from Louis that first time they met. Charlie kept the rest, and told John he only got $4,000 from Louis. Charlie told his cousin he had kept $1,500, when he really kept $12,500. That was no way to treat family. Louis thought Guys were into family. That's how it was in the movies, at least. Served John right, of course, but it was still a crappy thing to do to a relation.

Learning about Charlie's dishonesty was the first sign Louis had—or, more precisely, the first sign Louis noticed—that maybe Charlie was going to be a problem. The second sign took place in the waning days of Nationwide. They were still socializing, still friendly. But there was always an edge to the way Charlie dealt with Louis, a quick temper that he was doing less and less to keep under control.

Charlie was pissed about Fort Worth. He was not happy Nationwide was holding back on the commission money. It wasn't a lot, but Charlie was entitled to his share of it. The exact amount that Charlie was expecting wasn't fuzzy anymore. At Nationwide Charlie was getting at least $15,000 a month, and that was what he wanted. If Louis made more, Charlie wanted more. But if Louis made less, Charlie wasn't going to take less.

When Charlie made it known that he was expecting that much from Louis, he didn't react, didn't say anything. But there was this pain, deep in the pit of his stomach. This was what Charlie was going to get as his due, and there was to be no negotiation or discussion on the subject. He had done work for Louis, collected the money from the guy in Queens and visited those short-sellers. He had intervened with Black Dom—actually called his Guy, Barry, to intervene with Wild Bill and keep Dom from battering Louis to a pulp at Vision, when that scrub transferred AUXI stock away from the firm.

Why did he do it? Because he liked Louis's face? Because they were "friends"? Because he was a nice guy? Barry wouldn't have known Louis if he had passed him on the

Boardwalk or spilled clam sauce on him in Gargiulo's, where Coney Island wiseguys could sit among themselves and keep away from the dark-skinned people who crowded into that neighborhood. When Charlie went to see Little Benji Castellazzo at the Torrese Social Club, he wouldn't even let Louis come inside.

Barry and Charlie pulled Louis's bacon out of the deep fryer because Louis was partners with Charlie, because Louis paid Charlie, and because Charlie paid Barry. It worked that way up the ladder too. If Barry had a beef with Wild Bill or some other Colombo, he would call Chin Gigante, the Genovese boss, and Chin Gigante would call Alphonse Persico, the Colombo boss. That's because Barry paid Chin and Wild Bill paid Persico. The guys who reported to Barry, guys like Charlie, paid Barry, and the guys who reported to Wild Bill, guys like Black Dom, paid Wild Bill. Then Black Dom got people like Chris Wolf to pay money to him and Charlie got people like Louis to pay money to him. Chris and Louis were at the bottom of the food chain. Earners. The fools out in the hinterland were the grubs and sea turds.

That was how it worked. You did what you had to do to pay Guys, and the Guys were supposed to help you in a Guy kind of way. Those Guys paid other Guys. They weren't welfare workers. They weren't policemen. They weren't Godfathers. They weren't "Fathers"—that was the word the old-time boss Joe Bonanno used, in his modestly named autobiography *Man of Honor.* Guys didn't do "favors." Those were pipe dreams, for the scrubs and the saps. On the Real Wall Street and in Corporate America, it would be called spin—PR. Guys had the greatest PR.

Louis realized he was facing a situation in which Charlie was not going to sit back passively and wait for his share. He was going to get his money, and he was not going to tolerate any delay. After the dumb trip to Fort Worth, Charlie made clear to Louis the kind of thing that was going to happen if there was a delay.

"After Fort Worth I met him at the pizzeria. I was telling him about the money from Nationwide, how I couldn't get it. I was rambling and rambling. He was quiet, then he goes, 'I don't want to fucking hear it,' and he smacked me. Smack. And that was it.

"Before he did that, I'm thinking to myself, 'Wow. I'm the Man. I got the money. I got the Guy. I got the world by the balls.' Nobody's going to treat me disrespectful, because nobody did. And then he just killed that whole thing. I left there thinking like, 'What's this happening?' Now I felt like crawling out under the door."

What right did Charlie have, smacking him like that? Louis felt like killing him. Louis had a gun at home—he needed it, he carried around so much money—and he felt like taking it to Brooklyn and killing Charlie with it. But then, once the rage subsided, Louis had a second thought. Charlie had been nice to him when they last went out, a few nights before. Charlie had been to his home a few times. They were friends. Sure, he came up to the house to borrow Louis's Mercedes so he could use it for the weekend, and drop off his cruddy old Caddy in its place. Sure, he had a bad temper, but that's what Guys like him were like. They could still make good money together. Besides, it wasn't a hard smack. It didn't leave a welt and was more embarrassing than anything else, or would have been if anybody was around. It happened out by the kitchen. Nobody saw it.

So Louis decided to forget about the smack. There were more important things going on in his life, after all. He was moving to another firm. Getting married.

CHAPTER THIRTY-THREE

Louis was back in Staten Island now. He was living in a townhouse down by Tottenville, in a subdivision. It was a suitable place for a young couple to enjoy a blissful marriage.

Two nights before his wedding, Louis was at his new house with Stefanie, two others friends, and Sally Leads. Stefanie and the friends left. Louis went outside with Sal to move the cars. Sal put the Mercedes into the driveway and went back inside. Louis parked his truck.

"Freeze!"

Six guys with guns. They were wearing masks.

"Get in the fucking house!"

Louis thought it was a joke at first. "What are you talking about? Get out of here." One of the guys in the masks walked over to him and punched him in the face.

Louis fell on the ground and grabbed on to a tree in the front of the house. Five guys were stomping him, beating the shit out of him. They pulled him free of the tree. Louis yelled for help. But it was three o'clock in the morning, and this was a neighborhood where people minded their own business.

After dragging Louis into the house, two of them pinned him against the wall, while a third gave Louis a few hard socks in the left eye.

"Then they drag me upstairs, and meanwhile I'm spitting at them, telling them, 'You're dead tomorrow!' They take me upstairs, and Sally Leads is sleeping and so's my friend Carl. So they smack Sally Leads in the face, because he don't hear what's going on outside. Dumb bastard. I'm getting beat up all over the place, and he's sleeping! Five minutes after he parks the car, he's sleeping.

"They tie him up. Put his head in the toilet bowl. They got one guy with him, keeping his head in the toilet bowl. They got one guy downstairs and the other four guys take me upstairs to the third floor. Carl's still asleep. They kick him to wake him up."

Everything was happening fast. One of the robbers had a police radio, and Louis could hear it crackling in the background.

"On the way upstairs, one of them says, 'Where's your watch?' I'm saying to myself, 'How did they know about my watch?' So I say, 'What are you talking about? I don't have no fucking watch.' He goes, 'Where's your fucking watch?' And they're smacking me and shit. So I tell them it's on the kitchen table.

"They drag me upstairs and say, 'Let's go to the safe.' And I'm thinking, 'How do these fucking guys know about the safe?' It's ridiculous. So they take me upstairs. They throw me on the floor in front of my safe. They put me on my knees. There's two guys pointing guns at my head. 'Open up the fucking safe!' I had money in the safe. I didn't want to open up the safe. Fuck these kids. Meanwhile, they're kicking Carl in the head. Carl goes, 'Louie, open up the safe!' I go, 'I'm not opening up the fucking safe.' Then the big kid comes up to me and sticks the gun right in my face, cocks it. He's going to shoot me by accident, this fuck. I opened it."

The safe held $12,000 in cash and a gun, a 9mm Glock. His watch was a solid gold Omega. Custom-made. Had an extra dial. It was awesome.

"So they take the cash. And this fucking guy, this big guy stands me up and goes, 'Where's the rest of the fucking money?' I say, 'There is no money.' I say, 'You came on a bad day. Come back next week, I'll have more money.' That's exactly what I said.

"The guy says, 'Want to be a fucking cocksucker?' He grabs a screwdriver. Like an asshole I got a screwdriver laying around. He grabs the screwdriver, puts it point-down on the top of my head. Says, 'I'm gonna drive this fucking thing right through your head!' I say, 'Go ahead. I ain't got no more money. It's over. Take what you got and go. You're dead.'

"I start that shit again, and one of the kids's on the CB, listening to the police band. He goes, 'Five-oh.' They scatter now. They leave, except this one kid stays behind, and he goes, 'Give me that fucking ring!' I got this ring from my grandfather. Has a diamond in it. I say, 'I'm not giving you the fucking ring!' He tries to take the ring off my finger. I say, 'You got to cut the finger off. It's my grandfather's ring. It's not worth nothing. It's sentimental.' Then he smacked me again and left.

"Carl gets up now. He runs to the back of the house, kicks the screen out of the window. He wanted to see if maybe he could jump down from the second floor and catch them. We were going to chase them now. I go down the stairs, get two knives out of the kitchen, and go running out the front door. I got two knives in my hands and I'm bleeding.

"'Freeze!'

"It's the cops. I go, 'No, no, no, get the fucking car! They just left.' A cop says, 'Put the fucking knives down!' So I put the knives down and tell them I got robbed. Blah blah blah. They take me upstairs. Detectives come. I call my father-in-law. He comes down. Talks to the detectives. He got me out of the gun problem. It's an unregistered gun. It was left in my backyard. My fingerprints were all over it. So my father-in-law explains I have it in the house because I'm getting death threats and stuff like that. I got out of it. They didn't even write the gun down. They left the gun there.

"I looked for these kids. I found out where my watch got sold. They only got seven thousand for the watch. My friend Ronnie dealt with a jeweler who bought it, and it was my watch. He could have said who did it, but he wouldn't. I didn't tell the cops about that. I called the cops a month later and they had nothing. I figure they had no clues. The kids were wearing gloves, big work gloves."

Charlie was upset. He told Louis, "Let's find out who did it. I'll keep my ears open."

Charlie knew about the safe.

Louis remembered what Charlie had said about the "hostage situation" on Long Island, way back in the 1980s. "I knew he did a home robbery," said Louis. "It crossed my mind. Everybody crossed my mind. But I never suspected Charlie might have been behind it."

Louis never found out who robbed his house. In any event, he soon had more important things to worry about.

CHAPTER THIRTY-FOUR

Fade in on a wedding album swirling in space, as a male vocalist sings "If You Say My Eyes Are Beautiful."

The album opens.

Louis and Stefanie are walking, slow-mo, into the picture, as the song continues.

"You could say that I am a dreamer . . ."

They kiss.

"who had a dream come true . . ."

Bright-green titles are superimposed.

A PELICAN VIDEO PRODUCTION

STEFANIE AND LOUIS' WEDDING

SATURDAY, APRIL 27, 1996

A montage of freeze frames:

The wedding party arrives at the church in white stretch limousines.

The procession down the aisle. Stefanie and Louis: Stefanie

smiling, radiant, glorious. Louis smiling weakly, hesitantly. His left eye is puffy, the flesh surrounding it a bluish black.

The soundtrack switches to a female vocalist singing "The Chapel of Love."

More frames: Louis is "goin' to the chapel." Goin' to do you-know-what.

Nervous, a little distracted, as he recites the vows.

Stefanie, calm and serene.

George Donohue is best man.

Those bells are going to ring, says the song.

Stills of the catering hall.

That sun is going to shine, the song goes on.

Louis and Stefanie are dancing.

Charlie and Louis at the reception.

Charlie is deeply, evenly tanned, his gray Armani double-breasted suit razor-creased. His hand is on Louis's shoulder. Both are smiling, Charlie tightly, Louis broadly, as if they could hear the song:

> *. . . I'll be his*
> *and he'll be mine . . .*

They'll love until the end of time, maybe. Maybe not love but something better. And one thing was for sure. He didn't need the song to tell him this.

Louis would *never be lonely anymore.*

Another frame. Louis is relaxed, hands clasped in front of him in a gesture of triumph, maybe. Happiness. Success. Behind him, Charlie is beaming.

The freeze frames end and the video begins. Real sounds now. The guests arriving on a breezy, chilly day. The bridesmaids are Stefanie's friends; the ushers are Louis's—the beefy, boyish Benny, followed by a gawky Sally Leads.

Stefanie's parents are dignified and Middle American.

Louis's parents are exuberant, his mother cherubic, his father black-haired and mustached, youthful.

Louis is nervously chewing gum as he arrives at the catering hall, but he is more relaxed as the evening goes on, toward the end of the ninety-five-minute tape. He is in his element now, partying, horsing around with Charlie and his friends from Staten Island.

"I got a little song for Louie personally," says Stuttering John, bearded and disheveled, strumming an electric guitar. "This one's coming from Marco Fiore, personally wanted me to say this."

He sings to the tune of "Louie Louie."

> *"Louie got to tell you you're a real cool dude.*
> *I don't want this to sound so rude.*
> *But the chef's really pissed and I'll tell you why.*
> *It took a thousand steaks to cover up your eye!*
> *Louie Louie . . ."*

He doesn't stutter, not even once.

Now a great day, a great wedding, a great party is coming to an end. It had been a very American wedding, with no tarantellas, no Irish jigs. Louis and Stefanie are dancing, surrounded by their friends and family, who have formed a circle around them.

The camera shows the newlyweds and then moves down the line of people facing them—the misty-eyed parents and beaming relatives and friends, young and old, swaying to the dance music.

Benny mugging for the camera.

Marco prancing.

Frank Coppa, Jr., reserved and nondescript, self-conscious when the camera finds him.

Charlie, Bengal-tan, smiling, with his arms around his blond and wholesome-looking girlfriend.

The band is playing "That's What Friends Are For."

The video ends with Stefanie, Louis, and the wedding party climbing into their white stretch limousine and driving off.

FADE OUT.

It was cool how Stuttering John sang at his wedding and goofed on his black eye. Everybody was talking about it for months afterward. Stuttering John, that is. Definitely the highlight of the wedding. John sat at the wiseguy table, with his friend Marco and Charlie and girlfriend and Frank Junior. Frank Senior couldn't come, which was strange. "A few weeks before the wedding, Frank says, 'I'm looking forward to being invited to your wedding.' I got on the phone with Stefanie right away. 'We got to invite this guy,'" said Louis.

Frank Senior and Frank Junior gave $1,000 between the two of them, which was generous. At least compared to Charlie. He gave $300, which Louis figured was less than Charlie paid for his Cole Haan lighter.

No honeymoon. Not that he was in the mood for a honeymoon, after the robbery. But he really hated the idea of going away when he was moving to another firm. He just couldn't count on Benny. He was about to start a new job, at the World Trade Center offices of State Capital Markets. Stefanie was pissed about that. Tough.

State was Frank's idea. He knew the people there, and introduced Louis and Benny to the firm. They were going there to sell Chic-Chick. In theory. But Chic-Chick was as tough a sell at State as it was at Brod and Nationwide. Everything was tougher to sell. By now, regulation was getting a lot harder. The regulators were starting to crack down on "units," which were combinations of stocks and warrants, popular in chop house IPOs. Listing requirements on the Nasdaq were becoming more stringent. Things were starting to get sucky.

Louis and Benny made lunch money, about $15,000 each, selling the Chic-Chick private placement at State. Lousy. It was obvious after a few weeks that they were wasting their time there, and by now even Frank realized the thing just wasn't going to get sold, and he didn't raise a fuss when they moved to a firm called L. T. Lawrence. Louis and Benny each got a $40,000 sign-on bonus, which Louis promptly used for a down payment on a Ferrari. Model 348. Canary-yellow.

That was the good news. But then there was the bad news. There was a lot of bad news. It involved one of the two owners of Lawrence, Larry Principato.

"I didn't really know Larry or what his story was, and at first I thought he was running a half-legit kind of firm," said Louis. "When we went up to this place it was a great building, really nice office. Very professional. Everybody well dressed. Wearing suits. He told me that he had this stock, Echo Tire. I didn't get paid cash off Echo Tire. I think the common was three-something and the warrants were a dollar-something. The first month I think we did a hundred and twelve thousand in gross just off the warrants.

"I wasn't there too long before I had an incident with Larry. What I did was I put some of these Echo Tire warrants in my own personal account. I bought them off the bid. The spread was fucking sixty cents. It was ridiculous. So I bought some right above the bid and I crossed myself out at the offer, like I used to do with Stuttering John, and I made like forty, fifty thousand in my own account, a nominee account. And Larry just flipped out. He wanted me to give the money back. He gives me, like, a warning. 'We don't have that kind of shit here. Only for me.' So they canceled the trade and took the money back. It was the wrong place for us to work because Larry wanted to do the same kind of thing we wanted to do."

With Larry having that kind of attitude, there were obviously going to be limits on the kind of money Louis was going to be able to make at L. T. Lawrence. And that was bad, because his gambling wasn't getting any better. Gambling wasn't relieving stress and guilt anymore. It was causing stress. But Louis couldn't stop, and he was starting to have some trouble paying off his gambling debts. He always managed—somehow. But his spending was still out of control.

Not long after coming to Lawrence, Louis and his friend Ronnie—an old pal who just happened to sell drugs for a living—went to a local marina and put down a payment on a forty-eight-foot yacht. They christened it *CREAM*. The people at the pier might have thought Louis and Ronnie were dairymen, but they were actually borrowing the name from the Wu-Tang Clan rap group, which had a hit at the time called "Cash Rules Everything Around Me." Louis came up with half of the $62,000 down payment. Barely.

"I didn't have a ton of money because I was gambling at this point. I'd make forty grand and just gamble forty grand. I would take five grand to pay my bills and just gamble the rest. Nobody ever saw the money. But we got the money together for the boat, me and Ronnie. The guy at Staten Island Boat Sales probably still remembers me because I tried to pay in cash. It was a brand-new boat. Huge. Two full bedrooms, full kitchen, dining area. Had a big-screen TV."

He was doing well, making almost as much money as he did at Brod. But he was living month to month, gambling about as much as he made. Losing, winning, losing, earning.

"So now I lose a hundred and eighty thousand with a bookie in Staten Island. This wasn't a bookie to beat. Because Thursday afternoon, if I won ninety thousand, Thursday afternoon there was an envelope or bag with my name on it with ninety thousand dollars. If you lost and didn't pay, they would come get you.

"I knew this kid in Staten Island. Owned a gym. His name was Tom Cunningham. A big-money kid. He trusted me a lot. I'd been making good money for him through the bid-ask thing, figuring someday I could really set him for a score. So his time had come. He wanted to make some money with me in the market, so I made him give me two hundred thousand in cash, and I tell him, we're investing it in Chic-Chick. So he gives me the two hundred thousand and I pay the bookie. A couple of months go by. Tom's wondering, what's going on with Chic-Chick? Where's his two hundred thousand?

"It somehow gets back to Frank—maybe he called the company; I don't know—that I took two hundred thousand for Chic-Chick and didn't give him any. And it was bad. It was bad. Charlie calls me up and says, 'Louie, what the fuck did you do?' I say, 'What? What did I do?' He says, 'You took two hundred thousand dollars for Frank Coppa's name?' I say, 'What?'

"Now I'm shitting my pants, because just three days before this Frank shows up at L. T. Lawrence to talk to Benny. Without me, and that usually wouldn't happen. He would talk to us together. I kind of thought something was up but I wasn't sure. And it was. So I had to go to L&B Spumoni Gardens for a sitdown. L&B is in Brooklyn, on Eighty-sixth Street, near Marlboro Houses. Frank's always there. All benches outside, then a pizzeria where you get the spumoni ices, famous ices. That was his place.

"Now I got to go to this sitdown. And Tom's going to be there, telling him about the money. I go in, and I'm scared. I'm thinking I am definitely going to get whacked over there. I fucking robbed two hundred thousand from Frank Coppa. It's crazy. Charlie's there already. Frank's there. Tom's there. And this is the first time I heard Frank yell ever in his life. I wanted to say hello to him and he says, 'Louie, shut the fuck up and sit down. You're in a lot of trouble.'

"I sit down. Frank says, 'Tell me what happened. Tell me your story. And don't lie a word to me.' Now, I got no prep before this, I don't know what Charlie wants me to say, I don't know nothing. I don't know what to do.

"He might have told them something before I got there. They wanted me to speak now. They wanted nobody else to speak. Now, I'm very confident of myself at the time. I'm paying Charlie big money. I'm driving around in a Ferrari. I'm very confident of myself. I'm scared but I'm confident. So I kind of in a roundabout way deny it. I say, 'Frank, I don't know what he's talking about. This kid's a fucking liar.'

"And then he tells me, 'Don't call me Frank.' Everybody called him Mr. Coppa, you know what I mean? So I go, 'Mr. Coppa, I don't know what this fucking kid's talking about.' Charlie says, 'You don't know what this kid's talking about?' Crack! I get smacked for that. I say, 'Charlie, I really don't. What is he talking about? I didn't say Chic-Chick.' He goes, 'Did you take two hundred thousand dollars from the kid?'

"I don't want to admit I took two hundred thousand from the kid. I say, 'No, I didn't take two hundred thousand from the kid.'

"Charlie says, 'You're trying to tell me that this kid's here, in Brooklyn, at L&B, for no fucking reason but to lie and to say you took two hundred thousand dollars from him and didn't fucking give it back to him? You trying to tell me this kid's here for no reason?'

"I say, 'Charlie, I didn't take the money from this kid. Maybe this kid has other issues and other problems.'

"Charlie says, 'Frank, give us a minute.' We go outside, and I tell Charlie, 'Listen, Charlie, I'll give you fifty thousand in cash. I can't admit that I took this kid's money.'

"Charlie says, 'Louie, if I get you out of this fucking jam with this guy—I shouldn't even be here," he tells me. 'I'm not a fucking skipper. This guy's a fucking underboss. How the fuck do you get me here with this mess?' He says, 'You got me all over Staten Island and Brooklyn. My name is going to be all over the place. I'm a nice low-key guy, nobody knows me. Now you've got me sitting down with an underboss.' That's what I heard too. I never asked Frank, 'Are you an underboss?' but from my understanding he was the guy in charge.*

"We got back inside. Now they make us leave. Charlie says,

---

*The feds disagree. In court papers during his various scrapes with the law, Frank has been identified as a Bonanno family skipper—a "capo"—and not as an underboss.

'Tom, Louie, go outside. I'll talk to Frank.' So they talk a good hour. Tom and me are standing by the picnic tables outside. Tom says to me, 'How can you do this? How can you sit there and lie?' I say, 'I don't know what you're talking about, Tom. I don't know you. You got me here with this mess.' He could have just came to me. He didn't have to go through these channels. Because now it could be that I could be in a lot of trouble and pay back the two hundred thousand plus another hundred thousand, maybe. It could have been some type of major situation.

"We go back inside, and now Frank starts asking Tom to tell him the truth. Now I'm thinking in my head, 'What? Are you telling me that Charlie just told this guy that I was telling the truth, and that this kid's a fucking liar, and it worked?' I don't know what they talked about, but it worked! They beat him up. They beat up Tom, they smacked him around, right in front of me. Charlie goes, 'You fuck. You want to take this kid here, this reputable kid. You want to take this fucking reputable kid. This kid has a reputation.'"

Louis paid Charlie $50,000, and that was the last he ever heard of the subject. Years later he ran into Tom on Staten Island. They exchanged greetings. They chatted a little. Tom made no mention of the meeting at L&B.

CHAPTER THIRTY-FIVE

After the sitdown at L&B, Louis couldn't very well object when Charlie wanted his fifteen thousand a month—and more. Since that was about how much Louis spent on himself, and now Stefanie, every month, Charlie was now truly a life partner. Another wife. No—a husband. And Charlie was getting into his head, the way a life partner does. He was a spouse, a friend, a partner, and, now, a criminal-talent agent.

Over the previous few years Louis had perfected his skills as a thief, the lifelong calling that had found a warm and welcome home for him on Wall Street. Now Charlie was going to show Louis a new way to make money.

After L&B, after Charlie saved his life for $50,000, he couldn't object when Charlie wanted him to cash some stolen checks. And since he needed money to pay off his mounting gambling debts, he wouldn't have objected even if he could.

Charlie introduced Louis to a guy named Michael Basile, who had access to the checks. These were great checks—cashier's checks, and Mike had a way of getting people's names on the checks. All he needed was a check-cashing place that would convert them into bills, no questions asked. Louis had just the place in mind, a huge outfit in Bayonne, New Jersey, that was used by a lot of interstate truckers. Louis knew the guy who ran it.

They went to Bayonne. The check was made out to "Michael Decker"—an imaginary person to be portrayed by Mike Layden, for a cut—and the amount was $995,000. Louis was going to get $350,000. The rest went to the check-cashing guy, Michael Basile, and Mike Layden. It was September 17, 1996. They drove to Bayonne, happy as kittens chasing a newborn mouse.

"'Hands up! Get the fuck out of the car!" Oh, jeez. Local cops. I was sick to my stomach. I went to go out of the car, they threw me on the hood. 'You fucking scumbag! Hands on your head!' I say, 'Calm down! I'm not going anywhere.' They take my bag out and they find a gun. Cop says to me, 'What are you going to do with this, dickhead?' He's showing everybody, 'Hey, look at this!'"

This was serious. The gun charge was a felony. (It didn't help that the serial numbers were filed off, making it a "defaced firearm.") The check charges were felonies. A felony conviction ends, more or less automatically, any possibility of a legitimate, or even semi-legitimate, career on Wall Street. It wouldn't do his marriage any good either. And what about George—the ex-cop? Louis was shitting bricks, thinking about how George Donohue would react.

STEFANIE: "The night of the arrest people were calling me, trying to find out where he was. There were all these people looking for him, who he owed money to. And I guess this check was supposed to get his debts paid. This big score. So a lot of people were calling and calling. I called his mother—I don't think I called his mother until the next day. I just told her that I had to do some stuff, and I went with his mother and father to the court, and they set the fifty-thousand-dollar bail.

"I would do it, I'd post the bail, but I didn't have anything worth fifty thousand dollars. I had no properties, nothing that I could hock to get that kind of money. So my father just said to me, 'You can't give it, I'll give it. Your money is my money.' I said, 'I don't want you to do it,' and he says, 'No, if you're willing to do it, I'll do it for you.' I remember Fran coming to the house and crying, saying thank you, whatever. So me and my father went, got the check, went to the jail. I remember him coming but he didn't wait for Louis to be bailed out.

"That was the first time that I was made aware of how much in debt he was and how many problems he was having. In one sense it made my life even more horrible, but in the relationship this was probably the first time he was honest about anything that was going on. Instead of trying to hide everything, he was saying, 'Look, I have a serious problem. I owe a lot of money on the street. If I don't have that money, they're going to start coming to look for me.' He owed money to this one and that one. He didn't know what to do.

"Before, I knew he was gambling but I didn't know he had so many problems, that he owed so much money. It was a real awakening in a sense of who he was and what he was doing."

CHAPTER THIRTY-SIX

Louis had stock certificates in his briefcase. They were part of an upcoming cash deal. The FBI was expressing some interest in the check case, which they had the option to prosecute if they so desired. Louis expected the FBI might be interested in talking to him about the certificates. It would have opened up a huge can of worms.

Two agents from the Newark FBI office dropped by L. T. Lawrence a few days after the arrest. Louis wasn't there at the time, so they chatted with Larry Principato. They asked Larry a lot of questions—but didn't show the slightest interest in the stock certificates. When Louis found out, he almost dropped dead from relief and surprise. The surprise lingered, but the relief ended when he was fired. "After he saw the FBI guys, I came in and Larry says it's a difficult situation, he doesn't think I can work there no more. He says he can't have that kind of heat. I ask, 'What are you going to do, fire me?' He doesn't know."

Later the FBI came up again and asked Louis about the checks. He referred them to his lawyer. He was asked about the stock certificates. The bombshell.

He said they belonged to one of his clients. They nodded. They believed him. Why not? The certificates weren't listed as stolen. Perfectly credible. No law against owning stock certificates.

The interview only took a few minutes. After they left, Larry called him in and fired him. Too much heat. Louis would have to get out. Right now.

The firing was okay. Louis and Benny could find someplace else. But what wasn't okay was that Larry wanted his $80,000 in signup bonuses returned. They had only been there for a couple of months, so Larry felt that, since there had been such a mess, they should return the money. Usually brokers stay for a much longer period than two months, after all. But Louis and Benny felt that since they were getting fired it wasn't their fault that they couldn't stay longer than two months. As for that FBI visit—hell, whatever happened to innocent until proven guilty?

If this were a dispute in the Real Wall Street, an arbitration claim would have been filed at this point. As a rule, broker employment contracts require arbitration of disputes. And that was precisely what was going to happen in this case, whether they liked it or not. It was going to be "mandatory arbitration" in every sense of those words.

"Within like three, four days I get a call from Vinnie Corrao. Vinnie is Joe Butch's* son. He says, 'You know, we're going to have to meet up. We got some stuff to settle.' He says, 'Larry's looking for that bonus he gave you.' So I say, 'I'll have somebody get in touch with you.' He says okay, fine, give me a number. Joe Butch was basically Larry's Guy.

"Me and Benny weren't giving the money back, even if we had it. It was ridiculous. It's not as if we didn't want to work. Larry fired us. But we needed a Guy to sit down with Vinnie. If we used Charlie he'd have kept the money. He'd have made us pay back the money and took it. He wouldn't have been

---

* "Joe Butch" Corrao, a skipper in the Gambino family, had just begun a stretch in federal prison for racketeering. His son has been identified by law enforcement as a Gambino soldier.

reasonable about it. He'd have just said 'Eighty grand! Twenty grand for me.' Frank would have just done the same thing. Killed it.

"So we spoke to this guy John who worked for us at L. T. Lawrence and was Carmine Sciandra's* nephew. We figured Carmine is the best Guy to use in this situation. John says, 'All right, I'll have my uncle take care of it.' So now we got to go meet with Carmine. John set it up. He calls over the weekend and says, 'Let's meet at Carmine's. Tonight at seven.' He gives me the address, on Todt Hill in Staten Island.

"So that afternoon Stefanie's best friend Michelle was having a christening. Her baby was getting baptized, and they had a party at a restaurant afterwards. Everybody's hanging out, having a good time. I'm saying to myself, 'I got to get the fuck out of here.' I'm sick to my stomach. I didn't say anything to Stefanie, I just thought I'd say I got a call, and had to go somewhere for an hour. I figure if I told her she'd get all upset, that I was embarrassing her, blah blah blah. I was just going to disappear, go to the bathroom like I was sick, but then I thought, naah. I say, 'I got to go somewhere. I'll be back in half an hour.' Stefanie says, 'Why now?' I say, 'I'll explain to you later.'

When Louis arrived, Benny and John were there already. Carmine's house was tremendi—bigger than Paul Castellano's. He even had a Spanish maid, just as Paul did. They entered the house and in a room on the left, up a few steps, Carmine was sitting behind a big desk facing the door. To the side was a table the size of a pier. The office was all mahogany. "He had three chairs set up for us. I was looking around this office. Like, wow. He had this painted picture, of his father, maybe. The whole house was top-notch. He had a piano in another room, he had a game room. He had two kitchens, one for the maid. Everything was professionally

*Sciandra, identified in court papers as a Gambino skipper, was an official of Top Tomato, a grocery chain in Brooklyn and Staten Island.

decorated. He had an in-ground pool, trees. His basement was like Disney World. He had twenty arcade games, pool table, ping-pong table. He had three Mercedes. The house was just ridiculous."

Carmine was middle-aged and baby-faced, with tight, receding, slick-backed hair. Soft-spoken, quiet. Like a grocer. Hell, he *was* a grocer.

"After the introductions everybody sits down. Carmine asks me to explain the situation. So I did because Benny never does. 'He fired us. I feel we don't have to give it back,' blah blah blah. Carmine says, 'You're not willing to give him back anything?' He says, 'If you're not, just say you're not. And that's it. It's no big deal.' So I says no, I didn't want to give back nothing. He fired me. I'll still work there. Carmine says he can understand how he wouldn't want me to work there. I says I do too, but if that's the way he feels he has no right to get his eighty thousand dollars back.

"Carmine says, 'Okay, I'll see what I can do. I'll try to take care of it.' Thank you, and that was it. I explained the situation, and he talked back vague and rare. So then me, Benny, and John talk outside for another twenty minutes. John was like, 'Don't worry about it, we'll take care of it, we'll get in touch with Vinnie and we'll all meet in Brooklyn.'"

By the time he returned, the christening was coming to an end. Louis never heard the end of it from Stefanie.

The session with Carmine was just a kind of opening consultation, not the arbitration itself. That took place a few days later at the Top Tomato at 86th Street and Stillwell Avenue in Bensonhurst. It might have been the first time in Wall Street history, even in the history of Chop House Wall Street, that a broker-compensation dispute was adjudicated within twenty-five feet of freshly misted arugula.

"Carmine's got an office up some stairs at the store. A little office. Two couches, a desk, some chairs. Carmine's behind the desk again. Larry's there in his suit and tie. Him and me sit in the chairs in front of Carmine, and Carmine says, 'Why don't you explain yourselves to each other.' So Larry says, 'Well, you should give back the money I gave you,' and I go, 'Why should I? For what? It's ridiculous. You fired me. I'm not giving you back the fucking money. I did a hundred and seventeen thousand dollars gross and then I did another one-eighteen gross. You paid us for it and kept half the money. So you got that money back, if you really look at it.' So it went back and forth, he said we had to be there for at least a year, blah blah blah.

"Carmine asks if Vinnie has anything to say, and Vinnie says no, and Carmine's like, 'All right, I've heard both of your sides of the story,' and that was it. They'll let us know. Great. I could give two fucks, to be honest about it," said Louis. "And then they let us know. Later on I got a call from John. They wanted us to pay twenty grand back each, whenever we got it. Half. So I say, okay. No problem.

"I never had the money. They asked me for it. John would say, 'You got some money to pay back Larry?' and I'd say, 'I don't got it.' And John knew I didn't have it, and they didn't bust my balls for it. I think Benny paid it back, his half. I paid two, three thousand. Charlie never found out about it. Then he'd know I got a forty-thousand-dollar signup bonus, he didn't get a piece of it. That's ten thousand right there. It would have been a fucking mess."

Sometime later Carmine invited Louis, Benny, and John over for lunch. It was semi-social, with Carmine making small talk and finding out what John was doing with them. "That way John could never get beat," said Louis.

As often happens in arbitrations on the Real Wall Street, the Top Tomato tribunal left neither party very satisfied. Louis never found out how much Carmine was compensated for his mediation services, presumably some portion of the $40,000 that Louis and Benny were supposed to pay Larry through Vinnie. Carmine never pressed the issue. But Larry did.

"He sued me," said Louis. "I got sued by L. T. Lawrence. Like he didn't know whether to be legit or a gangster. He was confused."*

---

*It was an arbitration, actually—this time, a Real Wall Street arbitration, filed with the NASD. Louis ignored it and Lawrence won by default.

CHAPTER THIRTY-SEVEN

"You cursed his wife?"

Charlie didn't wait for an answer.

Bam! He smacked the guy Rob right across the face. That's how he did it. Fast. No time for Rob to react. You had to be fast, if you were going to smack someone across the face. Rob was crying. "You ever fucking call this kid's house, talk to his fucking wife," said Charlie, "I swear I don't care who's sitting at the table, I'm going to come personally to your fucking house and talk to your fucking wife."

Louis was sitting there, in a packed diner on Hylan Boulevard in Staten Island. A few months before he wouldn't have believed his eyes. Now he took it in stride. A sitdown, a smack in public. Charlie earning his money.

It was a money dispute. It was always a money dispute. And Charlie was going to bat for him. That was their relationship. Louis would come to Brooklyn, give him money, it wouldn't be enough, and he would get a beating. But when needed, Charlie would go to bat for Louis.

In this case, Rob had made the mistake of playing gangster and Charlie really hated the gangster act, unless he was doing the acting. Louis was his bitch boy now, and you don't curse the wife of a bitch boy.

Louis owed Rob money. Louis was always owing somebody money—Rob, Charlie, dozens of others.

It was 1996, and as the year dragged on it was turning out to be a totally sucky year, as Louis went from one firm to another. One firm would sour, and he would move on to another. He was in demand. But getting less money. Not a lot less, but enough less that he noticed.

More heat on the chop houses from the regulators. Less and less and less money and more and more and more pressure and sitdowns. More visits and calls and meetings with Charlie, who was getting to know the whole family.

STEFANIE: "I was upstairs and Louis answered the door. Charlie was with this heavy guy. I remember him sitting at the table, and I was sitting on the stairs. Charlie was yelling about something. Louis said, 'Calm down, calm down, calm down.' Charlie's yelling at me, 'He owes this guy money. He's supposed to have it and he doesn't have it. The guy wants his money.'

"Then they come upstairs and the heavy guy's sitting in my kitchen in one chair, and Charlie's standing there talking to me, and Louis was like two stairs up to the third floor. I'm sitting on the step.

"Charlie says, 'He owes him the money and he's not going to give it to him. This guy can't wait no more. He needs it. He's got to give it to his kids. He's got bills to pay and Louis owes him all this money.'

"Charlie says, 'You're lucky to have me' with Louis gambling so much—justifying that he's this good guy. Here's Charlie trying to make himself this good guy, and Louis is this big mess-up. 'Thank God he has me,' Charlie tells me.

"So then I just started crying. Then Louis says maybe he can get a couple of dollars to him.

"Charlie says, 'I don't want you to get upset, Stefanie. I just want you to know the truth here. You need to know the truth.

What's going on. He tries to hide everything from you. I want to let you know that he's my friend and I'm trying to help him out.' He says, 'I want you to be aware. He has a problem. He's gambling. He borrows money. You need to be aware of what's going on. He owes this guy money. He owes me money. I just want you to be aware.'

"I'm sitting there crying. And I remember the other guy says something like, 'Louis, I've had it. I'm not playing around. I need my money tomorrow. If I don't get my money, I'm going to be back here.' Louis says, 'Oh, no, no, no. I'll get you the money tomorrow.' And of course when they leave, Louis is like, 'He's out of his mind.'

"So we went to Brooklyn, around Charlie's neighborhood, so Louis could pay him the money. We parked the car. Louis got out and he walked over to Charlie. Before they even started talking, Charlie smacked him across the face. When he came back, I said, 'I don't understand. What the hell? Why did he do that?' Louis says, 'Oh, he's losing his mind. He's just pissed off and he's taking it out on me.' I says, 'This is your friend, huh?'

"I remember Charlie being there when his father was there. And I remember Charlie yelling about money or whatever, and Nick saying, 'Well, we'll get the money. We'll get the money. We'll get it somehow. We'll get it to you.'

"Everybody's intimidated by Charlie. I'm thinking you must be Italian to get it, that fear. Because I can be intimidated by people but it's not in that way. I figure it's an Italian thing. My father wouldn't allow a guy to intimidate him. And my father never dealt with Charlie at all. Charlie never called my parents' house but he called Louis's parents' house. He used to call their house and scream and curse. If he called my parents' house ever, he would use another name. And you knew it was him. You could tell his voice. 'Could you tell Lou to call Joey?' He would never say Charlie in my house. I'd hear from my mother, 'Some guy named Joey called.'"

NICK PASCIUTO: "One time I met Charlie in a bistro on Staten Island. It was a bar, club. Me and Louis went there. He's telling me how much Louis owed him. He says, 'This kid's doing all these crazy things. I got to stop them from getting at him.' He says, 'They want to get paid and I'm holding them off.' He says he's always helping him, keeping the wolves away from him. 'If it wasn't for me, he would be gone already.' I was going to say to him, 'Who are you kidding?' But at the time it wouldn't have mattered. It just would have made things worse. No way he was going to get away from him.

"I knew about this Charlie, not that he was anything big. I knew he was a knockaround guy and all that in Brooklyn. That's what he did for a living. Whatever—rob stuff, loan-sharking, gambling. Whatever he did, and extorting was probably the biggest one. I met him a few times. Louis was out with him, and he'd be there and I met him. Louis would go out with him, they had a couple of laughs, and he'd always be a ball-breaker. Talk down to you. Shit like that. That was part of the goof. That was part of the scene, I guess.

"I never really seen him in action, but based on his history, he was capable of doing nasty things. I knew he was involved in the Colombo wars, he was shot once. He said that. He used to say, 'I was in the Colombo wars. I survived that.' Blah blah blah. He looked like a normal guy. If you looked at him you'd think he was dressed up sharp. Clothes, jewelry. The way he talked, presented himself. You'd think he was an important person with somebody. Dressed sharp. Expensive clothes. Knits and stuff like that. Nails. The whole works.

"I was at Louis's house when Charlie was there with his friend Joe Botch. He was telling me that Louis took money from Joe Botch, he needed the money for his wife's operation, he needed it back. Some bullshit story. 'I'm going to fucking break his head,' blah blah blah.

"Look, I don't know. They're bringing me in. These people

are telling me this, you're telling me that, and Louis, because of his history, I couldn't tell if he was telling me the truth, in what he was telling me. Because he just lied so much. His thing was about lying and gambling. So at that point, based on his history, I didn't know who to believe. I tend to believe my son, but these guys are saying this, and I know what I was going through with him, so at that point I'm saying, these guys, maybe they have a beef, a legitimate beef, with him. I don't know.

"So after they left I ask him, 'Louie, what's the story? They need money for the operation.' And he says, 'No, that's all bullshit.' All right. So what do you want to do? I don't know what I'm going to tell you. You're getting me involved—and I don't have any money to give him.

"That was the time Charlie smacked him. He didn't punch him or anything, he smacked him. He smacked him in front of me. But then this other guy was there, and if I jumped in, they were ready. At the time I wanted to smack him too. So he deserved a smacking. [Laughs.] I never seen him really—if he got hurt worse than a smacking. I wouldn't stand for that. But he didn't do it, that one time he smacked him in front of me."

FRAN PASCIUTO: "I used to call him 'Charlie Macaroni.' He was about the lowest as far as I was concerned. I met him for the first time at the wedding. What did I think of him? That he was a gangster. You know, the way he was dressed, the way he acted. And then he called a few times, looking for Louis. 'Is Louie there?' I would say yes, no, or whatever. 'Tell him Charlie called.' He would have palpitations on the phone. He was always looking for Louis. He used to call, 'I'm going crazy. Where's your son? I'm going to kill him.' I used to say, 'I don't know where he is. Beep him.'

"At first he would just ask for Louis, and then after the arrest for the checks he started to get a little crazy on the phone, bad-mouthing him. I can't believe some of the things he said sometimes. I used to speak back to him. One time he told me how bad Louis was and I said, 'Hey Charlie, I don't want to hear that no more.' I said, 'An extortionist is talking?' I said, 'Here you are telling me everything my son does, what about you? What do you do? You take money from people. You sit, your feet up, and you take from everybody and you beat them up. You're an extortionist. How would you like if I called up your mother and told your mother how rotten you are and how you extort people, what you do for a living?'

"He says, 'Well, I work.' I said, 'Really? Where do you work? With your million-dollar tan and you never leave the house, where do you work?' I used to get, like, crazy with him and Louis used to go, 'I don't believe you, Ma.' I said, 'He got me on the phone. It's just some person calling me and I wasn't going to let him intimidate me in any way.' Charlie once said to Louis, 'Your mother's crazy.'

"When Louis was arrested for the checks, I remember he called me up. I don't remember his exact words, but it was something like, 'Your son, what is he, like, an informant or something?' I said, Charlie, please. He's in jail. What 'informant'? This is where he is. Leave me alone. He said, 'Is he really in jail?' I said, 'No, I'm making it up.' I told him, 'Call Jersey. That's where he is. Call him. Leave me alone.'"

From the moment Louis was arrested for the check scam, it became a continuing motif. An obsession. Charlie was preoccupied with the notion that Louis was a rat.

Louis wasn't a rat. But Charlie knew it could happen. Louis was facing serious jail time, or at least it was serious from the standpoint of someone who wasn't a Guy.

Hudson County prosecutors offered Louis a plea bargain in which he would have to serve three years in prison. It was, in the view of Louis's lawyer, a generous deal. It was the best he could do (or so the lawyer insisted when he wrote a letter to the judge, asking to be removed from the case because Louis owed him money).

Prosecutors were not aware that Louis had Guy connections, so—if they cared—they had no way of knowing that Louis could give up Guys. Louis never seriously thought about the idea.

But Charlie thought about it.

Charlie knew what being thrown in jail, deprived of your freedom, isolated—what that does to guys. Even guys who should know better. Hard guys. When they're young, unseasoned. A young kid up against an experienced cop? No contest. The cop wins. Charlie knew.

On March 4, 1982, Nassau County Detective John Majoribanks testified at a pretrial hearing in the case of People vs. Charles E. Ricottone. Majoribanks described what happened after he arrested Charlie for the home-invasion robbery in April 1981. He had just put Charlie in a police car when a conversation ensued:

"We asked Mr. Ricottone, 'Is that true? Do you want to cooperate?' And he said, 'Yes.' But he wanted to know what was in it for him. We advised Mr. Ricottone that if he did cooperate in helping us with the investigation, we would make it known that he had cooperated to the District Attorney's office and to the judge. . . . We asked him who the other two [robbers] were and where they were. And he told us that he would—he had just left them and he would show us where they were. . . . We got out of our car, got back into the Robbery Squad car, followed the Seventh Squad unit to a location. . . .

"Mr. Ricottone pointed to the house stating that was the house [the two other robbers] were in."

Later that day, Charlie gave Nassau County detectives a handwritten statement confessing his guilt in the robbery of the Polanski residence, describing the robbery in detail and implicating his two accomplices. Both were arrested. Charges against one were dismissed. The other guy fingered by Charlie, Anthony Cella, pleaded guilty.

It must have been a little uncomfortable in the Ricottone household back then. Cella was the boyfriend of Charlie's sister, and was living in the house, with the family, at the time they led him away.

It's not 100 percent clear from court records whether detectives would have found the other perps without Charlie's help. Maybe they would have been located anyway. It's that way sometimes with cooperating witnesses. Sometimes they are crucial. And sometimes they just make life easier for the cops, and themselves, when they turn rat.

CHAPTER THIRTY-EIGHT

The idea of cooperating was moot because Louis never thought much about the prison term that was hanging over his head. It was just another annoyance, another thing in the future. Louis never thought about the future. And even if he did, the idea of spending three years away from Stefanie and his cars and his gambling and his life—that was just inconceivable. Almost as beyond comprehension as being without Charlie.

Charlie was his Guy and he would just have to make the best of it, whether that meant taking his slaps or lying about the money he was getting or, when he couldn't avoid it anymore, paying the money. If you looked at it a certain way, maybe he really owed the money. Maybe, as Nick said, Joe Botch really needed an operation. Who the fuck knew? Nick didn't know. Nick had his doubts. And Nick didn't know that Louis owed Charlie his life, for the sitdown with Frank at L&B if nothing else. How much is a life worth anyway? The $50,000 he paid Charlie for speaking up for him with Frank?

As brokers, if not as human beings, the lives of the chop house kids were worth less and less. First the regulators, the polyester-suit guys, with their dumb restrictions cutting into deals and making investors wary. And now the press. The financial press had been puppy-dog passive when Louis was starting out. They were docile and stupid and blind. But now the publicity had begun.

In July 1996, *Fortune* published a full-length dissection of the decline and fall of Hanover Sterling, with several unflattering references to Roy. The story hinted at Guy involvement. Even though it focused on the short-sellers who profited from Hanover's decline—the red herring that was pushed by the Adler Coleman trustee, Ed Mishkin—it definitely was unwanted attention. Then came a *Business Week* cover story just before Christmas 1996, entitled "The Mob on Wall Street." It named Phil and Dom and Roy and Sonny, a Genovese skipper named "Allie Shades" Malangone and his sidekick Alan Longo. The story linked Roy to Longo and Allie Shades.

Louis and Benny weren't all that troubled by the *BW* story. It didn't name them. Except for Greenway, it didn't name any of the firms where they had worked since Hanover. They did a ritual burning of the issue when it came out, but they didn't get too upset because they knew that memories were short. Chop House Wall Street was as huge and anonymous as the city, and they could easily get lost in it, buried in the ever-shifting landscape of doors with pretty and patriotic names engraved on them.

With heat increasing from regulators and the media, they were going to have to work even harder to make a buck. Louis had a wife to support now. He had a lifestyle to support.

Louis's money hunger was like a never-slackening disease. Cash ruled everything around him. But cash ruled Louis too. He couldn't stop spending and he couldn't stop gambling. And losing.

It wasn't fuck-you money anymore.

As it became harder to make a dishonest buck, earning money on Chop House Wall Street meant greater potential for conflict. Conflict meant sitdowns. Except for the Carmine sit-down, which was a rare exception, sitdowns meant Charlie. And Charlie was getting harsher, more difficult to deal with, more unreasonable. Charlie was tired of being pulled into sit-downs. And he was throwing tantrums like a petulant child because deals were getting harder to pull off. A Brooklyn health care company looked promising at First Hanover, one of the firms he changed as often as whores changed tampons, but Louis and Benny—and Charlie—lost out when the stock promoter got cold feet. The reason was the heat, the publicity.

The *BW* story and other articles exposed the Guys and the chop house kids, but Louis and his pals didn't give a fuck and neither did the Guys. The money was just too good, even with deals harder to pull off. In fact, by 1997 Guys were doing more than just shaking down guys who ran firms, earners like Chris Wolf and Louis. They were running firms, the way Dom and Rico were running Vision, or acting as talent scouts, as Frank Coppa did when he introduced Louis and Benny to State Capital.

And now Louis was going to another firm, called U.S. Se-curities & Futures, because of a referral from another Guy in Louis's life.

The move to U.S. Securities grew out of another bullshit dispute. This one involved a Guy named Vinnie Nunez. Louis owed Vinnie about $80,000, and Vinnie was friends with a Guy named "Little Nick" Corozzo, a Gambino skipper who was about to go on trial for racketeering. Nick called Charlie. Same old ritual. Someone has a beef against Louis, calls Char-lie, and Charlie shakes down Louis. It was getting old.

"Charlie calls me up and says, 'You're going to have to pay this kid back some money,' which I knew was going to hap-pen. But I really didn't have the money, so I tried to deal with Vinnie personally, and it worked out better. Vinnie introduced me to a guy named Alan Saretsky and Alan's friend Ralph, who owned a catering hall in Brooklyn. Alan was in hock to

Ralph and this Guy named Phil Defonte. Alan had a deal—a company called Waco Classic Aircraft."

A simple idea. Louis would work off his debt, like some kind of sharecropper in the Old South. He would generate profits that would make Vinnie whole, and thereby lift from Louis the yoke of indentured servitude. To accomplish this task, Louis went to work at Alan's firm, Danalan Investments. When Danalan couldn't pull off Waco, the deal went to U.S. Securities & Futures and Louis followed. Waco made vintage aircraft for collectors, not that anyone cared. The product mattered—the warrants. Alan was in charge of the product.

Alan Saretsky was not a typical chop house broker. He was older than most. He had worked on the Real Wall Street, but his career had taken a wrong turn along the way. He was a Shearson broker back in the 1980s, but ran afoul of regulators and was barred by the New York Stock Exchange in the early 1990s. So now he was one of the dozens of former brokers who enjoyed a prosperous existence on the fringes of the securities business, brokering deals between unprosperous companies and chop houses. Alan was a "friend of a friend" of Vinnie's, the kind of networking that often resulted in jobs on both the Real and the Chop House Wall Street.

U.S. Securities & Futures was part of the Real Wall Street. It didn't just look like the Real Wall Street. It *was* the Real Wall Street.

For the first time since A. T. Brod, he was back—for a few minutes, at least—on the Real Wall Street. What was he doing there? The *Business Week* story had received a serious amount of publicity, and there were calls in Congress for the SEC to act. The chop houses were getting a great deal of unwanted exposure. But there it was—a legit firm housing a crew of chop house brokers. The proprietor was a man named John Hing, who traded bonds and futures and didn't seem to grasp the kind of people he was dealing with in Louis, Benny, and their friends. Instead of trading Eurobonds, these kids were pushing a company whose shares were about to be sold to the investors of America. It seemed legit at first glance, like most chop house schemes.

The Waco deal wasn't an IPO. It was a "15c2-11." Waco was a teeny-weeny company whose shares were going to start trading over the counter, which required filing papers. Form 15c2-11, to be exact. These kinds of deals were better than IPOs, because you had to file fewer papers before you could begin to steal—or raise money, in the case of a legit 15c2-11.

Louis and Benny were going to share a half million warrants as their reward for selling $1 million in Waco paper. It looked simple in theory. In practice, it was a fiasco.

"We're all ready and prepared," said Louis. "Our biggest client from way back at Todd, Ed Delano, he's invested. Tension's tight because we're waiting for the deal to come out. Nobody has money. Everybody's going to get warrants from this deal and we're all going to come out okay.

"So we raised all that money and the deal isn't going through. There's a holdup at Nasdaq. I have to go down to Maryland to see Shannon Johnson, and tell him we'll give him as payment twenty thousand warrants for his company, YBC Associates, if he'll get the forms approved. So I drive down there to Maryland with the 15c2-11 in a manila envelope, and handed it to Shannon. I didn't want to send it overnight so I drove it down. It was a fucking pain in the ass. I went down there in the worst car imaginable. A fucking 1984 Cutlass. I was uncomfortable all the way. By now the Benz is gone, the Ferrari is gone. I couldn't afford them no more.

"So the deal went through and everybody's trying to scam U.S. Securities. Everybody—me, Benny, Alan—all of us were running to get rid of our stock. But we couldn't raise enough money to cross ourselves out of this shit.

"This U.S. Securities is not anywhere close to a chop shop. It's an international brokerage firm. It's owned by Chinese people. There was always a problem. We were in Hing's office every fucking day. This guy called. That guy called. The clients were complaining.

"I couldn't believe the shit that was going on. Alan Saretsky is totally out of his fucking mind. He's trying to sell something like two hundred thousand shares of common stock. He's trying to cut John Hing in on it! I'm sitting in the room listening to Alan trying to tell John Hing that he can give Hing money under the table. John Hing says, 'I don't understand.' What was he doing? The guy's legit. I said, 'Let's look like we're doing this legit. If we look like we're doing it legit, we're going to pull this fucking shit off.'

"Then Charlie comes to the office like a gang-banger, looking to sell his fucking stock and get his money. Charlie came up there and smacked me and punched me in the face in the conference room of this legit Wall Street firm! I said, 'Charlie, you got to keep your voice down. This isn't like the other firms.' He goes, 'I don't give a fuck!' Bam! John Hing was right next door. Charlie went to talk to him. About his 'account.' His account? He had a fucking nominee account! He had it under his friend Sean. I go, 'Are you fucking nuts? What are you gonna tell him? You're Sean Dunleavy, you're going to tell him?' He did! He told Hing he's Sean fucking Dunleavy.

"So you got all these gangsters coming in and out and these U.S. Securities people are in suits and ties. They're fucking graduates of college. You got Charlie with a turtleneck and sports coat, tanned like he just came back from Florida, walking around with Joe Botch. They just look like fucking gangsters. They didn't belong there. The *Business Week* article had just come out. I used to tell Charlie, 'You're fucking nuts. You're going to get in trouble. You can't be coming up to the offices dressed like this.' He goes, 'Don't tell me how to handle my affairs.'"*

The Waco disaster was proof, not that Louis needed any, that Charlie was no businessman.

Waco wasn't a total loss. A little money was made from the warrants—much less than anticipated, but enough to pay off Vinnie, which was the purpose of doing the deal in the first place. He sold some of the warrants, before the Waco deal came out, to a cold-caller named Tommy Deceglie, an older guy who was Benny's brother-in-law. Louis put twenty thousand warrants in Tommy's account in return for $20,000 in cash.

Tommy expected that the warrants were going to rise to maybe $4.50, netting a $90,000 profit. Instead he wound up getting $3 for the warrants, but that was still $60,000. Not bad on a $20,000 investment, no?

No.

Another dumb sitdown. This one was at a restaurant in Bay Ridge.

"This old Guy with the Bonannos, Elmo, was representing Tommy," said Louis. "He was supposed to be Tommy's uncle. That's right—Elmo. Like 'Tickle-Me Elmo.' I was so disgusted I didn't think it was funny. Charlie used to make fun of it, though."

Louis won this one. At the sitdown it became clear that Tommy had lied to Elmo about the dispute. Not wise, as there was nothing especially cuddly or tickleable about Vincent "Elmo" Almarante, a convicted drug dealer. Louis—as would have befit a Real Wall Street arbitration—had brought along trading records that contradicted Tommy on major

*John Hing remembers Louis and Saretsky, but denies that they worked there or ever did more than "visit" U.S. Securities. Hing also denies Louis's account of an offer by Saretsky, or that gangsters congregated at the firm because of the Waco deal. He remembers a "Sean Dunleavy," but says someone else handled his complaint. Subsequent federal charges support Louis, and contradict Hing, by saying that Louis did indeed work at U.S. Securities and sold Waco stock there.

points. "Elmo tells Charlie he's sorry he brought us down there, it was a misunderstanding. I left and Benny told me the guy got smacked around after that. Every time I saw Tommy after that I made him miserable about it. Balls of the guy," said Louis.

A fair decision, not that he gave a shit anymore.

part five

FENCE JUMPER

CHAPTER THIRTY-NINE

It was time to kill Charlie.

When Charlie started to talk about Stefanie, he crossed a line. Niggers raping Stefanie? Uh-uh.

This whole niggers-raping-Stefanie stuff, and the resulting need to kill Charlie, was maybe the most unpleasant part of Louis's mid-career crisis. Here he was, twenty-three years old—an old man by chop house standards. When he left U.S. Securities in June 1997, Louis realized it was all over. He was through. The joy of stealing was gone. Now it was a struggle. Now he was just like everybody else, living from check to check, payoff to payoff, scam to scam. But there were no scams on the horizon, and the money he had was flowing out to Atlantic City and the bookies and loan sharks.

For the first time as an adult he couldn't afford stuff. First the boat and now the cars were gone. He couldn't afford the payments—and besides, Charlie had been using the Ferrari and the Mercedes as much as he was. He was down to one car, one wife (not counting Charlie), and soon he would have a child. Stefanie was pregnant. They both agreed that it was a bad time.

Charlie was pissed about missing out on the Waco warrants. Disappointment really brought out the worst in him, and Charlie's worst was unpleasant in many ways, some of them new. Louis theorized that maybe Charlie had some kind of deep-seated fear of rejection. But he didn't spend too much time analyzing it, and neither did Charlie. Instead Charlie did what psychologists recommend as healthiest for one's psyche. He kept in touch with his feelings.

"Around the time of the Waco deal he wanted money, I forget for what, and I didn't have it. I went to see him at his house. I took off my shoes, like I usually do, came into the apartment. I said, 'Charlie, I really don't have it.' He goes over to the stove and sticks his hand in this pot holder hanging by the stove. He took out a .38 revolver. I was shitting my pants almost. Took it out, put it right on my fucking head. 'I can blow your fucking head off right here.' At that moment I don't know what he's going to do. I said, 'Come on, Charlie, man, what the fuck are you doing, man? I'll have it. I'll have it.' He says, 'If next Sunday comes and I got to take this fucking thing out of the pot holder, I'm going to fucking use it.'"

But that was almost okay. Charlie was mad. He tended to get mad. That was Charlie. But Stefanie—no, that was off-limits. Louis was a man, and men don't let their wives be raped by niggers, even in theory.

"He started saying the craziest shit. Getting real abusive like. He says, 'I'll have six niggers come and rape your wife. How'd you like that? You lying scumbag.' I went, 'Charlie, that's out of line.' He says, 'Out of line, my fucking ass. I'll come myself.' I say, 'Now you're going to rape my wife? I don't understand. First you said you'd have niggers rape my wife. Now it's you?' He goes, 'Don't fuck around with me. Don't mind-fuck me.' He said that because I used to play with him sometimes. He says, 'Everything's a fucking joke. This is not a joke.' He's screaming. He was crazy.

"So Charlie's talking about niggers raping Stefanie, and I'm trying to make a joke out of it, and he's pushing it. He goes, 'She's probably fucking another guy. You're so fucked up she's fucking other guys,' and I say, 'Charlie, don't even talk about Stefanie. I don't give a fuck. Don't get too personal,' I told him. He goes, 'What, are you going to defend yourself over this thing?' and I say, 'Just don't talk about Stefanie and I won't have to defend myself.' It just died out. He kind of backed down a little bit. I would have raised my hands back to him that time. That's the only time I would have raised my hands back to him. I said to myself, 'If he raises his hands to me right now, I'm going to get the best of this motherfucker.' I would have taken out every frustration I ever had in my life on him."

After that, Louis realized he wanted Charlie dead. He deserved it. It was becoming torture. The phone calls. The beatings. Now Stefanie? Enough.

"I decided—that was it. But I needed someone to come with me. I was afraid to go alone. I went to my father. I talked to him outside the house. I said, 'Dad, I don't know if he's going to show up or not, but I can't live with me thinking he's going to show up. I got to kill him. Let's go to Brooklyn, take a fucking gun, ring his doorbell, shoot the motherfucker, and leave him dead. Nobody will care.' We'd get back in our car, and go away. Throw the gun in the fucking water. Nobody would even know. We'd ring the doorbell at seven in the morning. He'd think it's his fucking coffee. He'd open the door. *Pkowwww!*

"I'd be so happy. 'Aw, Charlie. Look at you. You're a fucking mess when you're dead. You idiot. You shouldn't have talked about the niggers fucking Stefanie. You fucking retard.' I swear I would have spit in his face. No remorse at all. But my father says no, don't do it."

Nick said he would talk to his old friend Butchie, the connected guy Fran didn't like, who was supposedly tight with Alphonse Persico, boss of the Colombos. Butchie knew a Guy. The Guy would talk to Charlie. And that would be that. The new Guy would say to Charlie, "Listen, you got to calm down and leave the kid alone."

Louis was going to get himself a new Guy. He was going to jump ship.

It would be a perilous move in any organization that values loyalty. But there can be valid reasons for moving from one part of an organizational chart to another. Louis figured the Guy world was like any other structured, logically run operation, with dispute-settling mechanisms and hierarchy. When he wasn't treated right at Hanover, he had gone to Roy to complain and Roy had been reasonable and agreed with him and moved him to another broker. Louis had his reasons now, even more than at Hanover. So Louis figured it would all turn out okay.

Butchie had Louis get in touch with a Guy named Robert Luciano, who ran a precious metals shop, My Way Gold, on Avenue S just off Stillwell Avenue in Bensonhurst. Luciano would be the one to deal with Charlie and keep Charlie away. So Louis went to the gold shop.

Louis went there one unseasonably chilly afternoon. He remembered it was chilly because Luciano began the meeting by telling Louis to take off his clothes. After checking for a wire and finding none, Luciano wasn't oozing with solicitude, but he was civil. He let Louis get dressed and asked Louis about his debts. Yes, he had debts, a couple. He would pay Luciano and Luciano would pay the debtors. Sort of like a credit counselor. He would talk to Charlie, assuming the role now of small-town family lawyer. He would tell Charlie to cease using coercive debt-collection tactics. The charge? No charge. It would be a favor. He was being nice. Luciano seemed to be a nice guy. He was in his mid-thirties, a bit pudgy.

Louis was happy after he left Luciano. Okay, he was jumping ship. Charlie wasn't going to like it. Well, fuck Charlie. You just don't treat a person that way and get away with it. You don't abuse their wives, even verbally. Now Luciano was going to be his Charlie, getting the cut that he used to give Charlie. Fuck Charlie. Fuck him.

The good feeling lasted a few days. Louis was between brokerages, so he was making the rounds, trying to find a place that might accommodate him. One day he went to visit a firm in Manhattan. It took about an hour. Louis came downstairs and there he was. Charlie.

Charlie walked up to Louis. He didn't hit him, which kind of disappointed Louis because he figured that he had it coming, that hitting him would be enough. Instead, Charlie just talked to him quietly. "He says, 'I'm just letting you know something. If you think this is gonna work, you're going to die.' And he just left. I was, like, 'Oh man. He's mad. I'm dead,'" said Louis. He called Luciano immediately from his cell phone.

"He just found me," he told Luciano. Louis could hear a sigh on the other end of the phone. It made him feel good, just a little. "Ah, that fucking guy," Luciano said. He said he'd call Charlie. He hung up.

Later that day, Luciano called him back. "He won't come near you no more," he told Louis.

For several nightmarish days, it was as if Charlie had nothing better to do but to call Louis's pager. He was relentless. The pager was constantly buzzing. It was almost as if his pager were some kind of malfunctioning circulation-boosting vibrator, the way it was buzzing constantly.

Louis didn't call him back. Luciano, while not exactly exuding warmth, had made it clear that he would get Charlie off his back. Louis figured that was going to happen. It might take a while, but it would happen. He still held that hope when he went to see Luciano to make a payment. He was a little short—he was supposed to pay Luciano $6,000 for distribution to his creditors, and he only had $4,000. But he figured that a partial payment would be okay, as this was supposed to be a friend of Butchie and Butchie was a friend of his father, not to mention his tightness with Alphonse Persico.

Louis went to the gold store on Avenue S, gave Luciano the $4,000, and Luciano proceeded to give Louis a slow, earnest, and methodical beating.

"He starts smacking me all over the fucking place, 'What the fuck are you doing?' I'm saying. He's goes, 'You fucking'—smack! He smacked me in my face a hundred times. I'm putting my hands up to cover my face and this guy's holding my hands down so he can smack me. He says, 'Keep the fucking four thousand.' He pulls out a knife. Fucking steak knife. He goes, 'I should fucking take this knife . . .' Meanwhile, I wasn't even all that scared because I was just thinking to myself, kill me already. I didn't care no more. Just get it over with. One of yas, you, Charlie, just kill me."

Louis decided, after that visit to Luciano, that maybe he had better try to patch up his differences with Charlie.

"I left there with the four thousand, smacked all around. Then I called Charlie up and I go, 'Charlie, sorry. I got money for you. Where do you want to meet? Get this guy away from me. He's nuts.' He was worse than Charlie! Charlie says, 'I told you! You stupid motherfuckerrrrrrr!' I said, 'Aw, Charlie, it was a fucking mistake. I'll just bring you the money I got, settle some of this shit, and just continue to work, all right?'

"When I saw Charlie he goes, real slow, 'You motherfucker. You fence-jumping stoolie rat motherfucker. I knew you'd be a fucking fence-jumper.'"

It was a bad time to alienate Charlie. Louis was still gambling whenever he had any money in his hands. By now his biggest creditor was a respected young man, intelligent and entrepreneurial, valued by many in the neighborhood as a purveyor of working capital. His name was Richie. Just as Charlie turned a local pizzeria into a very special place of his own, Richie was a constant and loyal customer of the Doo-Wop Shoppe, a music store, pool hall, and local hangout in a small stretch of stores on Arthur Kill Road, in a part of southwestern Staten Island noted for its landfill and penitentiary.

Louis would have to work off the Richie debt, just as he had worked off the Vinnie debt at U.S. Securities. Another sharecropper gig. Richie put him to work at a dumpy brokerage firm branch office in Woodbridge, New Jersey. Argent was the name. Richie's friend and associate John Mergen was going to come with Louis to Argent, to ensure that Louis worked hard and paid back what he owed. John was Turkish, real name Volkan Mergen. He was about five feet six inches tall, and built like one of the old-style multispout fire hydrants that were being removed from the streets by municipal authorities.

"I walked in and it was a real shitty office. Tremendous but shitty. Rugs are dirty. I just wanted to work there, pay this Richie back, and go away. I just went myself. No cold-callers. After U. S. Securities Benny went his separate ways. He quit the business.

"So now I'm working in the same office with this kid Mergen. Now, you got to understand, Richie is this major loan shark on Staten Island. All the kids in the neighborhood are intimidated and scared. The Turk, Mergen, was the muscle. I don't want to work with this fucking kid. He starts going, 'You got to pay my friend Richie back.' He goes, 'You're around us now.'"

CHAPTER FORTY

Do Wop

Louis wrote the words on a pad of lined yellow paper.

Do Wop 5,000

He was doodling on a pad of yellow paper in his shithole of an office at Argent.

Do Wop Do Wop

5,000

Do Wop Do Wop

Do Do Do Di   Di

Do Wop

The "5,000" was what he owed Richie, what he would have to trot over to Richie at the Doo-Wop Shoppe, after working at Argent for a few weeks. About $10,000 in gambling winnings brought his $20,000 gambling debt down to $10,000, and then he was able to pay Richie another $5,000 from his earnings at Argent, bringing his debt down to $5,000. That's all he owed. That's what he had to pay. Peanuts. To pay it off, all he needed was just a few more weeks on the plantation—maybe days, if he got luckier. Or maybe—fuck it—no days at all. Maybe he'd just "hang it on the limb," as Paul Muni did in one of those old chain-gang movies.

Louis had hit bottom, and he knew it. Or he hoped he had hit bottom. He thought he had hit bottom when the U.S. Securities warrant deal fell through. But Argent was worse. Nothing could be worse than this. He kept thinking of those old movies. Did they have Turkish overseers in the Antebellum South? At least he wasn't getting flogged. At least they weren't putting welts on his back.

Louis decided to hang it on the limb. He didn't have his heart in the job. He was too depressed. In the space of just a year, he went from being a sought-after broker, with sign-on bonuses and offices with TVs, to a guy in a shit office working off a debt with a Turk breathing down his neck. It was more than a guy could tolerate.

Mergen was in his late twenties and had spent a year and a half in prison on attempted robbery and weapons charges at Queensboro State Prison—the Guy equivalent of the New York Institute of Finance. Mergen's personal qualities were important assets for his broker-management work. He was squat, dark, and mean. It might have been nice to have Charlie in his corner at this time of his life, but Charlie was not feeling friendly toward Louis at the moment. Louis was not generating cash and had also recently displayed disloyalty of the most extreme kind.

At least he had company in his misery. It seemed that most of the other brokers and cold-callers at this Argent branch also had to make periodic trips to the Doo-Wop Shoppe.

Louis hung a sign on his wall: "An account a day keeps the Doo-Wop away."

"I used to tell all the cold-callers, 'Listen, if you don't want to have to deal with the kid at the Doo-Wop Shoppe, just open an account a day,'" said Louis.*

But Louis wasn't giving the fucking guy any more accounts, period. He stayed home—the chop house equivalent of heading into the swamps. Instead of the incessant din of bloodhounds baying, there was the gentle buzz of an ignored pager. Louis had made his bid for freedom as a matter of principle—he was tired of being a slave. And $5,000 was such a pissant sum of money. It was half of what he had spent to keep a limo idling for a few days in front of his building in Battery Park City just two years before.

It was a matter of principle for John and Richie too. Banks foreclose on tiny houses in bad neighborhoods when it doesn't make economic sense. Guys have to similarly act out of principle to maintain their credibility and standing in the community. But these Guys seemed to be taking their cues from *Fast Times at Ridgemont High* instead of *The Godfather.*

One day Louis came downstairs in the morning to find the air let out of his truck's tires. Not slashed. Deflated. Clearly the days of severed horses' heads had vanished, if they had ever existed. Louis had to pay $60 to get it towed.

Then the doorbell was ripped off his front door.

When Guys started acting like this, what could come next? Covering his mailbox with shaving cream? Short-sheeting his bed? Louis figured he was dealing with a new breed of Guy. Juvies were supposed to emulate Guys. But here were Guys emulating juvies. Louis would have laughed it off. But Stefanie was pregnant. She didn't need the stress, even from

---

*The owner of the Doo-Wop Shoppe, who declined to disclose his full name, hotly denied that his establishment was ever patronized by loan sharks or other unsavory personages.

bubble-gum gangsters. So he sent her back home to her parents.

Louis decided to move out too, and was with his friend Mike Fusco packing up when John Mergen crashed his car into the garage.

John was backing up and smashing into the garage door, again and again, and probably doing a hell of a lot more than $5,000 in damage to his car in the process.

"He's smashing his car into my garage, over and over again. So we went downstairs with a gun now, waiting for him to break through the garage. Mike says, 'I'm nervous!' and I go, 'Shut the fuck up.' Soon as he breaks through the garage, we're going to shoot this motherfucker. Fuck him. I had my father's registered gun. Big fucking .357 cannon. So I was going to say my father was living in my house, this guy broke into my house, and I shot him. Dead issue. I'm not in trouble.

"He never breaks through the garage. He leaves. I call the cops now. I say, 'Listen, some person just tried to smash through my garage.' I described the car. The cops start asking me, 'Do you owe the guy any money?' and I say, 'What's that got to do with it? He just tried to drive through my garage!'"

A couple of days later, Louis was almost finished packing and was moving a few personal belongings into the car. It was early in the morning. The movers had just left with the furniture. They were almost free. Almost gone.

Mergen and Richie paid a visit.

"They take me into the house and bring me upstairs. 'Where's all your shit?' I tell them I sent it to storage. I can't afford to live there. I'm moving. Richie says, 'You're moving your fucking shit out? This is what you do to me?' Pow. Hits me. I say, 'Rich, you don't understand. It's not like that.'"

At this point Mergen interjected with an offer—to smash a glass pot cover over Louis's head. But instead of doing that,

Louis's two creditors decided to bring him with them for a trip in their car.

"I say, 'Kidnap me? What you guys doing?' They fucking throw me in the back of Richie's truck. I'm sitting there, and I'm thinking, 'I'm going to jump out of this fucking truck.' I was just going to jump and run. But then they take me to this house where these Irish kids John and Jeff are living. They take my cell phone. They take my beeper. And they make John and Jeff watch me."

Louis stayed there all day in his makeshift debtors prison. While John and Jeff watched him, Richie and Mergen went to Louis's storage bin and removed his TV and VCR as a kind of payment-in-kind toward the $5,000 that was owed. Then they returned. Richie was upset. He discussed the matter with Louis outside the John-Jeff residence.

According to Richie, an incident had marred the trip to the storage unit. He had scratched his car while moving Louis's possessions. This was offered by way of explanation for what transpired—not that there had to be a reason, as Louis was learning.

The escaped sharecropper was flogged.

"Richie just beat the shit out of me. Started hitting me with a stickball fucking bat. I guess he blamed me for the scratch on the car. I got welts all over my back. He beats me up in the middle of the street. This was Huguenot Avenue and Woodrow. Right in the middle of the fucking intersection! There's cars going by every two seconds. Cars stop. John goes, 'What the fuck! Get the fuck out of here!' Telling that to the people driving by. One guy is like, 'Leave the kid alone!' John yells, 'Mind your fucking business!' Mergen tells the guy, 'You're next!'"

It was embarrassing, to say the least, and the idea of explaining everything to Stefanie was a prospect Louis did not relish, presuming he survived the experience. That was not assured.

"Richie takes me in the car now. I'm all beat up. John Mergen gets in the car and goes, 'I told you you fucked up,' and gives me a shot right in the eye. I'm bleeding. They drive me to the back of this school, IS 75. I get out of the car.

"I say, 'Rich, I think you guys did enough. I'll have the money in a few weeks. Give me a break. Keep my keys. Leave me the fuck alone.' Richie says, 'Nah, I don't think I'm going to do that. I think I'm going to make John take you in the woods to smash your fucking skull.'

"I go, 'You got to be fucking kidding me.' I'm begging the guy not to take me in the woods now. I say, 'Look, I really don't want the kid taking me in the woods. I'll pay the fucking money. I just want to get out of here.' So then Rich takes me for a walk-talk. 'I really didn't want to do this to you. But you have to pay the money.' I look at the guy. My eye's hanging off my face. I'm all beat up. I got welts all over my back. I say, 'In a few weeks I'll have the money for you.' He says, 'Don't leave or do anything stupid.'"

Do anything stupid? As he walked to the bus stop, Louis realized that there wasn't anything he had done for the past few months that wasn't stupid. But he also realized that there wasn't a goddamn thing he could do to find a way out, even if he wanted to be smart, or even if he could figure out what "smart" meant.

Stefanie didn't want to hear what happened. Enough.

STEFANIE: "I chose not to live in reality a lot. I chose—I still choose sometimes—not to live in reality, because it's okay to take a vacation from reality for a while in a sense. For the most part I could yell and scream about things, but then sometimes I didn't want to be bothered. Like when Charlie came up with that heavy guy and I'm sitting there crying. Or a phone call in the night he didn't want to answer. Or somebody ringing the bell in the middle of the night, and him not wanting to answer it. Him saying, 'Don't—just sit here.' And ringing the bell and ringing the bell and ringing the bell. And he couldn't look out the window, because if he looked out the window somebody would see him look out the window. And I'm like, 'This is ridiculous.'

"I remember lying in the bed, and the phone is ringing and ringing and ringing and ringing. I didn't know who it was. But somebody is calling at like three o'clock in the morning.

"After he was arrested for the check thing, the calls were nonstop. It seems as if the phone was always ringing, and he was always running out. He was always on the phone, talking to this one or that one. 'I got to go see this one.' 'I got to go see that one.' It was just overwhelming. I couldn't take it anymore. And I was never getting a straight answer about his problems or what was going on. Who he owed money to. He told me about some people but not all of them. One minute he'd have money. The next minute he wouldn't have any money.

"After the arrest Charlie started showing up more, Louis was always running out, trying to work but not really getting any money, and if he did—I don't think I ever saw him come home with checks anymore. He always used to come home with cash. He'd tell me he wasn't working under his own name, so somebody pays him in cash, or he pays me by check and then we cash it, but they're going to W-2 him at the end of the year. That was one of his big lines.

"I always knew they weren't on the up-and-up and I always used to tell him, 'Why don't you get a job at a decent place?' But at that point his record was so messed up from all the complaints and everything that he really couldn't.

"After he got arrested he got less money, and that made it harder to pay our bills, our rent. The landlord was pretty mean. I guess he had a right to be. Louis was lying all the time. 'Oh, yes, I paid him.' I'd get a phone call: 'Louis was supposed to come by with the rent. He didn't come by.' He'd borrow money from a friend or somebody to pay the rent.

We couldn't afford the house anymore. It was very stressful financially and emotionally because of all the problems he was having.

"I decided I was going to live at home."

CHAPTER FORTY-ONE

Louis realized he would never get rid of Guys. He would always have at least one Guy in his life. He developed a kind of Zen attitude. He would withstand the abuse, the pressure. He would focus on what was important, which was scamming, and try his best not to be driven off the edge.

Louis arrived at a firm called TYM Securities in Lower Manhattan in July 1997. He was happy even when Charlie No. 2, John Mergen, forced Louis to get jobs there for him and the other guys from Argent.

In his first week at TYM, Louis made $10,000 and was able to pay back the $5,000 he owed Richie.

He was back. A thief. He felt as if he were reborn. Yes, he could survive, he could make a living. Support his family. He had earned more money than some brokers did during their entire lives, and worked at three or four times as many firms. He had earned, and spent, millions already—he never sat down and counted it, much less accounted it for the IRS.

The days of wild living were over, more or less. His life was now a constant quest for money, interspersed with compulsive gambling, losing, using the few winners to pay for the losers, and scraping together enough cash to keep the bookies and loan sharks and landlord and Charlie off his back. Sometimes he just liked to disappear, to go away, when the pressure got to be too much. But he had hope, if not faith, that TYM would make him healthy.

The New York office of TYM Securities was at 2 Rector Street, way downtown. Familiar streets, familiar bars, familiar restaurants. Familiar people. Dave Lavender, one of his cold-callers from the old days (a year before), had told him about TYM and about the Guy who made it all possible, whose name was Ralph Torrelli.

As soon as he met Ralph, Louis knew that he was going to like him.

Ralph Daniel Torrelli was thirty-seven when Louis met him. Big and heavy. Very heavy. Tremendi. He was over six feet tall and weighed in excess of three hundred pounds. But he was soft-spoken. Reasonable. He was the kind of guy Joe Bonanno might have had in mind when he talked about "men of honor." Ralph kept his word. He didn't scream like the other Guys. He kept his voice low because his credentials preceded him and hollered on his behalf.

Ralph Torrelli was a sweet-dispositioned ex-drug dealer.

In 1989, Ralph was convicted of federal narcotics charges in the bucolic but drug-infested Gulf Coast of Florida. Ralph's arrest, trial, and conviction received little attention even in Florida. Some drug dealers from the north had come into town and gotten arrested. Not big news. This was the era of the War on Drugs, and Ralph was a POW.

"Five people were sentenced in Orlando federal court Monday for their involvement in a drug ring that manufactured speed and chemicals used to make cocaine," said the article on the second page of the second section of the *Orlando Sentinel,* March 21, 1989. "U.S. District Judge G. Kendall Sharp sentenced Ralph Torrelli, 29, to 10 years in prison and Glenn Crouse, 32, to six years. Last December, a jury had convicted the two men, both of Levittown, Pa., on drug-conspiracy and distribution charges." Ralph emerged from the federal prison system in April 1995 after serving nearly six years of his sentence.

In bygone eras, a Guy like Torrelli would have been able to find employment after prison on the docks, or in construction, or as a strikebreaker, or in the Fulton Fish Market. But in the 1990s an ex-con with the right connections had his best chances for getting his act together on Wall Street. Torrelli, sobered by his lengthy incarceration, moved from manufacture and distribution of controlled substances to manufacture and distribution of equity in companies.

Chop stocks were the crack cocaine of the New Economy, far less risky and almost as profitable, and there was no War on Stock Fraud when Torrelli set up shop at a brokerage firm called Amerivet. He organized a consulting firm called Effson, whose offices were in the same Rector Street building as Amerivet. He was now a full-fledged stock promoter, one of the investment bankers of the chop house world. Like Real Wall Street investment bankers, chop house stock promoters are middlemen between companies and brokerages. Stock promoters raise money for small companies by introducing them to brokerages, and get product for chop houses (and legit brokerages too) by introducing them to companies.

By the time Louis arrived, the Amerivet Rector Street branch office had a new sign on the door. It was now the TYM Securities Rector Street branch office.

Louis didn't know how Torrelli got into the chop stock business. But it made perfect sense. It was a thing that was being done at the time by Guys from all of the six families in the New York metro area and, now, Philadelphia. Louis was lucky to be hooked up with a Guy who was comparatively quiet, nonviolent, and reasonable, a degree of emotional intelligence not common in that walk of life.

"At TYM things started to get back to normal. Ralph got the OSJ [branch office] for TYM. He had a little office there. Computer, printer. Nice office. Ralph was in Pennsylvania his whole life, except for the time he was in jail. It seemed to me that what he was doing here was trying to get his life together. He had a family. Four kids. Ralph was low-key. He never gets in trouble. He's fucking hidden."

Ralph put the stock deals together, and was responsible for paying the brokers. He got the cash from a slick, well-dressed Russian named Alex, known as "Alex Versace" because of his taste in designer wear and good selection of wristwatches, which Louis estimated to be in the $70,000 range.

"After a while Alex started to talk about the money so I found out the money from the clients was wired to Israel, and then this Hassidic guy would come and then bring us the cash. One time I wanted to find out, so I followed Alex downstairs one payday. I left the office right after him, and I watched him get into this green van with a Hassidic Jew. I was curious where the kid got the money, because he'd come up with two, three hundred thousand in cash. It's not that easy. Even for a bank it's hard. You'd have to give a bank three, four days' notice. We would pay six percent off our money to get it in cash. That's the way it was. Well worth it."

Alex was what is popularly referred to as a "money launderer." A few years later, when terrorists destroyed the World Trade Center, a lot of attention would be focused on the kind of money laundering that sneaks cash into the U.S. from abroad. But for years, more complicated forms of money laundering were essential to the chop houses. The mechanics were complex but the aim was simple—to turn the proceeds from stock scams into untraceable cash. Ironically, considering the later association of money laundering with Islamic militants, the money laundering networks that benefited the chop house kids and their Guys were mainly operated by Russian Jewish immigrants and Israelis. Ralph had somehow developed good connections in that world.

Times were good with Ralph. Louis couldn't believe it. Unless he was missing something, which was possible, he had finally run into one of those characters he had only seen in the movies—a sympathetic, nice, not completely out-for-himself Guy. Ralph directly paid Charlie the money due from Louis, and even lied about the money Louis was getting, to cut into Charlie's share. "He was on my side," said Louis. And that was getting to be a rare thing, with Benny gone and Stefanie not around that much anymore.

Louis finally caught up with the Internet stock mania at TYM. By now, dot.coms, IPOs in particular, were generating crazy returns despite thin or nonexistent profits—kind of a chop stock pitch come true. TYM was pushing stock in a company called Internet Holdings. Great name. Great symbol—HTTP—the acronym for the hypertext protocol used on the World Wide Web. All it needed was a story Louis could sell. Not a business. A story.

HTTP had to get its story out to the public, and that was Ralph's job too. Like any promoter or investor relations professional involved in bringing stocks to the attention of investors, Ralph developed and distributed promotional materials that often were sent out to brokerage firms and to the financial press. After all, a favorable mention in the financial press can really light a fire under a stock.

In the summer of 1997, a white cardboard folder—somewhat cheaply labeled "Due Diligence Package"—came to *Business Week* from Internet Holdings Incorporated. Dozens if not hundreds of similar stock promotional materials come to *Business Week* each year. Inside the cardboard folder were promotional materials about the company. The material was undated but was apparently being circulated to the press in August 1997, at about the time Louis, Mergen, and the Argent brokers joined Ralph Torrelli at TYM. Included in the packet was a letter from a securities lawyer to Elton Johnson, president of Amerivet Securities Incorporated, listing the states where HTTP could be sold. There was also a handwrit-

ten note to Johnson. It was apparently included in this particular packet by accident. This is what it said:

Effson Consulting Inc.
2 Rector Street
10th Floor
New York, N.Y. 10006

Dear Elton,

Just wanted to send you this package for your review.
Please look it over. Call me.

Best regards,

Ralph

Unfortunately for HTTP, the packets weren't working too
well. The company wasn't getting any publicity, which probably
was because of the contents of that cardboard folder. An SEC filing in the company's due dilly package said it "presently has no
operations" and "does not currently maintain offices." The filing did have one bit of good news: "The company believes its
employee relations are good." There was one employee.

No offices, no operations. Not much of a company, but a
great stock! A terrific story! Louis sold $1 million of it to one
of his Whales.

"Name was Henry O'Keefe. I was practically guaranteeing
the stock to him. I told him it was an Internet company that
had a patent. Something that the phones needed, and that
every phone company in the United States would have to buy
over the next six months, or otherwise they wouldn't be able
to use their phones. Some shit like that. They had a monopoly
on this device and because they're changing all the lines from
analog to digital in the United States, 'if they don't buy this

device, they won't be able to become digital. You won't be able to use your phone. They got a monopoly!' Actually they had something to do with digital but they didn't have a 'monopoly.' They didn't even have the 'poly' in monopoly."

Somehow or other, Henry O'Keefe found out that HTTP wasn't all it was cracked up to be. Customers were getting smart—maybe it was all the press. They knew what to do when they got ripped off by a broker.

"One day I go out to my car and this guy shows up. Name is Steve. He says, 'I'm here for Henry O'Keefe.' I went, 'Who is that?' He says, 'You know damn well who that is, kid. You ripped him off for close to a million dollars.' He says he's Henry's 'friend,' and he's there to get the money. But this guy's a real broken-down valise. He's in his mid-forties, with an unbuttoned shirt, really cheap silky unbuttoned shirt with bad-material dress pants and these ugly beige Capezios. So I put him in touch with Charlie."

For Charlie, a complaining customer with "Guy connections" meant only one thing: payday. "Charlie goes, 'I got to get back to them. They want to meet.' He says, 'What do you think? Sooner or later somebody wasn't going to come over to you? You think you're going to get away with robbing people your whole life?' I say, 'Charlie, this is what I do for a living. I rob clients.'" Apparently the thought had never occurred to Charlie.

It sounded fishy to Louis. He suspected that this Steve was sent by somebody other than Henry O'Keefe, though he never bothered contacting O'Keefe to find out if that was true.

Steve eventually went away. But unbeknownst to Louis, there were other burned HTTP customers. And they were complaining. A client of one of Mergen's brokers complained to the regulators. Instead of being ignored, which was the routine in the past, she got a visit from two FBI agents. One was True Brown, head of the FBI's stock-scam hunters. The other was an agent named John Brosnan.

CHAPTER FORTY-TWO

Early in the morning of December 27, 1997—the lucky two-sevens were at work again—Stefanie Donohue Pasciuto gave birth to Anthony Pasciuto. He had Stefanie's cherubic face and Louis's strong will. Louis had mixed feelings about being a father. The timing wasn't too great. But he got into the whole expectant-father thing, which made the in-laws and parents happy. He participated in Lamaze classes. He was supportive, the way expectant fathers are supposed to be nowadays. After Anthony was born, Stefanie saw Louis actually cry one time. It is an emotional thing having a kid. More than just having another mouth, or Guy, to feed.

Now that he was a father, Louis tried harder than ever to hold a steady job. TYM could be a steady job. Stefanie had moved back in with Louis late in her pregnancy. Louis promised that things had changed. *He* had changed. He would change his ways. Stop gambling. Pay off his debts.

But it was hard, so hard. His favorite song was "Free Bird" by Lynyrd Skynrd: *"For I'm as free as a bird now, and this bird you cannot change."*

Louis was going to try to change. But he had to admit to himself that he couldn't. He gambled compulsively. He couldn't stop. He couldn't change, and he faced three years in prison for the check scam. He was keeping his mouth shut about Charlie, he had stopped trying to jump ship, and still Charlie was acting as if he were a pariah, a traitor, a rat. Charlie didn't help when John Mergen started to torture him again. Louis saw Mergen every day at TYM. Even though Louis had paid off the debt he owed Richie months before, Mergen was still trying to squeeze him for money.

The Mergen situation was straining his relationship with Charlie. It was a violation of the implied contract between Louis and Charlie: Louis paid; Charlie helped. Louis was still paying when he could, or more precisely when he couldn't get away with *not* paying. And Charlie was balking.

A typical early 1998 conversation on the subject:

"I want to go to Brooklyn to talk to you. I need help with Mergen," he told Charlie.

"No!"

"Every time you wanted me to come to Brooklyn for you to talk to me, I come. I want to come to Brooklyn to talk to you."

"I don't want to talk to you. What's it about?"

"I just said—John Mergen."

"Fuck that fucking Turkish pigheaded fuck. Tell him I'll smack him."

"If I tell him you're going to smack him he's going to kill me right on the spot. You just got to come here and smack him."

"Fuck him. I ain't fucking going nowhere. Tell him if he lays a hand on you he'll have to deal with me."

"That ain't good enough."

Charlie just didn't understand. Or he understood and he didn't give a shit.

Charlie might have forgiven Louis for the fence-jumping if he was generating cash. But he wasn't. By the spring of 1998 they were barely on speaking terms because the TYM branch office shut down. So much for stability. Louis moved to firm number thirteen, Barron Chase. The offices were getting crummier and crummier. He was on Maiden Lane now, a cruddy building on a grimy little side street a few blocks north of Wall Street. A kid named Lance Marino, who was related to a Guy in the Colombo family named Craig Marino, was running the place, along with Alex Versace and a few other Russians. It sucked. Louis didn't get along with one of the Russians, and Mergen and his crew followed him there too and made his life miserable. It seemed as if Mergen was going to follow him everywhere, forever. And not as his pal. As his boss.

"Now I go to Barron Chase and this kid Mergen thinks I'm going to work for him," said Louis. "I'm like, 'Get the fuck out of here.'" But Mergen persisted. Since Louis didn't tell Charlie he was making money, he couldn't go to him for help. "I couldn't say to him I made fifty grand and Mergen wants a piece of it," said Louis. "I was in a bad situation."

Louis had a plan to open his own branch office. If Lance Marino could do it, why not him? So he called Shannon Johnson, who happened to know of a firm that had a branch office available. "Shannon knew so many people, he could get me a branch office right away," said Louis. He flew Shannon up to New York and discussed it with him. But it didn't pan out.*

Nothing was panning out. Everything was turning to shit.

The Cunningham IPO was Louis's downfall. Not directly. One thing led to another, as it always did, and the other thing the first thing led to was always worse.

Cunningham was a printing company where Nick Pasciuto worked—Cunningham Graphics International. It went public toward the end of April 1998. A legit IPO for a legit company, and Nick Pasciuto wanted to invest in it. Louis didn't have any money to loan, so he put his father in touch with a

---

*Shannon Johnson was never implicated in any wrongdoing in connection with these events or the other work that he did for Louis and his friends.

broker and pal named Armando. Nick Pasciuto borrowed $40,000 from Armando and bought some shares in the IPO. A good investment. He wound up making about $20,000. But then something went wrong. Naturally.

Mergen found out that Nick owed Armando $40,000. So he wanted Louis to get that money from Nick—and give it to Mergen. Louis would just have to gain access to Nick's checking account. It would be simple. Louis knew what to do with checks. He had done that before. He had stolen from his father before too. It would be as easy as stealing rolls of quarters from the bedroom closet. Easier, maybe. "'We'll split it and beat Armando,' Mergen said. I said, 'No.' Then he starts threatening me, trying to force me to beat my friend."

Charlie decided to help this time. He called Mergen.

"Now John Mergen says, 'I don't give a fuck if Charlie calls me.' I call Charlie. He says, 'Tell him I don't give a fuck either,'" said Louis.

That was true enough. Charlie didn't give a shit. Louis was on his own. Mergen summoned him for a meeting in Staten Island. They went for a walk on the beach. "He grabs me and whispers in my ear, 'Go rob Armando by tomorrow morning, or I'll come to your house. You'll be dead.' I say, 'Okay, I'll rob him.' He says, 'Tomorrow morning, I want the money.' All right."

Louis knew what he had to do.

The next morning he drove to the Hudson County courthouse in Jersey City and asked a startled Judge Camille Kenny to revoke his bail on the check-stealing charge. He went to jail.

It was May 27, 1998. The lucky two-sevens were at work again.

CHAPTER FORTY-THREE

Louis's new home, the Hudson County Correctional Center, was a concrete-block structure about halfway between New York and Newark. Years later, after the September 11 attacks, it would gain some limited notoriety as a holding pen for illegal immigrants from the Middle East. But when Louis resided there it was steeped in obscurity. Even the gas station attendant down the street had trouble locating it for a visitor. From the outside it vaguely resembled a shopping mall, with a vaulted entranceway and exposed steel. But inside, from the inmate point of view, it had few if any virtues, except for a kind of heavy-handed, chemically induced germicidal miasma. Chlorine made it smell like a cross between a high school swimming pool and a public beach restroom.

When he arrived at the end of May 1998, Louis surveyed his surroundings with a kind of bleak indifference.

He could not leave. That was okay. Louis didn't want to leave. Most of the inmates were very upset about being there, which they demonstrated in various ways, but Louis was different. He was a volunteer.

Mike Basile was there. It was great having a friend in prison. Well, Mike Basile wasn't a friend, exactly, and if Louis had contemplated the subject much he might even blame

Mike for the whole check fiasco. But Mike was facing even more time at HCCC than Louis. He had just begun serving a five-year prison term for his role in the check nightmare. Mike had been to prison before. He read a lot. One nice thing about prison, if you like to read, is that you can catch up on your reading. Louis didn't like to read.

Mike and Louis—and a young car thief named Nick—were pretty much the only Italians, and the only white people, in all of HCCC. Or at least the only ones visible—and they were very visible—in C500 (Block C, Tier 500).

There was no "Mafia Row." There were no special privileges for these guys, no bribed guards, no steaks sizzling on hot plates. Unlike federal penitentiaries, which have large numbers of prisoners who had engaged in criminal activity requiring intelligence and finesse, the HCCC was less a place of punishment or "correction" than it was a solid waste facility—a receptacle for Hudson County's garbage, its muggers and burglars and street trash and bad-check-passers. Louis came to realize that he was now at the bottom. This time for real. He was in the can—the trash can.

Still, it was restful not having the beeper go off. Prison was the ultimate escape. He had finally escaped from Wall Street. Escaped to prison.

He thought a bit about the future now. He plotted ways of clearing up his license. Some weeks earlier he got a printout of his record from the NASD, which should have included any criminal charges, and the check arrest wasn't on it. But he figured it would show up there eventually.* He thought about getting a legit Wall Street job with a fourth-tier but clean firm like J. W. Charles or a J. B. Oxford, where a college degree wasn't required.

---

*The New Jersey conviction still wasn't on his NASD record—or in his Justice Department file, for that matter—years later. The reason could have been a screwup by Hudson County court personnel. Louis's name was misspelled as "Pascuito" in the court records, and the mistake wasn't caught even after motion papers filed by his lawyer spelled his name correctly.

But Stefanie wanted him to quit the Street. He did not blame her. His way of life was coming to an end. Just a few months before, the first trial of a chop house exec was concluded in New York State Supreme Court in Manhattan, when the mousy-looking controller of a chop house called A. R. Baron was tried for something called "enterprise corruption." That is the New York State equivalent of the federal racketeering laws. John McAndris, a middle-aged, soft-looking accountant, was sentenced to five to fifteen years in a state prison where he'd be lunch and breakfast for the hoods there, if not isolated in protective custody.

The feds were a more imminent threat than the Manhattan DA. In 1997, federal prosecutors began to get indictments of Street-linked Guys, among them the ones behind a cash deal Louis remembered very fondly—HealthTech International. He had done some HealthTech a few chop houses ago.

State regulators were showing a lot of moxie too. It was a bandwagon, people were climbing on it—and it was barreling down on Louis and the chop house kids.

All these things were hurting business and making it hard to make money, but Louis never expected that any of this stuff would ever adversely affect him personally. Neither the feds nor the regulators had ever charged him or named him in any indictment. And it wasn't as if they hadn't known where to look. The SEC had conducted an investigation of Nationwide after it closed, and he gave off-the-record testimony that pretty much laid out what had happened (except for the Guy involvement). But the SEC never followed up, as far as he could see. And the NASD had done nothing to Louis in his nearly six years on the Street—except give him a license to sell stocks.

Sitting in prison gave him a chance to think about all this stuff. And after about a week, almost magically, he got a visit—from the FBI.

The agents wanted to talk with him, again, about the stock

certificates they had found in his briefcase at the time of his arrest. It was good timing.

He never made a conscious decision to cooperate with the authorities. It was simply the most obvious and natural thing to do. He had hit the lowest point of his life. His misery was real, and so was his guilt. So he didn't blow off the FBI agents this time. He didn't refer them to his lawyer. He didn't give them any bullshit about the certificates belonging to customers.

This time he told them the shares were in his briefcase because he was being paid to sell stock. A cash deal.

"There were three agents. One guy was supposedly a Mafia expert. They start questioning about the certificates. I said to myself, you know what? It's time. I was done. I can just end it all here. I told them—these are my exact words—'You have no idea of my value in helping you with any type of crime on Wall Street.' I basically told them if they want my help I'll give it to them. I kind of hinted I would go back on Wall Street and work there and be like an inside guy," said Louis.

The agents did not seem very interested, but said they would get back to him. Louis went back to his cell at HCCC and resumed his thinking. He waited for the agents to call. He had nothing to do in prison, so he waited, and waited. They never returned. "It was amazing. I could have worked for them for the next five years. Nobody would have had any idea, because I wasn't arrested on stocks, I was arrested on the checks. They were so goddamn dumb," said Louis.*

With his career as an informant going nowhere, Louis started thinking about the next event in his life—his sentencing, which was coming up in a few weeks. The offer of a three-year sentence was still on the table. A good deal, considering the gravity of the offenses—passing a bad check,

---

*Louis never found out why his offer to cooperate was ignored by the FBI's Newark office. When he told John Brosnan, the FBI agent handling his case, "he just laughed," said Louis.

carrying a firearm with a defaced serial number. Louis would have to get used to the idea of spending at least a year in prison, even with the most possible time off for good behavior. It was the best he could do.

Like hell it was. Louis wrote a letter to the judge.

It was a dumb move. Defendants rarely can get anywhere by writing letters begging for mercy, pleading to get cut loose. But that was exactly the letter that Louis wrote. His new lawyer—he had the public defender now that his previous lawyer had quit over nonpayment—would have advised against it. But he didn't ask. He just wrote the letter.

When Louis appeared before Judge Kenny for sentencing on July 24, 1998, his letter was in front of her. Fran was in the courtroom and so was Stefanie. And so was Anthony, seven months old.

"It was a sincere letter. I told her I got involved with the wrong people, that I was sorry, that I wouldn't do it again. She took it to heart. The judge, Judge Kenny, was very sympathetic. The prosecutor could hardly believe it. The judge said, 'I don't believe he deserves state prison. He wrote me a beautiful letter, and I trust that he's sincere.' That's what the judge said, 'I trust that he's sincere.' In the courtroom. My mother and Stefanie were in the courtroom, and they couldn't believe what they saw.

"The judge said, 'Do you have anything to say before I pronounce sentence?' And I got choked up and I cried a little bit, because my son was in the courtroom. I was really upset. I wasn't going to see him. I hadn't seen him for two months now. I wasn't going to see him for his first birthday. I got choked up, and she actually told me, 'Please.' Like she got choked up, this woman. My mother said, 'I can't believe you had that effect on this lady.' She let me go. She let me out of jail. She did not want to send me to state prison.

"But I meant what I said. When I went home I wanted to do the right thing."

In imposing a sentence of three years probation, Judge Camille M. Kenny recorded the following four "Mitigating Factors" in his case file:

1. The defendant has no history of prior delinquency or criminal activity and has led a law-abiding life for a substantial period of time before the commission of the present offense.
2. The defendant's conduct was the result of circumstances unlikely to recur.
3. The character and attitude of the defendant indicate that he/she is unlikely to commit another offense.
4. The defendant is particularly likely to respond affirmatively to probationary treatment.

Louis was released.

"I wanted Louis to get a good job," said Stefanie. "I told him, 'You need a job where you get paid every week.' I told him we need money, and we need to know it's coming every week, so we know how much money we have to spend. We have to know how much rent we can pay. And we'll budget our money. And if we have to spend every night in the house, eating pasta or whatever, that's what we'll have to do. It's no big deal. Everybody has to start at the bottom, and work their way up. I said, 'So what? You started at the top, come back down to reality and start where everybody else starts. At the bottom. And hopefully in ten years you'll be better off. That's how most people do it."

For eight years Stefanie worked part-time at a Kids "R" Us in a Staten Island shopping mall. She was paid peanuts. But she liked to work. It was something people did. It was how she was brought up. Even when she was spending weekends in Miami, she would drive to the Kids "R" Us in the Beemer. Then she got a job as a brokerage house assistant through an employment agency. By coincidence—small world that Wall Street is—Stefanie was placed at a firm called William Scott, a chop house run by a scary-looking Colombo family associate named Frank Persico. Stefanie quit Scott after a few months.* She later found work as an elementary school teacher in Brooklyn.

Louis was willing to try anything, at least for a while. After coming out of prison, he went to bartender school for a few days. Naah. Got a lead on a job selling cars in New Jersey. Went for an interview. Naah. Then he got a real opportunity. A good job. A job a lot of young people would kill for—an opportunity to learn a trade that had made a lot of enterprising, hardworking guys rich. If he kept at it, it was a job that could mean a comfortable, even luxurious lifestyle.

Louis was becoming a plumber.

---

*Interestingly, Stefanie was never questioned by authorities, even when Scott's principals were indicted in mid-2000.

CHAPTER FORTY-FOUR

An old Pasciuto family friend, Leo, did construction jobs—"roughing the building," putting in the cast-iron pipes. It was hard physical labor, carrying eight-inch pipes. Hard labor but honest, clean. The kind of work the Pasciutos and Surrobbos had done since they came off the boat from Sicily nearly a century earlier. It was the kind of hard work the Donohues had always embraced.

Louis didn't like to work. But Stefanie was pushing him, so he took a job with Leo as an assistant plumber, working off the books.

For a month or so, Louis led a normal life. Most of his neighbors on Staten Island lived that kind of life, and Louis was amazed when he found out how absolutely shitty it was. You get up early, so early that the sun isn't out even in the summer. You ride out to a miserable, filthy, disgusting work site somewhere. Even the worst shithole of a chop house was no comparison to a muddy slime pit of a construction site, even when it was right smack on Park Avenue. Didn't matter where it was. You got a shovel from some slimy, unshaven turd and you had to dig and carry heavy iron pipes. Louis was in great shape but at the end of the day his muscles were aching and he was dead tired.

This is what most people did, and most people did this all their lives.

Louis was different. He was better than that. He proved that to himself when talking to his landlord one weekend. His landlord noticed that Louis was being picked up every morning at an ungodly hour by a guy in a pickup truck, so he asked Louis what he was doing for a living.

Louis didn't hesitate a moment. He instinctively knew what to say. In a millisecond his brain was active and the old Louis was back.

"I said, 'I do renovating. We do kitchens, bathrooms.'

"He said, 'I want to redo my bathroom. Think you can do it?' I said, 'I been doing it nine years.' My whole fucking life I been a plumber. I gave him a price. He said, 'I could get it done for a couple hundred less.' And I said, 'If you want to get it done for a couple hundred dollars less, it's not going to be professional. I'm going to come in there and do a professional job.' I sold the guy."

So Louis became a plumber. He cut out a few steps—such as the several years required to learn the trade—but that was okay because the money was great. He knew how much plumbers could earn from renovation work. That was really the only information he needed.

"I went up there and I didn't know where to start. So I just started ripping tile down. But I did it. Took me like a month, but I did it. Had to gut the bathroom, rip out the toilet and sink. Had to retile the walls, new toilet, new sink, new bathtub. Caulk the shower stall. New tile floor. It came out looking awesome, though. I had to rig things a little. I figure by now the shower door fell off. I knew I didn't put it on right. If he just leaned on the shower door, it's falling down. Because I leaned on it and it fell out. I put in some more glue and figured it would stay at least a month.

"I read instructions! That's how I did it. When I had to put in the sink I couldn't find no instructions, so I went to Home

Depot and asked the guy. He drew me a little diagram. I had no tools. None of the proper tools. Instead of using a monkey wrench for the pipes I'm using pliers. Leo thought it was ridiculous. I told him I was doing a side job, and he said 'Get the fuck outta here.' He said, 'You're gonna get sued.' But he was nice about it. Helped me take a pipe out. One of the pipes was rusted, and I spent hours trying to take it out. Hammering it, trying to hack-saw it off. Nothing worked. Leo came over and took it off in like seven seconds. He took the monkey wrench and went *kwitcccch!* Came off. Felt like an idiot. Me and my friend Glenn were standing on the wrench, trying to turn it. We were probably turning it the wrong way."

Louis might have had quite a career as a plumber. He especially liked the terms, with money paid up-front before the job was started. A guy who cut corners could just line up side jobs and walk off with the up-front money. But Louis figured he might get people a bit too pissed off. He decided to make the landlord job the last one. He kept on going to the work sites every morning.

He was finishing up a job in Manhattan one afternoon when Louis saw him, waiting outside the construction pit.

Charlie.

When Louis got out of jail, Charlie had taken half of the $6,800 Louis had had with him when he was arrested. Then he went away for a while. He stopped beeping. Maybe he had gotten used to Louis being away for a couple of months. But here he was again. He missed him, maybe.

Charlie got right to the point.

Louis was making $300 a week. Charlie wanted $100 of it.

"'You're going to do this to me?' I told him. 'I just came home, and you're going to take what I'm earning every week as a plumber for my wife and kid?'

"He goes, 'It don't matter because you'll have no wife and kid to support. I saved your life. You owe me your life. You don't pay me for your life, I'm going to take it.'"

It was a sucky job anyway. Getting up early. The digging. The hauling pipe. Louis was almost relieved when Leo pulled up the next morning and Louis told him to take a hike. He was going back to sleep.

CHAPTER FORTY-FIVE

Louis faced several problems as he prepared to reenter the Street in August 1998. The felony conviction was a big obstacle, and even if his record was whistle-clean he'd have had a lot of trouble. Closer regulatory scrutiny of deals, and involvement of law enforcement in the fight against securities fraud, were making life miserable for everybody on his side of the law. "By this time IPOs were, like, shit, and the authorities were catching up with the cash deals. You couldn't even get a 504* registered anymore. It was impossible. They changed the regulations. The companies actually had to have money in the bank or their stock couldn't get registered," said Louis. The nerve.

Paper was always a problem. Dumb forms. Dumb filings. Dumb criminal records. Selling stock left a paper trail. Even the cruddiest stocks resulted in SEC filings and trading records, with all the incriminating stuff they often contained, and brokerages piled on their own mountains of processed pulp. Brokers had records that could be searched, and the

---

*That is, an offering of under $1 million in securities under SEC Rule 504. The rule was aimed at helping small companies get their stock on the market, and was often used to bring chop stocks before the investing public.

NASD by the late 1990s was allowing members of the public to access broker records through its website.

Louis hooked up with a firm, First Fidelity, that had found a solution for all that. He was referred by an old friend, Eddie Talmeni. "I called him and said, 'Eddie, what are yas doing, because I'm fucking dying. I'm being a plumber. I can't take this shit no more. I got to go back to Wall Street. What's going on up there?' He was doing First Fidelity. First Fidelity was a straight 'I'll take your money and I'm going to a party' rip," said Louis.

First Fidelity said it sold stocks to its customers, but that was a fib. It didn't really do that. It took its clients' money, and didn't buy the stock for them. A simple idea, and an old one. First Fidelity was a bucket shop—the most ancient scam on Wall Street. Bucket shops didn't produce much paper. No paper, no problem, at least in theory. You can't regulate what you can't see, at least in theory.

First Fidelity was pushing, of course, an Internet stock, Exchange.Online. Louis used the name "Bruce Follick." This was a broker with a clean record. By using Follick's name, he didn't have to worry about anybody finding out about that felony conviction, or somebody suing Lou Pasciuto for what some Follick guy did. Since Exchange.Online didn't trade but was a private placement like Chic-Chick, it had no stock symbol with pesky shares that had to be sold and boxed and cleared. First Fidelity was, itself, a "public company" whose "stock" actually "traded," though its "stock symbol" belonged to another company.

Just about every day was a payday—$1,000 one day, $3,000 the next. It made Charlie happy. It made the bookies happy, and Louis was able to pay down his mountain of debt. He was at First Fidelity through the beginning of 1999, clearing something in the neighborhood of $200,000, which wasn't bad for a few months' work.

Louis barely looked up from the phone during the market

tremors of October 1998, when tech stocks took it on the chin. The market bounced back anyway. It always did. It was a permanent bull market, after all. It would never end.

But the glory days were ending for Chop House Wall Street, as its leading figures were arrested, one by one. In September 1998, a federal grand jury in Brooklyn indicted Jordan Belfort and the other bosses of Stratton Oakmont, the Long Island counterpart of Hanover Sterling. Three months later, another bombshell, also from the Brooklyn feds. On December 17, 1998, the target was a slew of brokers who used to work at Hanover Sterling. By the time the arrests were completed, fifty-five brokers and their Guys were thrown in jail—including Roy Ageloff and Bobby Catoggio. Louis's old pal Randy Ashenfarb was arrested, and so were Rocco Basile and his former boss John Lembo. There were some omissions. Rico Locascio was arrested, but his partner Black Dom was not. Chris Wolf was not named in this indictment. A broker named Brent Longo was arrested, but not his stepfather Alan Longo, the Genovese skipper and Fulton Fish Market Guy whom *Business Week* had identified as a Genovese family connection to Hanover.

Louis was sad and pissed when he read about the arrests. Roy was God, the reason why he and the rest of the chop house kids were making money. Roy had created the pitching style, and his management techniques were emulated everywhere there was a rip. Rocco was another role model, a salesman to copy and cherish. All the guys at Hanover taught him everything he knew about selling stocks, and managing kids, and spending the money that came from it all. And they were starting to go to jail.

When the FBI came up to First Fidelity, Louis was calm. Everyone else was panicking. Not Louis. He realized there wasn't a damn thing he or anybody else could do about it. More shit luck. Shortly before Christmas 1998, New York police raided the 5 Hanover Square office of First Fidelity. Somebody had smelled the odor of burning crack. The FBI took over the case and eventually followed a paper (or powder) trail to the office at 110 Wall.

When the FBI agents came to 110 Wall, Louis was at his Play Station, enjoying a video game with Eddie Talmeni. Two of the four agents entered his office and politely interrupted the game.

"Hi, how are you doing? FBI."

"How you doing, guys?"

"What are you doing here?"

"I just use this office."

"Who you work for?"

"Myself."

"What do you do?"

"Consulting."

"What kind of consulting?"

Louis had to think a moment before answering, "Securities consulting."

"Interesting. What's your name?"

"Robert Gro."

"Have you got ID?"

"No, left my wallet at home."

The FBI guy made Louis print his name and sign it. He wasn't sure how to spell his name, as he had just made it up. G-R-O-W?

"I didn't know how to spell it. I think I spelled it G-R-O," said Louis. "Eddie put down some Spanish name. Nobody had ID. Nothing they could do. I cleared out that afternoon."

Louis had to figure out some way to get cash. He looked to his family. He had helped them when times were great. Now times were not so great.

STEFANIE: "One time I was changing the baby and I remember taking off my ring. And my ring—my engagement ring—disappeared. Louis says, 'You probably flung it some-where,' but I didn't fling it. I ripped the whole house apart. I went through dirty diapers. Every single diaper, because I thought maybe it fell into the diapers, and I had a pail of dirty diapers. I remember going to meet my mother for lunch one day with the baby, and my mother noticed that it wasn't on. My father said something to my mother, 'Why isn't she wear-ing her engagement ring?' and I said I can't find it. So he says, 'If you want, I'll come down and help you.' But I think they knew what was going on.

"Louis swore up and down he didn't take it, he didn't take it. It took a long time for him to say it. I knew he took it, whether he wanted to admit it or not. There was no way I lost the ring. I put it down to change the diaper because I had to put cream on my hands, to put cream on the baby or what-ever. There was no way. I didn't lose it. I didn't miss it till the next day. It was a year before he fessed up. I never got it back. He hocked it. I got past it without him admitting it, but my biggest thing was, 'If you needed it, you could have told me. And if that's the case, at least you could have given some money to the house.' That was my biggest thing. 'If you had asked me, I would have given it to you. It's only a ring. You don't have to steal.'"

NICK PASCIUTO: "I shouldn't have helped him after the first ten grand I gave him. But you're a father, you have a son, you believe in him and you trust him. Meanwhile, he had a wife. I mean, I love her. She's the mother of my grandson. She's my daughter-in-law. Partly because of her I had my grandson. I love him as any grandfather would love a grandson. There was a lot of shit and it wasn't her fault. He cheated on her, he gambled. It was wrong in my eyes. It wasn't right what he was doing. Let's put it that way. It hurt me. It's not good.

"My son's never going to lie to me. My son's never going to hurt me in any way. This is his word. His promise to go by. At the time I was wrong. He became a mad, degenerate gambler. With the money he made, he'd be well off, way well off. He got a good piece of the action. But he'd get $20,000 and he'd bet on the Mets to win. Who does that in their right mind?

"He'd get in a jam, and we'd help him. That's what I felt. You think you're doing the right thing and taking care. 'If I don't get this ten thousand dollars on Tuesday, I'm getting killed on Thursday.' What are you going to do? I'll get the ten thousand for you, Lou. Is it over now, Louis? Is it the end of this? He'd say, 'After I get this cleared up,' but he's still gambling. How's he going to get it cleared up?

"He took us for a beating. Not that he, at the time, robbed us. I was giving it to him. Taking care of it. The credit cards that we had, I don't know what the credit rating was, but we had AAA credit. And it just went down the tubes, because it was all overextended. We couldn't pay anymore.

"When he moved to Battery Park City, I signed the lease because my credit was impeccable. I had an American Express Platinum Card. I was making fifty thousand a year. It wasn't based on my income. It was based on my twenty-five years, my credit history. If you applied for it, you needed to make a lot more than that. So I signed things, and that was that. He wasn't paying. My name. Kill it. And they did. They killed it. Bigtime.

"When I claimed bankruptcy I think I had five hundred thousand dollars in debts. Three hundred thousand was because of him. With the boat and Mercedes. The Mercedes, I signed for that, they repossessed that, and I'm battling with my lawyer. I want to make sure there's no lien on my house. They took the car back, but they're still suing me for eighty thousand. I don't understand that part. You got the car. They're saying it's because the car was worth X amount, one hundred thousand dollars. They sold it for, whatever, forty thousand. And you owe sixty thousand plus penalties and interest and all the bullshit lawyer fees, garbage. They piled everything on. They got the car. They repossessed it. You didn't sell it for what you want, you shouldn't have sold it. That's the way I look at it.

"You have no idea. It's, like, insane. It's my fault too because I kept on doing it, like a jerk, I kept on doing it, doing it, doing it. But still, you got to smarten up. You figure, like, the word of your son. The promise of your son. If you can't believe that, what can you believe?"

GEORGE DONOHUE: "After I bailed him out for the check arrest, I just washed my hands of the whole situation. Him and I were finished. That's it. It's like a disease. Like a drug addict. You can't believe anything they say. You got to hide everything. Because you're just so afraid that they're going to do anything. Forget it. You can't leave the keys to the car. It's a terrible feeling. Not being able to trust somebody at all. I just turned my back. That's it, buddy.

"I knew Louis's personality, so I knew he was scared to death. No matter how you look at it, he was a Staten Island kid who went to a Catholic school. He might have been a little punk guy in his own way, but he wasn't a hard-core. He was in the big times—and he was lost."

CHAPTER FORTY-SIX

Every number on a pager can mean something, if you want to be creative. Lovers sometimes signal each other with 214—February 14. Valentine's Day.

Charlie would begin by entering his phone number on Louis's pager. By the late fall of 1998, Louis was not responding to that. So after paging with his number and getting no response, Charlie would enter his number and then 123123. That meant "hurry up."

By early 1999, 123123 wasn't working, so Charlie would tap in 123911. Hurry up. Now. Emergency.

When that stopped working, Charlie started using 911911911911. Then 666911. Die. 666. The devil.

"By the time I called him back, I knew he would be foaming out of his mouth. I'd call, the phone wouldn't ring even once. It would go, 'ring—' He'd pick up and go, 'You cocksuckerrrrrr!' I'd go, 'What the hell's the matter with you? I had to get to a pay phone.' Meanwhile I'd be like smiling and laughing.

"'You fucking laughing at me! I paged you forty fucking times!'

"'All you have to do is beep me once. It comes into my beeper. As soon as I get to a pay phone, I'll call you back.'

"'All the money you fucking rob, you can't buy a cell phone, you cocksuckerrrr!'"

Louis had a cell phone, but wouldn't give him the number.

It was a ritual now. The beeper. The screaming. The passive-aggressive defiance. It wouldn't take a legion of psychologists to conclude that maybe Charlie wasn't being very effective, that he wasn't getting anywhere, that his harassment was feeding into a kind of deeply rooted rebellious streak in Louis, developed in childhood and honed in parochial school.

But Charlie had one advantage over the priests at Sea. He had Louis convinced that he could never quit.

So the rituals became a mutually chanted mantra as their relationship disintegrated, following Louis's departure from First Fidelity and its promise of a steady income. Charlie would scream and Louis would bait. Charlie would threaten and Louis would reason. Charlie would page and Louis would not respond. It was more than just defiance—it was good sense. The less he had to do with Charlie, the less money he had to pay.

Louis didn't read the papers anymore. His friends and mentors were getting indicted while legit guys his age were getting rich by day-trading and starting up dot.coms. He wanted to go over to these nerds, bending over their fucking computers, and bash their heads in. Here he was, caught in a time warp with a brown-tanned ex-con tapping psycho messages into his pager.

As the countdown to the millennium reached 365 days, Louis was back with Ralph Torrelli, briefly. Louis had a new crew of cold-callers, mainly kids who'd been with him from TYM. They were friends, or friends of friends. Good salesmen. But they might just as well have been selling condoms to convents if they couldn't lie. You had to lie if you were going to sell an oil company, Anglo Gulf Oil, when oil was passé and dot.coms were hot. This was 1999, not 1979.

It was no use. Ralph was adamant. "I wanted to do it like 'anglogulf.com.' I said, 'Let's make it a real estate investment trust for oil wells.' It was a good idea. I said I could raise money on that. But he didn't want me to do it that way. He wanted me to do it legit. So I said, 'I can't do it, Ralph,'" Louis said.

Louis and Ralph parted ways. It was sad. What made it even sadder was that Charlie wanted Louis to work for him. Charlie said he had control of the New York branch office of a firm called Aaron Capital, through his pal "Stevie Two Guns" Mignano. "He says, 'Stevie works for me. I got control over this firm,'" said Louis. "He said this to me on the phone. Charlie would talk on the phone. I would say I didn't want to talk on the phone, and he would get annoyed. I guess he figured no one was listening."

Aaron was a fiasco from the start. Charlie arranged a meeting at Zio's in Bay Ridge. The guy who was supposed to be running the office, a Russian kid named Mike, obviously owed Stevie a lot of money. It was obvious because as Louis walked into the restaurant, Stevie and Charlie were roughing up Mike. The meeting went downhill from there—downhill into the sewer. Louis was supposed to be in charge, but Charlie wouldn't let Mike give him any information that he needed to run scams. "I wanted to know if he could run trades without money in the account. And right away when I said 'money in the account,' Charlie said, 'What money in the account? Who has money in the account? You have money in the account at the firm?'"

Even before Louis settled into his new shithole of an office at 30th Street and Madison Avenue, he realized he had to get out. He started up his own firm. It would be another First Fidelity, only better, because Louis was going to run it.

A good structure was essential. The firm would have to have a bank account, it would have to make believe it was a brokerage, and it would have to not be registered with any governmental or regulatory entity in the world. Louis had learned at First Fidelity about the power of a good name, so a properly conceived company was another must. United Capital Consulting Corporation had a good ring to it, and it sounded vaguely familiar, which was good. A legit firm with that name used to exist. The bank account would be at Dime Savings Bank. Louis didn't trust banks, but he needed a bank account so customers had a place to wire money.

Louis started working on United Capital during his few weeks at Charlie's branch office—yet another common feature of the entrepreneurs Louis was hearing about. They worked for themselves. Louis needed his own firm, and he didn't want Charlie to have anything to do with it. Charlie would have to fend for himself from now on.

While he was still at Aaron, Louis started putting his clients—clients who were supposed to be buying Aaron's house stock, Matco—into United Capital's "stocks."

Louis didn't tell anybody. But Charlie found out. Instantaneously. For others, it took a lot longer. Such as, for example, a man by the name of Dennis Gordon who lived out in Texas and was president of Aaron Capital.

Years later, Gordon didn't remember anyone named Charlie or Stevie or Louis. But he remembered meeting some guys, tough-looking guys. They wanted to open an office of his firm. He said no. That was, he thought, the end of it.

According to Gordon, there was a break-in at Aaron's New York office not long after that. Someone stole business cards. Account information. And then—complaints. Stock was sold that was never delivered. Stock in the Goldman Sachs IPO, with money to be sent to an account at Dime Savings Bank.

"They stole the business cards from our brokers and the customer account information, and took it to their office downstairs, calling our clients, representing themselves as a broker of our firm," said Gordon. "The clients already had a trust in the broker, so when this fake broker told the customer to wire money to Dime Savings, on behalf of some other company, some consulting firm, they did. So we called the FBI, SEC, NASD, and washed our hands of it."*

By mid-1999, Stefanie and Charlie had remarkably similar complaints. They both thought that Louis was uncommunicative, dishonest, and disloyal. They suspected betrayal. In Charlie's case, the suspicion was confirmed. The Luciano fence-jumping incident still burned him.

For Charlie, divorce was never an option. He was going to make their marriage work. But Stefanie had had enough.

After hearing from a friend that Louis was seen cheating on her, and then seeing his car parked for what appeared to be a tryst, Stefanie walked out on him. His denials meant nothing. His credibility was not too great at this point. One day, while Louis was at work, Stefanie and her family hauled away everything, even the furniture. Louis came home that night to find the apartment empty except for a mattress on the floor.

Now his personal life was as fucked up as his life on the Street.

In June 1999, as Louis finished drafting the United Capital private placement documents, the feds launched another assault on Louis's friends and their Guys. This time he was really shaken up. His old pal and mentor, the strung-out Hanover-Greenway superbroker Chris Wolf, was indicted by a federal grand jury in Brooklyn on multiple counts of securities fraud and money laundering. Named in the indictment were Chris Wolf's two Guy patron-tormenters—Black Dom Dionisio and Enrico Locascio. So were twenty others, nailed by the same tenacious Brooklyn prosecutors who had gone

---

*The criminal charges later brought against Louis, however, say that Louis was "working at" Aaron Capital and sold Aaron's house stock, Matco. Louis, who was not involved in setting up the office, says it is possible that it wasn't an officially sanctioned Aaron office. Aaron itself was not able to shed any more light on the subject. Gordon was no longer an official of Aaron, and the firm's NASD-listed phone number was disconnected.

after Roy and Bobby and, previously, Jordan Belfort of Stratton Oakmont. One of the chop houses named in the indictment was Amerivet, Ralph Torrelli's firm before TYM. Torrelli was not indicted.

At about the same time as the Wolf-Dionisio bust, Phil Abramo and a bunch of his confederates were taken down in a twenty-one-count Florida indictment. Later Phil was hit by another indictment nailing the entire DeCavalcante family hierarchy. It was perfectly timed—a TV series about New Jersey Guys, *The Sopranos,* had become wildly popular. The feds were competing over which Guy or chop house scalp they could produce on a platter. Since the chop houses had offices and trade-processing facilities around the country, jurisdiction was nebulous. It was chaotic stuff—if this was the Mob, there definitely would have been sitdowns.

By mid-1999, the Eastern District of New York, under soft-spoken but aggressive U.S. Attorney Zachary W. Carter, had racked up the most indictments. But Wall Street was in the Southern District of New York. So far, U.S. Attorney Mary Jo White had been little heard from. Was the short, cropped-haired White a lame "nothing happens here" wimp like her predecessor Otto Obermaier? Or would she aim for the jugular, the headlines—and, maybe, higher office—as did her other predecessor, Rudy Giuliani? Through most of 1999, that just wasn't clear. There were rumors of major investigations and imminent indictments from the Southern District. Louis heard the rumors. But that's all they were.

What was obvious was that the feds were getting nearer and nearer to Louis and the people around him. But if that dawned on Charlie, it seemed to make him even more violent, even more unreasonable. Louis didn't know what pressure Charlie was getting from the Guys above him, but it must have been every bit as brutal as the pressure Louis was getting from Charlie.

Things were simple now. Illusions were out the window.

Louis was taking money from his customers in return for nothing, and Charlie was no longer making believe that he was doing anything for Louis in return for his money. He was collecting a debt that Louis owed him—Louis's existence on the planet—and Louis was going to be paying for the rest of his life.

"After Aaron I didn't care no more," said Louis. "I was getting wise with him. I used to just totally irritate him. I used to know exactly how to tick him off. He'd say, 'I'm coming to your house.' I'd know if I said, 'No, Charlie don't come!'— he'd back off. But I didn't say that no more.

"I'd say, 'You come here, it's not going to get me to Brooklyn any faster. In fact, it would be better off if you came here. If you come here I don't have the money, and if you come to Brooklyn I don't have the money, and I'm not leaving my fucking house. So if you want to come here, I'm here.' He'd say, 'You're therrrrre! You're therrrrrrrrrre!' I'd say, 'Right here. I don't know why you're yelling about it.' I'd be a wiseass. I just didn't care no more. I'd hear the phone dropping on the floor. I could see him foaming at the mouth.

"I'd just tease him now. I'd say, 'Charlie, you're getting crazy for no reason. You're really going to make your blood pressure go up, pal. You shouldn't be acting like this. You're a grown man.' That's what I used to say to him."

It was a game of chicken. They were both rushing to the edge of the cliff. One of them was going to have to jump.

CHAPTER FORTY-SEVEN

"According to our most recent investor survey we have determined that everyone who possesses the knowledge and the wherewithal would like to take advantage of the many opportunities that are currently available in this industry. We believe this creates a desire for our primary service which is finding top quality companies in targeted industries."

—from the private placement memorandum of United Capital Consulting Corporation, dated July 15, 1999

It went on like that for six pages, single-spaced, describing what United Capital was going to do for its investors. It was so good. There was a little problem in the section describing key executives. Louis had to tell a little white lie and say he "graduated" from the College of Staten Island, and he inflated his position a tad from unregistered cold-caller to "investment banker with Hanover Sterling." Louis figured that nobody would have paid much attention to the indictments of Hanover principles, which were all over the papers. But this much was true: "Following a successful stay at Hanover he went on to build such small cap firms as AT Broad [sic], Nationwide Securities and has successfully placed and participated in 20 successful IPOs." He certainly built those firms, though he did have to take down Brod as well as build it up. But nobody would know about that.

Nicholas Pasciuto, "managing director of international and U.S. manufacturing at Hudson printing for ten years," was down as vice president. Once again, Nick was letting Louis use his name, figuring that this time Louis was getting into business for himself, a legit business, and would finally pull himself up by his bootstraps.

By the summer of 1999, Stefanie was trying to reconcile with Louis—and reconcile the Louis of 1999 with the Louis she'd known years ago, the skinny kid at the gas station. Stefanie was facing reality now—the reality of Louis, and the reality of the world in which he and she were living.

Louis was making promises now. He admitted stuff too. He had problems. They were fixable. He would change. Lynyrd Skynrd—fuck them. *This bird you can change.*

She believed him. She went back to him in time to see him off to Arizona for his meeting with Joe Welch. At last, a legitimate moneymaking opportunity.

The blackjack cracked Louis on the skull. Louis leaped out of the car and ran onto Fingerboard Road, toward the Verrazano-Narrows Bridge. Louis didn't know where he was going. Maybe he would head to the bridge. Maybe he would jump off it.

He owed $5,000 to John and Jeff, the kids who had watched him for a day while Mergen and Richie looted his storage unit. He had started gambling with them. No hard feelings. That is, no hard feelings so long as he paid what he owed. He now owed $5,000. That seemed to be the magic number—$5,000—the threshold that got Guys to haul out their blackjacks. John and Jeff had taken him for a ride in their car, and the blackjack was their way of commencing the discussion.

Blackjacks are venerable methods of nonverbal communication. They are black, leather-covered, flexible devices, typically filled with lead or some other heavy substance. Blackjacks can be easily concealed in a jacket pocket. They were formerly the standard equipment of New York City police detectives and other plainclothes police, but had fallen out of favor over the years, to be replaced by a flexible metal rod called the asp. But blackjacks were still available for purchase on Staten Island and over the Internet, and they still worked well, as evidenced by the tiny droplets of blood Louis was leaving on Fingerboard Road.

It was early October 1999. United Capital had lived up to his expectations, grossing $360,000, of which $100,000 went to Charlie. The remainder, of course, went to the bookies, to satisfy previous indebtedness and finance further wagers. All told, Louis was short $5,000, hence the car ride and the blackjack usage.

"Jeff holds back and John's right behind me. There's people all over the place. People on the bus stop. I see a door open and I run into some lady's house. Some Chinese lady on the corner of Fingerboard and the service road. I was bleeding. I run in, and this Chinese lady is flipping out. I slam the door and lock it. She's yelling, 'Nooooo!' I say, 'Calm down.' I say, 'Somebody just jumped me.' She goes, 'Get out!' She goes to open the door. I say, 'What, are you fucking nuts, lady? They're right outside.' So these kids go into the backyard and try to get into the back door. I had to lock the back door. And this lady is flipping out. 'Get out of my house!' I go, 'Shut the fuck up. Call the cops. Tell them you're getting robbed.'"

The police arrived.

"I try to walk over and talk to them. They go, 'Hands up!' I go, 'Listen, you don't understand.' The cop that was there happened to be a friend of mine I went to high school with.

He went, 'What happened?' I told him I was waiting for the bus, two guys jumped out and beat me up. I went to the hospital. The white of my eye was ripped. I looked like the Elephant Man for a few days."

He had to pay these kids back their $5,000. So when he got the checks in his hands, he had to cash them. It was that simple. He had done it before. He knew how. It would have to go better this time, not that he cared much one way or the other if it didn't.

A stock deal had fallen through, and checks were going back to the customers. One of the checks was for $7,500, and the other was for $25,000. Real money, just like the money he used to get in the paper bags on Tuesdays.

His friend Rich Dacunto knew a friend at a check-cashing place who would cash the checks for them. On October 13, 1999, Louis and Rich went to United Check Cashing in Carteret, New Jersey, cashed the checks, and walked away. No cops this time.

The only problem was that the checks were from a Ralph Torrelli stock deal.

part six

ESCAPE

CHAPTER FORTY-EIGHT

Ralph was annoyed, very, very annoyed, about the checks. And Charlie was furious, even though he took most of Louis's share of the proceeds. Charlie insisted that Louis pay back to Ralph the money he stole from the clients—without deducting what he had paid Charlie. It was a kind of penalty for stealing.

Charlie was taking a minimum of $12,000 a month, no matter what Louis was making. By now that meant Louis was paying up to 80 percent of his monthly income to Charlie. He was almost twenty-six years old. He had a wife and a child. He was a man. And here he was, getting belted around, and giving away most of his money. One day a note appeared in his mailbox.

YOU CAN'T ESCAPE

Charlie denied he sent it. Louis figured it didn't matter. Charlie, Joe Botch, John or Jeff, or somebody else he had pissed off—what difference did it make?

The note raised a good point, though. He had to escape.

He made the decision on the sidewalk in front of Lundy's. That's a restaurant on Sheepshead Bay. It was a cool, clear, crisp day, sunny and windy. You could practically see all the way up to Canarsie Pier.

The seagulls were floating lazily overhead when he saw Charlie approaching. Louis was leaning against the railing, smoking a cigarette, looking out over the small bay, with Manhattan Beach beyond. It was a weekday and the street was clear. The fishing boats were docked, but no one was hawking fresh-caught bluefish in little tubs on the sidewalk. Damn, was it a great day. It had gotten to the point that Louis couldn't enjoy a day like this anymore.

Charlie was supposed to get $7,000. Louis had $6,000.

"Walk this way," Charlie said. He was in a windbreaker and cap. Slumming.

"Do you have the money?"

Louis gave it to him.

"I'll have the rest in a couple of days."

"Tomorrow."

"All right, tomorrow."

Charlie walked away without saying a word.

Louis called out after him.

"You're welcome, Charlie. Don't worry about it."

Charlie didn't react.

"You want some clams? They should be on you. I'll treat you if you want."

He kept walking.

"Thanks. I'll come here anytime you want. Bring you money. No problem. I'll be right here. Sitting right here to-morrow. Take care."

Charlie kept walking.

Louis watched as Charlie walked away, toward Brighton Beach. Soon people came between them and he lost sight of Charlie, with that bouncy walk of his. He watched after him and suddenly his eyes were filled with tears, and he was think-ing thoughts he couldn't control.

"This is the last time I'm giving that motherfucker a

penny," Louis said to himself, over and over again. When he stopped the thought, it came back again, unchanged. He had no second thoughts.

Louis went back to where he parked his car. He didn't have the truck anymore. He had a Toyota Camry. A nice car. Better for traveling with the baby. Solid, dependable, but nothing fancy. Reasonably priced but still expensive—$400 a month. He got into the car and went home.

He never saw Charlie again.

CHAPTER FORTY-NINE

Louis had never written a résumé. That involved planning, which he didn't do. Now, right before him in black and white, there it was. The United States government had drafted it for him, and it was not the kind of curriculum vitae that most employers would embrace.

Count One was Conspiracy to Commit Mail, Wire, and Securities Fraud. Counts Two and Three were Securities Fraud. The entire document was fourteen pages long and signed by Mary Jo White. There were so many firms, so many stocks and scams, that they were broken out in a chart, a spreadsheet of crime, beginning with Hanover and ending with United Capital.

It was not so much a criminal complaint, or even a résumé, as it was the broad outlines of a life.

Louis pleaded guilty to his résumé, and his life, a few days before the end of the millennium. He then went to work. The FBI kept him busy.

Late in 1999 and early in 2000, Louis paid visits to his old friends and acquaintances on the Street. He just materialized out of nowhere. It had to be nowhere, because Louis assumed that Charlie and John and Jeff were looking for him. John certainly was. He rang the doorbell of his parents' house. Louis wasn't home at the time.

If anybody wanted to know what Louis was up to, all he had to do was go to the federal courthouse on Pearl Street. Although the multicount "résumé" indictment was sealed, the one-count criminal complaint that was filed against Louis on the day he was arrested, October 20, was right in the files. A check of the courthouse computer would have found an entry for December 20: "ORDER as to Louis Pasciuto, dismissing." Why were the charges suddenly tossed out?

It's a good bet that no one ever bothered looking there. So much for the vaunted ability of Guys to ferret out secrets.

Louis signed a cooperation agreement in which the government pledged to make its best efforts to put him in the federal Witness Protection Program. But first Louis had a bit of work to do.

January 21, 2000, was a freezing cold day. FBI agents John Brosnan and Kevin Barrows picked him up at noon. They put a tape recorder in his Frye boot—it was a microcassette job but sizable, uncomfortable. They pulled the wire up the leg of his jeans and taped two microphones to his stomach, just above the belt. In his jacket pocket they placed a transmitter that would radio the conversations to the van. Then they drove to Manhattan. The idea would be for Louis to set up shop at a chop house and open accounts for his "customers"—federal agents. He would sell them stocks and get paid by the firm in cash, just as he had so many times before, only this time it would all go down on tape. Then he would go away and the feds would come in, eventually, and bust the firm for the cash deal.

His first stop was a firm in Staten Island. But it was a no-go. He had a friend there who knew him, and he wasn't in. Louis went back in the van and shut the tape off. They drove to another firm.

Louis had been at this firm twice before in the preceding few weeks, but never managed to talk to the right people. He was irritated that the feds had strung out the visits. "I kept on explaining to them that if I go there on a Monday I have to go back on Tuesday," said Louis. "They know I'm not the type of kid to wait a week to go back somewhere. If they tell me they're going to pay me cash, I'm going to do it right away."

When Louis got there, he immediately saw that things weren't right. "This guy Jackie is there. He motions to me from his office—'I want to talk to you.'"

Louis felt the microphones cold on his skin and his stomach juices started churning. "I'm really nervous. I don't know this guy Jackie, so why does he want to talk to me? Nobody's expecting me. What's going on?"

"I go into his office," said Louis, "and he says, 'I know you're a big broker. I know you raise a lot of money. But I made a couple of phone calls and somebody told me not to deal with you. You're shady.'" At that point two large men walked into the office and closed the door.

"You do scandalous shit," Jackie said.

"I thought by shady that he meant I'm a rat," said Louis. "My stomach is in my feet. I'm in the back office of this guy's fucking place! I could be killed. The two guys were monsters. Italians. Bodybuilders. The two guys just stood there and listened. Said nothing. I got defensive. 'What are you telling me? What do you mean, scandalous?'"

Jackie explained that by scandalous he meant "'the way you sell stock.' So he starts to explain I'm a cowboy on the phone. He says, 'You take it to the next level of lying.'"

Louis could relax now. The rest of the conversation was good. Pretty damn good. This firm was offering Louis a 50 percent payout, meaning that he got to keep half the money he was getting from customers.

Money. That was what the man said.

Being a cooperator sucked.

For weeks, Louis had been living in other people's apartments and subsisting on other people's money. It was humili-
ating. Ridiculous. Sure, it was better than jail. But all the
bullshit about witnesses being paid by the feds was a crock. At
least, it was a crock as far as Louis was concerned. Maybe he
just didn't get a good deal. Or maybe he was lucky not to be
in jail.

But none of that mattered now. Here it was. The goddamn
millennium year. Chop houses were supposed to be dead.
They had dropped out of the headlines. But here they were.
Still operating. And here he was, wearing this stupid wire.

Jackie was promising cash. It was all Louis had lived for.
And now he had none.

He felt like going into the bathroom and ripping out the
fucking transmitter, sitting down and making calls. Just a couple. He could say the transmitter malfunctioned, or something. Then he could come back and get the cash.

It would mean going back to the old days, and the old days
weren't over. They would never be over.

Louis thought about it while Jackie talked.

He had heard enough. He could have kept the conversation
going, but it wasn't necessary. Brosnan and Barrows would
have enough. They would be happy. He went out on the
street, turned a corner, turned another corner, and climbed
into the van.

epilogue

Shortly after seven-thirty in the evening of June 14, 2000, Charlie Ricottone was led into Courtroom 5A, 500 Pearl Street, the U.S. District Court for the Southern District of New York. Charlie appeared in court unshaven, jail-ready in a pale gray sweatshirt, scuffed Nikes, and blue jeans. He was tan. His bald spot was undisguised, lest the communal shower result in an embarrassing mascara-like run. He entered the courtroom with difficulty because he was chained hand and foot, as were the other defendants who were led into the courtroom with him. It was a routine procedure, enforced by the burly U.S. marshals who were everywhere.

Earlier in the day, Mary Jo White had proven that she was no do-nothing Otto Obermaier. In a packed press conference that made headlines around the world, White announced the biggest securities bust in recent memory. A total of 120 defendants, Charlie among them, were arrested by FBI agents around the country.

Louis had supplied information for three of the courtroom minuets that Mary Jo White had choreographed that day, and others that were still in rehearsals but would soon have their premieres. In addition to nailing Charlie, Louis had helped the feds build a case against a three-man crew that was running a private placement scam Louis had worked in 1999, involving a Staten Island gym called Future Fitness. Louis also had furnished information leading to the roundup of the First Fidelity crew. All eighteen of them were led into the courtroom, as Charlie was, bound hand and foot. In all, Louis had helped the feds in cases that were brought against 22 of the 120 Guys and brokers who were paraded before the TV cameras on that day.

Louis had never heard of most of them. White's prosecutors had thrown together, in a single press release and press conference, a grab bag of twenty-two largely unrelated cases. Thirteen of the cases had something to do with a Manhattan stock-promotion firm called DMN Capital, run by a Bonanno skipper named Robert Lino. Nine—including the three in which Louis was a cooperating witness—had no connection at all to DMN.

DMN was a fairly typical Guy-run stock promotion firm, and it was similar to, if more sizable than, Ralph Torrelli's Effson Associates. White made it out to be a cross between Merrill Lynch and the Hole-in-the-Wall Gang. It was terrific publicity.

This was war—a war for media attention—and the Eastern District had lost. Compared to the Brooklyn feds' Hanover Sterling and Stratton Oakmont indictments, the Manhattan feds' June 2000 cases were small potatoes. Eastern District U.S. Attorney Zachary Carter, and his successor Loretta E. Lynch, were both fine prosecutors. But they had a lot to learn about the art of the press conference.

Louis had been waiting anxiously for Charlie's arrest, and he was relieved that he was behind bars. Charlie was charged with two counts of loan sharking. Unlike most of the other defendants, Charlie was detained without bail on the grounds that "there is a serious risk that the defendant will endanger the safety of another person or the community." They didn't say who the "other person" was. But Louis's identity was soon made known to defense counsel.

Charlie was arraigned and pleaded not guilty. His case was soon moved to the Brooklyn courthouse, and lawyers swiftly began pressing for his release on bail. Louis was upset, but he was assured by his FBI handlers that Charlie would likely remain behind bars.

In support of their application that Charlie be held without bail, prosecutors had submitted excerpts from intercepted phone conversations showing that Charlie had made threats against people who owed him money. In a letter to Judge I. Leo Glasser dated September 8, 2000, Charlie's lawyer Michael Rosen made a number of observations. To begin with, he noted, the charges against Charlie were lodged in February 2000, but were not unsealed until June. If Charlie was such a threat to society, why was the case kept under seal so long? A fair question. The answer might have been that the feds wanted to give Louis a chance to continue his undercover work—or give Mary Jo White another case to announce at the June 2000 press extravaganza. Or both.

Rosen went on:

> We learn from the bail hearing before Judge Daniels on June 23, that the alleged "victim" is a confessed stock swindler who, with the aid of the FBI, made telephone calls to the defendant on three days in October 1999. He continues to be under the aegis of the FBI and has been safe from the Fall of '99 to the present. . . .
>
> To be sure, the language captured on tape is tough and graphic. Yet, perhaps due to my thirty-five years in this profession, I do not regard the words used as unusual for an alleged "loan shark"—most of whom are admitted to bail. Judge Glasser, I am not downplaying the seriousness of these cases, however, I believe that there are substantial bail conditions that can

be imposed even on someone alleged to be a "loan shark." . . .

Defendant's convictions for robbery were over eighteen years ago. His conviction before Judge Raggi in 1992 occurred because of a stupid struggle when he was intoxicated and resulted in a four-month sentence. I respectfully submit that this conduct speaks more of "interference with" rather than "assault on" a federal officer.

Charles Ricottone is 42 years old and works in his father's window business. He is a diabetic and suffers from carpal tunnel syndrome. . . . Charles Ricottone is not a danger to his community but, instead, is a contributor. He serves as a volunteer in the *New York City School Volunteer Program*, helping children read, as evidenced by the attached documentation.

Attached to the letter were identification cards indicating that Charlie had been a member of the School Volunteer Program at PS 177, Brooklyn, during the 1997–1998 and 1998–1999 school years. Also enclosed was a letter from a neighbor who said that he had known Charlie for fifteen years. He described Charlie as:

. . . a very nice person and good neighbor. He is very helpful and caring, attentive to all his neighbors and especially the children who live on West First Street. He has volunteered to help children to read at the local grammar school. He never was mean to anyone on his block. Always had a helpful hand to anyone who needed it. He has always been kind to my children and myself. Charlie is a very caring person. If I ever needed help with anything he was there. I hope you will consider his bail.

It worked.

With the agreement of Brooklyn prosecutors, on September 21, 2000, the child-loving, diabetic, good neighbor Charlie Ricottone was released on $800,000 bail. He was kept under house arrest except for visits to his lawyer's offices and to work with his father as a window installer. It wasn't clear from the court records whether he was able to continue in the School Volunteer Program.

Charlie was given no list of Guys to avoid. The days of hit teams and Mob wars were over. That was proclaimed repeatedly in the media. The Mob was dead. Massive gang-bang prosecutions, such as Mary Jo White's June 2000 indictment-fest, were credited with destroying the very core of organized crime, forever, everywhere.

Or at least, for the time being on West First Street.

In October 2000, Brooklyn prosecutors brought additional gambling and loan sharking charges against Charlie and fourteen additional defendants, including Stevie Two Guns, Charlie's cohort at Aaron. Louis didn't supply any information to authorities on the gambling charges. There were probably other cooperators. It was a popular thing at the time.

Elsewhere in the Brooklyn courthouse, other Guys were being brought to justice with little fanfare or publicity. On March 2, 2000, Frank Coppa and eighteen other Guys and brokers were indicted for their alleged control of State Capital Markets, where Louis and Benny briefly peddled Chic-Chick.* Rocco Basile was again indicted, as was Joe Temperino. So was supersalesman Al Palagonia, for allegedly working in concert with the State Street brokers. Gene Lombardo, Frank Coppa's craggy henchman, was named as well. In June 2001, L. T. Lawrence principals Larry Principato and Todd Roberti were indicted in Manhattan.**

The takeover of U.S. Securities spawned no indictments,

---

*Neither Frank Junior nor Chic-Chick were implicated in any wrongdoing.
**Larry pleaded guilty. He had not been sentenced as this book went to press. Todd pleaded not guilty and was awaiting trial.

but by mid-2001 Alan Saretsky was serving a prison term on fraud charges unrelated to U.S. Securities.

Then came the guilty pleas—Frank and Rocco and Al and Gene and—just about everybody else. Then a drumroll of sentencings that droned on through the end of 2002. The chop house kids and their Guys were shuffling off to federal detention. Rocco Basile went to prison, and so did Chris Wolf, and so did his tormentors, Dom and Rico. The days of lenient white-collar sentences were over. The days of bullshit SEC sanctions were over. John Moran would have probably been tossed in the clink if he had been prosecuted a decade later. It's a fair guess that Bob Brennan and Meyer Blinder would have faced the blast furnace of the criminal justice system, instead of skipping daintily over useless SEC lawsuits. And maybe, just maybe, the chop house era wouldn't have happened. We'll never know.

Louis was relieved that he would never have to testify against his old mentor Roy Ageloff—and neither would anyone. Roy had copped a plea.

Roy pleaded guilty to one count of racketeering, and he spent months dickering with prosecutors over a suitable deal. The rumor was that he was cooperating. The rumor was false. On August 15, 2001, he appeared for sentencing before Judge Raymond J. Dearie.

Dearie was handing out stiff sentences. Some months earlier, Bobby Catoggio, burdened by a previous conviction, was hit with a twelve-year prison sentence and ordered to pay $80 million in restitution.

Roy must have been nervous. But he didn't seem nervous.

Roy was true to the code. He was Roy to the end. A guy who wanted to be a Guy and was facing his punishment like the Guys of old, like Sonny Franzese. Roy wasn't ratting out the people he worked with, like his counterpart at Stratton Oakmont, Jordan Belfort. Roy was keeping his mouth shut.

It was a slow news day, but this was the Eastern District so reporters weren't summoned and there was no publicity. Even if reporters had gotten a heads-up, Roy's sentencing would not have gotten much attention. The bull market that had spawned the chop houses was a memory now. Memories were short. Hanover and Roy were forgotten, even as one of the techniques perfected by Roy at Hanover was coming back in popularity.

In 2000 and 2001, the financial press was ablaze with news of SEC inquiries into manipulation of Internet IPOs—particularly the "prepackaging" of IPOs, in precisely the way it was done by the chop houses. That is, forcing customers to buy IPO shares after the stock went public, which artificially boosted their prices. (Real Wall Street had its own term for that—"laddering.") News reports indicated that "boiler rooms" had migrated overseas. The era of the chop houses was over, it seemed, but that summer their spirit lived on in the IPO mess.

In that Brooklyn courtroom in August 2001, Roy's concerns were more immediate—keeping his time in prison to a minimum. Half of Judge Dearie's courtroom was filled to overflowing with friends and relatives of the defendant. The other half, sparse like a wedding between families of far different social strata, contained barely a dozen or so prosecutors and federal agents.

Roy was in fine form. He was manicured, confident, his slightly simian head topped with an expensive haircut, his stocky features encased in a tasteful gray suit. In recent years he had been an investor in Hollywood productions, and had even appeared in small acting roles a few times. He knew how to hold an audience. But he was producing this show for one man—and Judge Dearie was a tough crowd.

It would take the sales presentation of a lifetime to get his sentence held to a minimum.

Roy's pitch lasted into the afternoon.

A young cousin testified that Roy was "my second dad."

A doctor testified that lengthy incarceration would impose a hardship on the Ageloff family, even though Roy was divorced.

Roy's lawyer said Roy was such a devoted parent that he would not curse in front of his children.

The head of an AIDS foundation, a recent beneficiary of Roy's largesse, testified that Roy was a "compassionate, caring individual." Roy became so compassionate (after his guilty plea) that he had volunteered to supervise counselors at a camp for kids with AIDS. He was due at the camp that very day.

His ex-wife testified that Roy loved his children, and vice versa. Under cross-examination, she denied questions implying that Roy had sometimes hit her. "I probably hit Roy and in the process got hurt," she said.

Roy stood directly before the judge. Dignified. No hard sell. "I would like to say how sorry I am and how much I regret what took place based upon greed, stupidity in my life," he said.

The judge listened, his face immobile. He was impressed, he said. Moved, he said.

But he wasn't buying what Roy was selling.

Roy certainly loved his children, but there were other kids who weighed more heavily on Dearie's mind:

"This sentence sort of brings to mind all of the young folks—and, granted they got on the bandwagon too and they saw the easy money. But I saw so many young men, many with barely a high school education, who got on that sort of gravy train, full of excitement, full of fast money, whose careers, certainly in the securities field, are ruined, that you had a hand in leading astray.

"I think you have to understand that there are some real victims here. Not only the people who lost the money—they line up by the scores—but you've got to take some responsibility, in my view of it at least, for some of those younger people who were here."

Judge Dearie refused to cut Roy's sentence because of his family obligations and philanthropy. He sentenced Roy to eight years in prison, and to pay $8 million in restitution.

Roy's lawyer pleaded to give Roy a few weeks to say goodbye to his children. Roy apparently expected this request would be granted, because his burly black bodyguard was waiting, hands clamped behind him, right outside the courtroom doors.

Judge Dearie wanted Roy in jail now. "Defendant is remanded," he barked. As his relatives cried, the marshals swiftly cuffed Roy's hands behind his back and led him to a door at the far corner of the courtroom.

Roy's composure wavered. He gave a quick look toward his family as they led him away.

Benny and Marco weren't part of the June 2000 festivities. But Louis knew their day was coming. He was going to see to that. He had no choice. You had to go all the way when you were a cooperator, just as you couldn't be a little bit pregnant.

Throughout 2000, Louis had been giving the FBI, NASD, and SEC information on Nationwide as well as the other firms where he'd worked. It was only a matter of time before the feds acted. On December 12, 2000, the inevitable happened. A five-count indictment by the Manhattan feds. The list of names in the indictment was headed by Benny and Marco, and included his old associate Tommy Deceglie, who had lost the Elmo arbitration, Sonny's guys Howie Zelin and Glenn Benussi, Louis's pals Frank Piscitelli and Dave Lavender, and, sadly as far as Louis was concerned, Charlie's brother Mike Ricottone. Mike had gotten a job as a cold-caller and had made very little money at Nationwide. "They just put him there to get at Charlie," Louis said. The feds fought dirty.

The guilty pleas for the Nationwide crew began in August

2001. Howie, Dave, Tommy, Frank. Kid brother Mike. Marco.

Benny.

When Louis heard about Benny's guilty plea to two securities fraud counts, on August 13, 2001, he felt a pang. Relief that he would not have to face his old friend in court. And that familiar old feeling, the one that he had ignored for so many years.

He could live with it. He had no choice.

On June 4, 2002, Marco was sentenced to fifty-one months in prison by Judge Lewis A. Kaplan. Appearing before the same judge three weeks later, Benny received a forty-nine-month sentence. He was ordered to undergo substance-abuse treatment while in prison.

Louis had no role in Benny's other legal troubles. Benny was arrested again by the feds, in May 2001, for his alleged involvement in a Brooklyn drug ring after he left the Street. Benny pleaded not guilty, and the charges were pending as this book went to press.

Drugs also proved a heavy burden, in every sense of the word, for Robert Luciano, the gold-shop proprietor who was involved in Louis's fence-jumping incident. In 2000 he was nabbed by the feds for importing a tractor-trailer load of marijuana. By then, the gold shop had morphed into an Italian ices stand.

Louis never had to face Charlie in court. On November 29, 2001, Charlie pleaded guilty to reduced charges in the June 2000 case and the subsequent gambling indictment. He was sentenced on April 16, 2002.

Charlie's family and friends were not in the courtroom. John Brosnan, blond and lanky, dressed in a polo shirt and khaki pants, lounged at the prosecution table, impassive, as Michael Rosen put his case before Judge Glasser, who was gaunt and scowling and faintly resembled Martin Landau in the role of Bela Lugosi. Brosnan's blank-faced partner Kevin Barrows, wearing dark-rimmed glasses, was in the very rear of the almost empty courtroom. An elderly man sat in front of him.

Charlie was deeply tanned, wearing a white shirt and black pants. His hair was close-cropped. His hands twisted nervously behind him as his lawyer argued and Glasser occasionally made a biting and unsympathetic rejoinder. A tough judge. Retribution time. Chickens coming home to roost.

Much discussion of the dispute at the Canarsie pier ten years before. The altercation. The police officer's sprained thumb.

The threat to the prosecutor back then.

No, it was not at all humorous, Rosen readily conceded. But no, it would be so unfair, so unjust, so *disproportionate* for that little brawl on a pier to result in declaring Charlie a three-time loser, a career criminal, thereby justifying a much higher sentence under the federal incarceration guidelines.

Judge Glasser was unmoved, rigid. "A legal argument of a very shallow order," he said at one point, driving a stake through one of Rosen's arguments. Rosen persisted. That 1992 pier brawl, that drunken expression of unleashed Guy bravado, "should not be the fulcrum that makes this the third strike" and converts Charlie from a mere multiple offender into a career criminal.

Not with all that he had done, all that he had strived to do, all the people he had touched so very positively. The young lady who had written the judge a letter saying that Charlie had saved her from a life of drugs. The young man, now a high school football quarterback, who had nothing but good things to say about Charlie. The senior citizen, the one in the back of the courtroom, who was ready to get up in court and tell the judge, right to his face, all of the things that Charles Ricottone had done for the people of Brooklyn. Positive things.

Rosen continued to plead for his client.

He is a decent person. He has a checkered and regrettable past. He has made some disastrous choices, but he is a school volunteer now. He does give back. He works with children. "That should be a plus," said Rosen.

Charlie spoke. His hands were behind his back, and he wore glasses now, and his stocky build and tieless white shirt/black pants combo gave him the fleeting appearance of a cross between Al Jolson and a waiter.

"I deeply regret the life that I have chose," said Charlie. Not that he wanted to make any excuses for his behavior. Given a chance he would lead a life that would be productive for himself and his family. He did apologize for his actions. If he could take them back he could. He never seemed to make the right choices.

He stopped. Time for sentencing from a judge whose glower seemed capable of reducing the hardest Guy into a quivering mess.

The judge began by very slowly expounding upon the definition of assault. This had some bearing on whether Charlie's 1992 thumb-spraining altercation could count toward him being declared a career criminal. Causing a physical injury would put Charlie over the top.

The judge read several definitions of physical injury. A sprained thumb didn't appear to fit the definition. But it didn't matter. Judges have discretion and this was one angry judge. He had seen so many defendants, people like Charlie, stand before him as their lawyers read letters saying what wonderful people they were. But this judge saw through all that. The people who wrote those letters had no idea of the other side of the defendants' lives. Judge Glasser did. He saw right through Charlie like an X ray.

"You beat people up. That's what you do. That's what loan sharks do." He wasn't buying a thing. Rosen might just as well have saved his breath. And so it seemed, right up to the moment the judge said he was not designating Charlie as a career criminal, and was sentencing him to four years in prison.

Then came a tongue-lashing. Charlie might not be a career criminal, but if he was not going to get a heavy sentence he was certainly going to get some pretty heavy words thrown at him, to shame him in front of the assembled lawyers and FBI agents and court clerks.

"Let me tell you, Mr. Ricottone. In some respects you are pretty lucky, because you've been standing before judges for the greater part of your life, and every time you appear before a judge you make the same speech . . . I want to tell you that if you half believe the things you say, you might want to give consideration. . . ."

The judge went on in that vein for a while. A tough speech from a tough judge. Maybe Charlie listened and maybe he didn't. He had heard it before, and he would probably hear it again.

Charlie was remanded to custody immediately. That had been a big problem for Roy Ageloff. Not Charlie. He didn't care. He could do the time. He took off his bracelet and neck chain and gave it to the old man in the back of the courtroom.

Then he went to jail.

In the summer of 2002, Louis began reading the papers regularly for the first time in his life. There was plenty to read. Enron, WorldCom, Arthur Andersen. Wall Street analysts lying. Investigations. Indictments. Convictions. During his years in the chop houses, Louis had always believed that he just wasn't good enough—not polished enough, not well-educated enough—to cross that unbridgeable gulf into the Real Wall Street. But now, as he read the papers, he knew he had been wrong. He'd been in the Real Wall Street all the time.

Nothing in the papers about chop houses anymore. Not even the guilty pleas and sentences. So Louis didn't feel that he was missing out on anything, that if he hadn't been caught he could have kept up his old lifestyle. Louis was pretty sure of that until one day in July 2002, when he ran into an old friend from Staten Island who was opening up a chop house in downtown Brooklyn.

He offered Louis a 30 percent payout. Cash.

Good money. Tempting. So painful to pass up.

This much was sure: Louis would always have temptations and he would always have to pass them up.

Louis's life was very different now. He wasn't always happy about it, but he was coping. The cars were gone; the expensive restaurants and nights in the strip joints were a thing of the past. No more gambling, no more drugs. Stefanie saw to that. Their relationship was still rocky at times, and they weren't always together. But they were trying. They didn't have much choice in the matter. As 2001 gave way to 2002, Stefanie realized with a mixture of joy, surprise, and chagrin that she was pregnant with their second child. Just as it was when Anthony was born five years earlier, the timing wasn't terrific. Maybe it was a message from—who knows? Louis was still an atheist. But he began to realize that nothing in his life was totally under his control. He began to realize that maybe something more than pure chemical interaction placed Amanda Pasciuto on this planet on August 4, 2002.

Now that he had a second kid, Louis knew that he couldn't fuck up anymore. He had to focus on rebuilding his marriage and being a father, and preparing for whatever the government might demand of him—whether that meant being a witness against his former associates or serving time in prison for what he had done.

No more Guys meant no more torture, but it also meant no more clout. He would have to handle disputes himself. When a neighbor was acting unreasonably, complaining about noises and making false claims of drug use, Louis for a moment missed the days when a call to Charlie would have ended that problem quickly. But when a friend wrote for him a strongly worded letter to the building management, something miraculous happened. The problem ended. The neighbor apologized.

Louis made other discoveries in his new life. He found that if he collected the loose change that was left over at the end of the day and put it in a jar, at the end of the month he had as much as $50. He would take the jar of loose change and bring it to the bank, which would convert the coins into clean, fresh greenbacks. It was good money, fifty bucks. He would count the bills fast, with his thumb, like a teller.

Louis knows people are looking for him. He knows because they have said so in their own special way. His sister was threatened. His mother's car was burned in their driveway. Nobody was hurt. That was the important thing. His mother called the police when the car was torched. The FBI paid the suspected perpetrator a visit.

Louis is careful. He takes precautions to assure his safety. The Guy world is weaker than it ever has been—but it still exists. It's dying, it's on the ropes, the good guys have won. Blah blah blah. But it will never go away. Guys will kill when provoked, such as the time in October 1999 when two stock promoters, Alan Chalem and Maier Lehmann, were shot dead in Colts Neck, New Jersey. It made front-page headlines at the time. The Mob was on Wall Street. Imagine that.

Louis knew Alan slightly. Alan once offered him a job. He had no idea why the two guys were killed. Maybe they reneged on a debt.

To the Guys who used to run his life, Louis reneged on a debt too. He owed them his life. It was his life, and he has taken it back.

It was his last score.